More pra
Breakdown Matters

'In this philosophically masterful book Read reminds us that anthropogenic climate change and ecological collapse pose a grave and imminent threat to human civilization. Collapse is not a potential "black swan" event he explains, but a *white* swan, an *expected* event. His analysis is tough to read. He aims to wake up his readers to reality, and demands we re-examine our lives. But he also provides radical, active hope; a route towards transformation that requires the jettisoning of shallow optimism and futile fantasies. A powerful read.'

Ann Pettifor, author of *The Case for The Green New Deal*

'This is what philosophy written down on Earth – rather than adrift in the stratosphere – looks like. This is philosophy that is eco-logical, grounded in reality rather than in dangerous fantasies. This book explains the origins of our troubled times, and offers a guide on how to transform a civilization that is on the brink of collapse. Please read it.'

Giorgos Kallis, co-author of *The Case for Degrowth*

'This is a timely and thought-provoking book that forces the reader to think deeply about the true implications of the climate and ecological crises. Even the most environmentally literate reader will be challenged to consider aspects that, perhaps, they had not considered before.'

Craig Bennett, CEO of The Wildlife Trusts, and
former CEO of Friends of the Earth

'I might paraphrase this book this way: climate change represents a kind of final exam for humanity. If we pass, we move on to a new and interesting life as a species. If not, well . . .'

Bill McKibben, 2014 winner of the Right Livelihood Award,
and founder of www.350.org

'Rupert Read is one of the few honest philosophers writing about the climate crisis. He makes it clear how confronting breakdown matters not just for saving our skins, but for saving our souls – for re-igniting the human spirit which has burnt so nearly down to the socket in these desperate times.'

John Foster, author of *Realism and the Climate Crisis*.

More praise for Rupert Read

'Rupert Read is more than just a brilliant thinker. He is a determined and responsible campaigner for a better country and a better world. I've known him since the legendary Newbury bypass protests over a generation ago now. He has never abandoned his political commitments, or his commitment to humanity and the rest of the living world.'

George Monbiot, author of *This Can't Be Happening*

'In the absence of grandmothers and grand uncles, modernity is depriving us of intergenerational precautionary wisdom. Thankfully, Rupert Read is stepping in to fill in that role, with clarity...and courage.'

Nassim Nicholas Taleb, author of *The Black Swan*

'There are not too many people on this planet, even among those most alarmed about global warming, who are actually living as though they believe that the climate is in genuine crisis and that every promise and hope we have ever extended for future human flourishing is in doubt as a result. Rupert Read is one of them.'

David Wallace-Wells, author of *The Uninhabitable Earth*

'Rupert Read is one of the few people of my generation who brings an emotional intensity to the page that recalls an older existentialist attitude toward philosophy. Read is a living reminder that ideas matter.'

Steve Fuller, author of *Humanity 2.0*

'Rupert Read is one of the world's leading climate activists.'

Claire Perry O'Neill, Former Minister of State for Energy and Clean Growth & former COP26 President-Designate

Why Climate Breakdown Matters

Why Philosophy Matters

Series editor: Professor Constantine Sandis, University of Hertfordshire, UK

Why Philosophy Matters focuses on why a particular philosopher, school of thought, or area of philosophical study really matters. Each book will offer a brief overview of the subject before exploring its reception both within and outside the academy and our authors will also defend different provocative outlooks on where the value of philosophy lies (or doesn't, as the case may be). Why Philosophy Matters is accompanied by an ongoing series of free events (talks, debates, workshops) in Bloomsbury. Podcasts of these events will be freely available on the series page.

Books in this series

Why Iris Murdoch Matters, Gary Browning
Why Medieval Philosophy Matters, Stephen Boulter
Why Solipsism Matters, Sami Pihlström

Also available from Bloomsbury

The Ethics of Climate Change: Right and Wrong in a Warming World,
James Garvey
General Ecology: The New Ecological Paradigm,
ed. Erich Hörl with James Burton

Why Climate Breakdown Matters

Rupert Read

BLOOMSBURY ACADEMIC
LONDON • NEW YORK • OXFORD • NEW DELHI • SYDNEY

BLOOMSBURY ACADEMIC
Bloomsbury Publishing Plc
50 Bedford Square, London, WC1B 3DP, UK
1385 Broadway, New York, NY 10018, USA
29 Earlsfort Terrace, Dublin 2, Ireland

BLOOMSBURY, BLOOMSBURY ACADEMIC and the Diana logo
are trademarks of Bloomsbury Publishing Plc

First published in Great Britain 2022

Bloomsbury Publishing Plc does not have any control over, or responsibility for,
any third-party websites referred to or in this book. All internet addresses given
in this book were correct at the time of going to press. The author and publisher
regret any inconvenience caused if addresses have changed or sites have
ceased to exist, but can accept no responsibility for any such changes.

A catalogue record for this book is available from the British Library.

A catalog record for this book is available from the Library of Congress.

ISBN: HB: 978-1-3502-1202-2
       PB: 978-1-3502-1201-5
       ePDF: 978-1-3502-1203-9
       eBook: 978-1-3502-1204-6

Series: Why Philosophy Matters

Typeset by RefineCatch Limited, Bungay, Suffolk
Printed and bound in Great Britain

To find out more about our authors and books, visit www.bloomsbury.com
and sign up for our newsletters.

Contents

Preface

Once upon a time there was a species that was asleep. Efforts were made to wake it, but to no avail. It seemed more comfortable dreaming.

But as the situation got more dangerous, and started to become undeniable, those efforts became more frantic. Finally, it started to stir. It started, reluctantly, to wake up. And as it stirred, through a glass darkly, it saw the doom that it had already created for so many other species. And it saw that it was now trapped on a path that led towards self-imposed destruction. It foresaw its own doom and it trembled in fear and wept.

But then it realized that it wasn't fully awake yet. There was a further step it had to take to become truly awakened. And that was to realize that it was no spectator of this. This story isn't over yet. It's wrong to tell it as if it's over. We can rebel against this path to extinction. But we will be successful only if we can take the time to see clearly what we've done, the predicament we're in, and the different possible paths ahead. This is the beginning of how this doom might yet be averted. Because we're *not* spectators. We are agents. We are potential agents of change and we have no idea what we are capable of until we try. We can rebel against our present path. If we dare to look the reality of what we are doing to life on Earth and to our very climate in the face, then two things can happen.

First, we can prepare for our possible doom. If we fail to prevent it, as looks objectively probable, then we'd better get on with preparing to meet it.

Second, we can try to prevent it. The one thing that might fully wake us up is fully facing the doom that awaits us if we don't so awaken.

This book is about those two closely connected kinds of preparations. It is about sufficiently serious adaptation to this possible coming fate. And it is about the heroic attempt to avert, or at least mitigate, that fate. This book is about how, while it looks like we're doomed, it only looks like that if we do *nothing other than* look. If we wrongly picture ourselves as spectators.

If only, instead, we'd act . . .

For if, instead of gazing as if from outside, we step into our full power as agents of change capable of extraordinary things, then objective assessment of probabilities becomes moot. Let us embrace the freedom to create something new, historic and glorious right in the very teeth of the darkness of this time.

Whenever something awful happens, it always has a silver lining if we are willing to respond to it authentically. Improbable though this may sound, I really do mean always. That is built in for human beings. Our very awareness of how dreadful the situation is itself now the mother of all motives.

Self-evidently, this book is about why ecological and climate breakdown matters. And what we find is that it matters most of all because of the way it can come to matter more deeply and widely to us in the very course of facing it. Because that process of waking up can make us matter more. It can give our lives meaning. And that might even make this worst of times into a best of times.

This book is a guide through the dark dream we are living. These pages reveal the power of a paradox: in the very darkness, in the very danger, is the dawn. If we are willing to see, and to feel it completely, then we can make real the best that we can now realistically hope for. I believe that we have a power in us stronger than we have yet dared to dream. Glimpses of this have been visible in Greta Thunberg, and in the authentic communications and creations of Extinction Rebellion. I hope that this book can help liberate you for the struggle ahead, dear reader.

The choices we are starting to have to face are truly tough, and in some cases almost impossible to deliver on. Yet if we don't face them, we will be continuing merely to kick the can down the road so that even tougher choices must be faced further later. The gradually looming end-game is a no-less-than-apocalyptic possible (likely?) future that at times I have to make visible in these pages.

Right now, there is not a lot of hope. If there is to be hope, then it's only on the back of a much more dramatic and active shift than most of us have yet contemplated. *Don't read this book unless you are ready to stretch to the very limit what you are willing to contemplate and countenance.* (And don't say you weren't warned).

I don't hold back, here. If some people write me off for it, so be it. I can do no other. I won't be a bystander.

It has hurt me to write some what I have had to say in this book. I feel bad having to say some of it to you. I just can't hide away my grief (Chapter 5) and disillusionment, as people in this field nearly always have done (until very recently). I don't want you to, either. I invite you to bring all you are feeling, all you are thinking, all you *are*, to your reading of these pages – and your action, beyond them. When we do that, then something new and grand is possible.

All significant human activities are collaborative. This book is a striking example. *Why climate breakdown matters* has been made possible – made visible, real-ized! – by the massive and invaluable research and editorial assistance of my young colleague Atus Mariqueo-Russell. I dedicate this book to *him* and *his generation*, who will inevitably face the fires of climate breakdown more even than me and my generation will have to. To the young generation in general then let me say this: meeting so many of you in Glasgow at COP26 from all around the world was a tremendous and a heart-rending experience. You have moved me (and inspired me) and stimulated me to love more deeply.

I wish you all the courage and strength that you can and will become.[1]

Prologue: The Attention-shift from Climate to Corona – and Back Again?

Other than possibly the Cold War, the coronavirus pandemic has been the first global experience in living memory of universal vulnerability and emergency. In 2020, public attention shifted almost unyieldingly from everything else to the coronavirus crisis. We became wrapped up in a planet-wide crisis of human mortality. At time of writing, we are still not out of it, and we have been alerted to the fact that it could happen again all too easily.

Given that, *why does climate breakdown (still) take precedence? Why does it matter most?*

At time of writing, we have, over the past couple of years, been living through history. We have lived through a vast 'experiment'; on whether we as humans can adjust intelligently to an emergency, a threat that has unsurprisingly almost completely consumed our attention. COVID-19 has systemically shifted our attention from the many things that we were concerned about, including crucially the 'long emergency' of climate and ecological breakdown, to the much more immediate concern of avoiding death (especially perhaps, the death of our parents or grandparents) at the hands of the virus.

Nevertheless, amidst its horror, coronavirus conceals a great gift. It has given us the chance to experience and reflect on this remarkable period of global semi-stopping, and to reassess the sort of society we have created (Read 2020e).[1] This globalized society, through its dislocation of our climate, its destruction of wildlife habitats and its hyper-mobility, has co-created the COVID-19 pandemic (Read & Shrivastava 2021). The coronavirus crisis was caused by, and is a part of, the climate and ecological crisis.

Now, as we start to emerge from this historic challenge, is the time to decide whether to be real, or to continue trying to shut out the facts (Sinclair & Read 2021). Now is the moment to get serious in asking how and why we have allowed ourselves to become collectively so vulnerable; and how we can care for our most vulnerable right now *and* in the longer term.

The vulnerability story – the story of our under-acknowledged vulnerability to existential threats (threats that pose a risk of human extinction), the story that needs to land with most humans if we are to have any chance of not crashing civilization – is now present. Like the virus itself, it has suddenly leapt from the periphery to centre-stage. (If organizations such as Extinction Rebellion, Fridays For Future and Parents For Future can resonate with the felt-vulnerability that has traversed the world in the last couple of years, then that will matter more than any specific direct actions, however striking. For it is our vulnerability to true emergencies of whatever kind, and above all to the underlying climate and ecological breakdown, that needs, above all, to be felt).

We need the intellectual resources and strength to challenge the vast energy poised to flip us back to the normal that was killing us. That's partly why we need to dare to imagine the post-corona reset we desperately need (Read 2020f). We need to dare to imagine a better future, a transformed normal: one with much less commuting, much less air travel, much less noise and pollution, much less unnecessary economic activity; but one with much more care and love, a much more localized economy, much more prepared for future existential risks, as well as much more attention to root causes of our troubles, and with much more protection of nature...We need to do this in spite of the emerging evidence that the post-Covid 'recovery' emerging in most places is not taking this form. We need to change history.

Yes, I'm asking a lot. I'm asking us to either rise to our largest possible selves, or to give up this one and irreplaceable gift that the virus has brought us. This is an historic time of choosing. And I'm reminding you that you cannot justify giving up on this chance by claiming that it's unrealizable. Every time we are tempted to plead for time out and retreat into smallness, we need to remember that before COVID-19, so much of what has recently happened seemed completely politically impossible. Impossible that the world reputation of the US and UK could plummet so far so fast, as it did in 2020.[2] Impossible that so many could decide to value care and love over economic growth. Impossible that the fabled 'magic money tree' could be found to fund the COVID-19 response. Impossible that some countries would exercise the imagination that they actually did to protect their populations. Impossible that we would shut down entire economies to protect our most vulnerable.

We need to protect ourselves against future pandemics by addressing their causes. And this brings us to the clear importance, in the context of the obvious importance of the coronavirus crisis, of the topic of this book.

We need to be ready to imagine future ecological/climate disasters and catastrophes – and to plan against them. These plans need to take a precautionary form. We need to move *ahead* of the threats.

Let no one ever again say that such things are impossible.

Only if we really envisage the full gravity of the threats of breakdown (of climate, of ecology, thus of society) now facing us, might we be ready to do enough to stop the situation from running away with us.

I think we need to reflect about all this too in terms of the very difficulty we have in even thinking about it. Why is it that we find it so difficult to face this kind of terrible possibility which may soon become a reality?

Here, the coronavirus precedent is strikingly both hopeful and discouraging. Hopeful, in that when the need was pressing and urgent enough, we changed everything, fast. Discouraging, in that, in the majority of the world, even with the crisis staring us in the face, we didn't change everything fast enough. Only in certain forward-looking places such as Vietnam, South Korea, Taiwan (all of which, notably, had been previously subject to the threat of SARS), New Zealand (which learnt from these east Asian countries once it became obvious that no leadership on the coronavirus would be coming from other Anglophone countries) and some African countries[3] (which, notably, had been previously subject to the experience of Ebola) was the response deep, wide and swift enough.

How much tougher, then, the slow-burning climate 'emergency'. On the one hand, we have far more time in which to act (though of course much of that time has already been squandered); but on the other, this very luxury of time lulls us into inaction.

This brings to mind the notorious frog-in-boiling-water syndrome, of which most readers are probably aware. If you put a frog in warm water and gradually heat up the water, eventually the frog will be boiled. The question of course is: why didn't the frog jump out when the water started getting really hot? The standard answer is that because the temperature went up so gradually, the frog barely noticed. That is precisely the situation that we are in as a species.

Now I want to tell you something unexpectedly hopeful. *It's not true.* Most frogs exposed to such a situation – even if the temperature is turned up very slowly – *do* actually jump out. I think we should take some new hope from that. If frogs are smart enough to sort this out, then surely we are too.

What would such smartness, such wisdom, on our part, actually involve? We have to try to imagine how different the future will be if we get to the point, which we may well get to well within your lifetime or mine, where it becomes clear and unavoidable that for the foreseeable future *each generation is going to have a worse life than the generation that came before it*, in terms at least of the physical threats and (un-)natural disasters that will have to be endured. This is going to force an enormous change in human consciousness.

To even contemplate – let alone address – this likelihood requires deep reflection and courage. I'm not talking merely about a reduction in GDP. That's no great hardship, provided the transition to a post-growth or degrowth economy is undertaken in a just fashion (Blewitt & Cunningham 2014). I'm talking about an ongoing semi-permanent reduction in actual quality of life, at least in material terms, however well we organize ourselves. And I'm talking, to put it bluntly, about possible mass-death, that could even make the coronavirus death toll look small.

For so long, we have thought that what life was essentially about is: having a good time and bequeathing a better life to the next generation. It's going to be an enormous psychological, philosophical and value challenge, to bracket this assumption. And to instead be caught up in a long rearguard action, of trying to stop things from getting unfathomably bad.

The coronavirus crisis absorbed our attention for a long time. It showed us that when we don't imagine deeply enough, our elders die.

It was part of the broader ecological and climate crisis. That crisis will kill far more of us and our non-human kin, unless conceivably we get busy imagining what is coming and how we can respond truly to it. And what's worse, those it will kill will be disproportionately our young.

Climate and ecological breakdown matters so very much because of this. It is high time to take the lessons from Covid and bring them to bear on the matter under direct discussion in this book.

Introduction: On Climate, Ecological and Societal Breakdown

The way up and the way down are one.
Heraclitus, *The Fragments of Heraclitus of Ephesus* (1889)

A place to start

Probably the greatest philosopher of recent times, Ludwig Wittgenstein, wrote that philosophy isn't really about teaching us new things or theories: instead, philosophy is about *reminding* us of the things that deep down we already know (1958, §127). Reminding us of matters so basic that we tend to forget them. Things that are so obvious that we don't even notice them, because they're there all the time. Like a pair of glasses. Over time you become unaware that you are wearing them, and don't consider the possibility that perhaps you might even see better without them (Wittgenstein 1958, §103).

Sometimes we need to be reminded of fundamentals. We need to examine our very ways of seeing and being, and be prepared to trade them in for truer – more fundamental – ones.

I invite you then to consider a surprising new vision. A new – actually, a very old – place to start. In the thought that perhaps we need to re-root ourselves on this blue, borrowed planet to which we are in truth deeper-than-deep wedded. We need to remember where we come from, the only place, so far as we know, that we can live.[1] We need to be reminded that we are embodied beings who come from (and dwell in) somewhere. We begin and end in Earth. And specifically, we are mammals: those that suckle their young. Even more specifically, human beings: those that know and must seek to understand ourselves, together. Remarkably, we tend to forget all this. The desire to forget our origins is almost compulsive among modern 'civilized' humans. We don't want to remember these elemental truths. We want to 'rise above' them. That desire turns out to be deadly.

And so we need reminding.

If politics and society have a first virtue, then perhaps it is this: taking care of our young.[2] We are not lizards that, because they do not care for or recognize their own young, are perfectly capable of eating them. We take care of our children. *That's what we do.* It is fundamental to who and what we are. And this care, if taken seriously, ramifies into the future. If we really are going to take care of our children, then we have to stop doing things that compromise the conditions for their descendants to have a good life too. Or indeed: a life, at all. As I detail in Chapter 1, the worst thing we can do is risk the very future of our descendants.

Let me mention a couple of real historical examples of this, to make this topic real to you, reader.

Times when we almost destroyed the world

It is well known that during the 1962 Cuban Missile Crisis, the world came perilously close to nuclear war. Perhaps even closer than we realize (Kikoy 2018). Had the missiles been launched, pretty much everybody's future would have been destroyed. Possibly everybody's, if the action induced 'nuclear winter'.[3]

Not so well known is that in 1983, we came even closer to nuclear war. This was instigated by a flock of geese flying across the edge of the Soviet Union. The USSR's radar systems misidentified this avian excursion as a series of incoming nuclear missiles. It was only due to the prompt action, or (if you will) inaction, of an intelligent and calm Russian officer (not even a very senior officer), that nuclear missiles weren't released in response to those geese. Against protocol, he delayed authorizing a retaliatory strike, until the looming threat was unmasked as simply birds. This episode is documented in a film called *The Man Who Saved the World* and the title is apposite: he did.

Less well known still (and possibly even more disturbing) are the following facts. Currently we have a hole in the ozone layer which is gradually recovering. It opened up because we did not proceed slowly with the mass rollout of chemical CFCs commonly used to cool fridges.[4] These chemicals found their way into the atmosphere and eroded the ozone layer. As scary as this is, it turns out that we had actually been fortunate in the choice of CFCs. Because it was basically luck that we had chosen to cool our fridges with CFCs rather than bromine. Had we opted for this seemingly attractive rival chemical instead, then things would have been unfathomably worse. For it turns out that bromine-based refrigerants are somewhere between ten and 110 times more effective at destroying the ozone layer than CFCs are. If we had used bromine to cool our fridges, and rolled them out at the same speed, then we probably would have created a hole in the ozone layer so vast and fast that we wouldn't have had time to grasp what we were doing before we had absolutely devastating consequences on our hands. We may have serendipitously escaped destroying ourselves by selecting CFCs over bromine.

That is the kind of threat that we have exposed ourselves to in the past. And our technological innovation rate is only escalating. If something as seemingly innocuous as fridges can imperil our civilization, then we must wonder what new threats are lurking, without our realizing, in what we are currently doing.[5]

Climate and ecological breakdown are chief among what we as a civilization are currently doing. 'Chief among' because, as I'll set out in Chapter 2, they – unlike our other self-imposed existential threats (including even nuclear, which is very much still a live danger) – are firmly on course to do us in. The challenge to us, then, is to think about how to become safer again. To think through how to build down the burden of flawed civilization that creates these threats.

This book is my contribution to thinking through that challenge.

What this chapter introduces to you

I begin that thinking by introducing the subject matter and key themes of the book to you at some length. I first sketch exactly why this book uses the dramatic, scary term 'breakdown'. I then lay out briefly how the escalating biodiversity crisis (the extinctions crisis) cannot be disentangled from the climate crisis. We face an intersecting, deeply imperfect storm of human-triggered ecological degradation. I outline how we got into this desperate situation: one in which we must be brave enough to acknowledge the likelihood of some level of ecological *and* societal collapse (a common theme of several of the chapters of the book).

What does it mean to talk of (eco-driven) societal collapse? It means something like an 'uneven ending to our current means of sustenance, shelter, security, pleasure, identity and meaning'.[6]

My approach differs from most other popular books about climate change/ breakdown, which tend to emphasize (or to presuppose) how we can supposedly be pretty sure of preventing the eventuality of collapse. They tend to pose the bogeyman of apocalypse as something that we will avoid because we must; or even that we should not discuss at all, for fear of demoralizing ourselves. That risks being a variant of 'soft denialism'; avoiding and denying the full truth of our predicament. By contrast, this book takes the possibility of some level of collapse for granted, and suggests moreover its *likelihood*.[7] By stressing the tragic likelihood of collapse, the book includes and frames discussions around how best to prepare for and respond to potential collapse in a poignant, appropriate and effective way. By shifting the focus from solely prevention of breakdown to a serious focus on adaptation too (especially, transformative adaptation), this book offers something that is more novel than it should be. Too many activists, scientists and writers are still unwilling to discuss adaptation seriously. They fear that doing so plays into the hands of those who want to avoid their responsibility for reducing climate-deadly greenhouse gas emissions.[8]

I next sketch briefly the positive psychology of the honest approach that I strongly recommend. Finally, building on my previous books critiquing the ideology of a narrow-minded techno-science-worship[9] that still has our societies in its thrall (Read 2012b), I indicate how we could conceivably escape from this deadly mindset.

The main point of this introductory chapter is, in sum, to outline[10] what climate breakdown means and amounts to. This frames and feeds into later discussions about why climate breakdown matters and what we can do about it. In particular, I stress and work through the paradoxical-sounding but crucial thought that unless we are willing to honestly confront – together and with the whole of our feeling as well as thinking being – the likely scenarios lying ahead of us, then we will not be able significantly to change them, nor even to ready ourselves emotionally for them. We need to apply a rare and sometimes 'brutal' honesty to our situation. That has become my trademark in recent years; it is unleashed here perhaps more than it ever has been before.

And what I hope you will then find is that the cure is contained within the very dis-ease.[11] The very things that are hurting us now, in incipient climate breakdown – such as the climate disasters we are already experiencing, and the terrible emotional toll being taken on many of us by our changed planet – are exactly what may yet save us, if saved we can be.

Why does this book matter?

The body of this book contains seven chapters about the climate and ecological crisis; it is about *us*[12] and our role in fuelling climate breakdown. Together, those chapters articulate the basis of an accessible 'deep green' political philosophy that is sensitive to the reality of climate breakdown and honest about our prospects for averting it. While 'climate change' is frequently discussed now in media and politics, there is generally an understatedness to the level of urgency in the way it is talked about. Even the language most often used betrays a form of 'soft' denialism and obfuscation. A 'change' can be for better or worse. By contrast, a systems *breakdown* seems unambiguously and seriously negative for those affected by it.[13] It is first and foremost for this reason that I have called this book *Why Climate Breakdown Matters*.

And make no mistake, the stakes simply could not be higher. Our economic, political and social systems are in the process of making our planet uninhabitable (at least for us, or at least for anything like our civilization), and successive governments have signally failed to address the ecology- and climate-wrecking effects of their policies . Despite broad scientific consensus, for decades, on the climate and ecological emergency, we are in the absurd situation now of living in a world warmed by 1°C according to the Intergovernmental Panel on Climate Change (IPCC), while hurtling towards a predicted warming of 1.5°C or greater within the next ten to twenty years (Shine 2018). By the end of the century, the hike in temperature may well reach 3–5°C (Spratt & Dunlop 2019). That's a civilization-terminating level of over-heat.[14]

And, as I'll explain below (and in Chapters 2 and 3), if anything the IPCC is likely to be under-estimating how bad things will get, even now.

The 2015 Paris Accord, which is the international agreement touted as the most 'successful' attempt to date at getting policy makers to face up to the climate emergency, is an entirely voluntary treaty that relies upon conservative estimates of likely over heating scenarios. Worse yet, the agreement counts upon the technophilic fantasy of widespread deployment of 'negative emissions technologies' (i.e., sucking carbon dioxide out of the atmosphere) in order to effectively take global CO2 emissions *to below zero* in the latter half of the century.[15] Carbon capture and storage (CCS) is the technology that is supposed to be able to take the lead on this. But there are currently only a handful of CCS plants, which have only a negligible impact on removing carbon from the atmosphere. Furthermore, there is no proof of concept that they can be safe at storing carbon in the very long term.

In May 2021, John Kerry, the US Climate Envoy, declared in full confidence that half of all the emissions reductions we need will come from technologies that don't yet exist. In his words, 'This is reality' (Murray 2021). When last I looked, reality was stuff that you could rely on, and ideally even see; not will-o-the-wisps that come from our fevered sense of how brilliant we are.

These technologies that we are told will save us are not available, even conceptually, to anywhere the scale needed to meet the Paris targets; and it is to say the least unclear whether they ever will exist and ever be safe to use at scale (Paul & Read 2019). We are at risk of relying on technologies that we have not yet even developed to solve problems that we know will cause widespread ecological and social collapse within the century, and probably within the next few decades, if left unchecked. This is gambling our civilizational survival on our faith in extreme technological progress and innovation.

Paris (and its successor, Glasgow) is therefore an agreement that I'll argue is destined to fail because it does nothing to challenge our dominant economic, social or political models, and instead pretends that technology will mostly fix it for us. The reality is that, collectively, we are failing to take meaningful action to halt, significantly slow, or even adapt to, the broadly predictable climate and ecological disasters and potential catastrophes that are unfolding today.

The world's governments failed us at Glasgow in November 2021, at the conference charged with devising a ratcheted-up successor to the Paris Agreement that would do enough. They mostly just put the task off for another year. But we have reached the point at which delay is equal to disaster and death. Our situation is thus truly beyond scary.

It's time to face up to the fearful fact that no one is riding to the rescue. There are no adults in the room, at the top table. We're going to have to deal with this mess as best we can, ourselves.

Let's drill into the particularly clear and present threat we face from the rising tide of climate chaos and climbing temperatures. I work at the University of East Anglia, where we have some of the world's leading researchers in environmental and climate science. What they tell us is extremely grim. The work of such scientists suggests that unless our civilization manages to dramatically turn itself around, then the future will be unrecognizably worse (Lenton et al. 2008; Lenton et al. 2019). It's actually even worse than that; because if one manages to talk to them off of the record, in the pub for instance, as I sometimes do, they tend to say things like, 'Well you know actually in my papers on this I've been pretty conservative … it could be a lot worse than I've said. What do I *actually* think? I'm genuinely scared for my kids' futures; and maybe my own'. The IPCC reports are notoriously conservative (Knorr 2020; Harrabin 2021), but even the less optimistic papers underlying those reports are probably on balance significantly too conservative, because scientific methodology consistently leans toward the side of 'least drama' (Brysse et al. 2013). Scientists are wary of stating in their work what they cannot definitively prove.

One of the few who is not generally so conservative, however, is Kevin Anderson of the Tyndall Centre. He dares to say what he actually thinks near-unexpurgated. Reading him is a sobering experience indeed (Anderson & Nevins 2016; Anderson 2017), as is reading the great James Hansen of NASA (Hansen 2009).

Above all, scientists are typically concerned with avoiding false positives, 'false alarms' (O'Riordan & Read 2017). That is why they are so risk averse in their scientific work. Hansen and Anderson are rare in being willing to risk 'false positives'. That is: they might end up being shown to having been more pessimistic, more alarming, than the situation warrants. But that's a good thing, for the risk for society of 'false negatives' is far worse than that of false positives. One's shining scientific reputation is of little importance compared to possible complicity in the self-destruction of human civilization! We should be more worried about damaging society than about damaging our own academic reputations. Most climate science, and virtually everything said by the IPCC (especially in its summaries, *which are edited by governments*), probably understates the threat to which we and our children are now subject (Bendell & Read 2021, ch. 1; Spratt & Dunlop 2018; Harrabin 2021). When our collective exposure to harm is very high, normal scientific methodology is inadequate.[16]

Over the past few years, this situation has finally (though too gradually) begun to change. The IPCC report that was leaked in summer 2021 is significantly more shocking and worrying even than the impressive '1.5°' report from 2018 (Read 2018g). A climate-scientist colleague made a good point to me about this shift. He questioned whether this new, franker report will cut through without scientists and the IPCC openly saying, 'We're sorry we didn't say this clearer, earlier. We soft-pedalled, and were too slow. That was a strategic error. We're genuinely sorry'.

Climate is only the canary in the coalmine: On the need for eco-logical thinking

At this point it is important to note that, while this collectively self-imposed [17] dire climate threat that I've been describing is at least now getting some proper airtime, it is actually only one key element of an even bigger picture. A more accurate way of understanding our time is that what is actually happening is: ecocide (Higgins 2015) – the killing of ecosystems and of biomes, that puts at risk, Gaia. According to the authoritative work done by the Stockholm Resilience Institute, the breaching of planetary boundaries by humanity is even worse *vis-à-vis* biodiversity/extinction than it is *vis-à-vis* climate (Attenborough & Rockström 2021)!

Dangerous anthropogenic climate change is one symptom of our world out of joint. The reason some people are obsessed with climate at the expense of the broader aspects of what we have done to our planetary home, the Earth, is principally because it is the most obvious short-term problem for us humans and (seems to) lend itself to possible technocratic solutions (or at least forms of carbon accounting).

I cannot take this topic to the extent the issue merits in this book,[18] but I must stress here the danger of any such anthropocentric and technocentric 'carbon-fundamentalism'. The rest of this Introduction includes some further examination of the ideological biases that lead to such blinkered, self-congratulatory self-obsession on the part of humanity.

Our primary focus in this book is climate breakdown as a likely route to societal breakdown, as the sword of Damocles we've dangled over ourselves. But bear in mind throughout: climate is only the canary in the coalmine. I will seek therefore to contextualize climate as often as possible within the broader ecological emergency. As Chapters 6 and 7 of this book make crisply clear, *our actual task is even larger and more challenging than tackling the climate crisis.* We need an even wider perspective, ultimately, than the one I most focally bring to bear in this book; we need a perspective that very thoroughly includes other animals and indeed the whole web of life. And the inclusion of them ultimately needs to be for their own sake, not only for ours.[19] Until we attain such a perspective, we risk being locked in a paradigm of selfishness that will neither make us happy nor even give us secure life for long.

My approach in this book is, in this way, far from being remotely extreme; it is actually itself at risk, if anything, of being too conservative! ...

So why does climate breakdown matter? Surely the question doesn't even need to be asked? Surely the answer is too obvious for words? Surely the stakes are clear, and we understand now that climate breakdown means societal breakdown?

So the title of this book might seem even a little silly. A kind of overkill. Dwelling needlessly on the most likely cause of a tragic but likely self-imposed literal overkill to come during this century.

But wait; look slightly closer.

Consider a slightly different question: 'Why does *societal* breakdown matter?' Now that really *is* a question which doesn't need asking. It's (beyond) obvious that societal breakdown would matter. Horribly. By contrast, we can still, just about, ask 'Why does climate breakdown matter?'. There's something to be learned from that difference.

But now notice a slippage here. I found myself substituting the word 'would' for 'does'. It is too uncomfortable to even ask the question 'why does societal breakdown matter?' Doing so presumes that such breakdown is already underway, which is too awful to contemplate. (Some are willing to (at least seem to) contemplate it. In some cases, perhaps slightly too willing, if it tacitly means that they are giving up. Or if it means that they are assuming that such breakdown as is already present in our society/ies is the kind of thing I am talking about. People sometimes say to me, 'Our society is already collapsing'. To which I reply, 'I know what you (mean to) mean; but you ain't seen nothin' yet. If collapse really comes, it will be orders of magnitude different from what we currently have. It will almost certainly mean multiple megadeaths').

Whereas we don't feel the need to change 'Why does climate breakdown matter?' to 'Why would climate breakdown matter?' In other words: *we are tacitly accepting that climate breakdown is already happening.*

And this is not unreasonable. Since 2016 or so, our climate does indeed seem to have started spinning out of control.

It is, however, terrifying. I mean; it is terrifying that we are now accepting that climate breakdown is happening – and yet not changing everything as a consequence.

For the onset of climate breakdown means that everything has to change (and, one way or another, *it will*). As this book will set out:

- It means that we have to seek to implement an emergency programme of 'mitigation' (the radical reduction of climate-deadly greenhouse gas emissions).
- It means that we have to try to adapt to climate decline, something that has hardly even begun to be taken seriously, and which, as you will see, is a key focus of my work now. Such adaptation needs to be transformative, and deep (Bendell & Read 2021).
- And it means that we have to contemplate going further. We have to be willing at least to contemplate desperate measures such as seeking to 'engineer' the climate. (I'll argue in this book that we should reject most such measures completely. But we cannot avoid at least contemplating them, discussing them; the urgency of the situation is that severe).

And this, of course, is another way of understanding precisely why climate breakdown matters. It matters because it throws a stark light on *our failure to act as if it matters as very much as it does.* It matters because, it changes everything – or ought to. If we are sane. If we really are rational animals. And if we really love our kids. And indeed ourselves.

And all this is why it is well worth a philosopher writing a book called 'Why climate breakdown matters'.

I wanted to call this book 'Why ecological breakdown matters'. But the sensible people at Bloomsbury didn't want me to. They worried that such a title would sell less well. They're probably right. But that in itself is disturbing. Humanity is slowly, painfully, waking up to its self-imposed climate nightmare. But it is considerably behind in facing the nightmare of habitat-loss, of ecosystem-destruction, the nightmare of the (anthropogenic) sixth mass extinction. Actually, as I've noted, the climate emergency (properly considered) is a subset of this ecological emergency. This book, despite its climate-y title, will sometimes address both. For until we understand the way in which the climate emergency is just *part* of the ecological emergency, we are doomed to be unable to confront its real nature, and so to be unable to act on it adequately. We will be doomed to repeat the vast failures that have led toward climate breakdown, if we don't take in the still vaster nature of the ecological emergency, and the flawed paradigm of how to live and be that led to its gestation.

How did we get to this pretty pass?

How did we – as a planetarily hegemonic civilization of progress-oriented liberal individualist capitalism, a civilization allegedly based on 'Enlightenment' values and insights – get into the situation where we have failed to act on what amounts to an existential threat to our society, and perhaps even to our survival? A full examination of this question is beyond the scope of this book,[20] though I trust that its chapters will turn out to have contributed toward it. But we can safely say that part of the reason for inertia on the biggest crisis that we face has been the litany of false information about the certainty of the crisis itself that, via certain less salubrious (but very profitable) outworkings of capitalism, has bedevilled us for so long. This is most notable in the United States and Rupert Murdoch's Australia (ironically, given how hard the climate axe is falling on that continent), where even today an alarming (though falling) number of the public simply fail to believe the stark science on climate, instead paying attention to a series of well-funded nefarious 'think tanks' and the sections of the corporate media that legitimate their 'research'.[21]

Overt climate denial is like a vampire, or a zombie: while dead *technically*, it remains somewhat undead.[22]

Of course, there is no ambiguity in the scientific community about the fact that, if current threats are left unaddressed, we are facing climate-induced catastrophe (Lenton et al. 2019; Gabbatiss 2019; Marvel 2018; Pistone et al. 2019; Steffen et al. 2018) – in other words, a breakdown. That breakdown may already have begun, judging (for instance) by what has happened to the jet stream in the last few years, with consequences such as the terrible, unprecedented, unanticipated 'heat dome' that sat over northwestern North America for several weeks in the summer of 2021, bringing death to many hundreds, in the heart of the 'developed' world. (This was followed immediately by the hugest floods in German history). And that's before we even discuss the various climate disasters unleashed with much worse consequences already for the lives of many in the Majority World, the global South, who typically have very little responsibility for the carbon bomb, and much less capacity to cope with its consequences.

The world's weirding weather of the last few years, and especially the off-the-scale north American heat dome of summer 2021, strongly suggests that the models used by climate scientists are probably underestimating the direst actual consequences of climate breakdown (Harrabin 2021). When we consider the climate emergency, we should take very seriously the 'lower probability' outcomes that suggest a far larger scale of ruin for humanity and its habitat than average predictions forecast. These lower probability events are so catastrophic (Wallace-Wells 2019; Lynas 2007; Taleb et al. 2014) that we ought to be proactive in doing everything possible to minimize their chances of coming to fruition.

On 'soft' denialism – and *adaptation*

Even in countries where denial has been less overt, it is still common to encounter a systematic downplaying of the seriousness of the emergency. This 'soft denialism' is now the real enemy. It is so entrenched even in most of academia that, while discussion of the science is abundant, discussion of the social, political and economic ramifications of taking the science fully seriously is typically far more marginalized. For instance, most of 'Political Science' and of Sociology still simply ignore the way that the ecological crisis will entirely transform our world in the lifetime of students now studying these subjects at university. Browsing through the latest issues of top philosophy journals reveals a similar lacuna in the discipline, with some notable exceptions. This is insupportable and unethical. But it is part of a wider trend.

The conversation about climate and ecological collapse has been hijacked by calming and obscurantist language that seems cherry-picked to present potential ecological apocalypse in as palatable or unthreatening a way as possible. Honest words like 'catastrophe' and 'extinction' are, even now, often shunned[23] (often with nothing more than a tired vague pseudo-justificatory gesture such as saying 'Martin Luther King said "I have a dream", not "I have a nightmare"'). Discussions about societal collapse are often suspiciously dismissed as unhelpful 'alarmism', and the conversation still revolves mainly around the academic evaluation of rival 'solutions' to this emergency – as if we hadn't already scarred this planet irreparably and the crisis could simply be 'solved'. There is no 'solution' to this long emergency. Sure, there are without doubt better and worse ways to respond to impending climate and ecological collapse, but the reality is that we have already locked ourselves into disasters, and into a certain degree of environmental catastrophe.[24]

Hard climate denialism is no longer the main barrier. The numerically much greater problem is not those people influenced by it, but those who accept most of the climate analysis and even perhaps, in principle, the need for all kinds of action – but who still hope for 'solutions' to this 'problem'.[25] Evading the need for more than cosmetic or merely reformist changes. In other words, they are climate-aware but still 'have to' fly for work, and make no real effort to convince their bosses that they should not fly at all; they still go on holidays on the other side of the world because they want to experience different cultures (before those go under); they still have relatives on other continents who they really want to visit; they still do not vote for Green parties, because what's the point? – in most countries (except Germany) they can't really influence government policies very much; and they still buy all kinds of stuff for their children, because otherwise the children would feel excluded from group activities with their friends, and so on and on and on.

This soft denialism – this hope for a reprieve, this (understandable) difficulty in facing the future – is principally what I aim to offer methods for moving beyond, in this book. I do so in part by drawing attention to the systemic aspects of the crisis. This is not a 'problem' for us to 'solve' as isolated individuals; it is a condition that we need to seek to modify and cope with together.[26]

A key like-minded attempt to turn attention to the academic (and much more) blind spot of (not) discussing or planning for potential collapse is Jem Bendell's paper 'Deep Adaptation' (2018) (now republished in updated form in the book I've edited with him, of the same name (Bendell & Read 2021)). He argues that, given what the science is telling us about the ecological and climate crises, and given our collective inaction thus far, we should conclude that we are facing 'inevitable collapse . . . and possible extinction'. Once we are realistic enough to accept that some level of collapse is to be expected (not, in my opinion, yet certain, but to be expected), our political priorities around climate inevitably must become broader. No longer can we focus solely on reducing emissions and preserving habitats; we must also implement policies to adapt to the increasingly hostile climate that we have brought upon ourselves and our fellow beings.

The deep adaptation (Bendell 2018) and 'collapsological' (Servigne & Stevens 2020) analyses are too often dismissed as doomism, even by people who follow the science and should know better (Read 2021d). They are rather *post*-doom. They contain a willingness to undertake a full-spectrum active response to what leads 'doomers' by contrast to give up and to resort to desperate rants and survivalist 'prepping' only. Discussing the full spectrum of necessary modes of adaptation (including at the societal and global levels) in response to definite disasters and potential catastrophe is necessitated by taking the science – and precaution – seriously. It is key to liberating ourselves from naive optimism about climate and ecology and their knock-ons. To borrow a phrase from Winston Churchill, when Bendell and myself and others make claims such as these, we are not being alarmist at all; we are *raising the alarm*. Much of this book focuses on how injecting more honesty into discussions of our predicament can serve as an antidote to the head-in-the-sand attitude that is still too pervasive. More than one chapter in this book will help us consider how we can prepare for likely ecological collapse. (Part of such preparation of course being: to make it less bad! To *mitigate* it, in the true sense of that word).[27]

The idea that some level of collapse may be becoming almost inevitable can be harrowing to hear and process. It can spark feelings of grief and hopelessness; emotions that are sometimes uncritically dismissed as unnecessary and unproductive (more on this crucial matter later, especially in Chapter 5). But this reaction doesn't stop the position of Bendell and others from being alarmingly credible. Although note that my stance unlike his is designed to resist any possibility of attribution of doomerism; I take care to assert, unlike him, that we cannot know that collapse is inevitable (Read 2018g & 2021d). Disasters are inevitable (Chapter 4), but eco-driven societal collapse is, so far as we know, not (yet!). Unlike Bendell, I regard deep adaptation not as a necessary response to inevitable collapse but as a necessary part of our response to increasingly likely but uncertain potential collapse; I take it to be a kind of insurance policy against something we cannot now rationally avoid hedging against.

Our children, as they grow up, will be very clear with us about what matters at the present time. They will have only one question for us: 'What did you do, while there was still time to prevent collapse, or at least to soften our landing?'

But there is another question that emerges at this point: what can adaptation even mean for the kind of climate-degraded future that I am expecting? For it is true to note that some scenarios present a future that cannot be adapted to. (David Wallace-Wells speaks of an Earth that might become progressively uninhabitable for humans and similar animals. I prefer to speak of *the unimaginable Earth*. We need to be brave enough to seek to imagine futures currently way beyond our ken. The likely unending, permanent emergency will be mitigated adequately only if we rise to meet those possibilities).

But all too often, the fact that humans may not be able to adapt to some 'high-impact' desperate possible climate futures has, to date, been used as an excuse for not thinking or doing adaptation at all. That attitude is no longer acceptable, no longer viable. What we need now is to think and do adaptation that is without illusions. And this again marks an unusual feature of this book: that in what follows, I am out and proud about placing what is called adaptation centrally in my proposals for what we ought to do now.

To be clear though, I'm not proposing the pseudo-adaptation of traditional shallow, incremental, defensive adaptation, that tries hopelessly to perpetuate our current system of would-be endless economic growth and boundless technology-based 'progress'. Too often, that is what 'adaptation' has been taken to mean – merely building higher flood-defences within which we try to keep our current failed civilizational model staggering on for longer. What I'm talking about is a progressively deeper adaptation. This means adaptation to the possibility of a full-scale collapse. Deep adaptation now must be undertaken for the simple reason (which should by now be obvious) that collapse cannot be ruled out, and a collapse for which we have not prepared would be far worse than one for which we have readied ourselves. Alongside this, we need *transformative* adaptation (Foster 2019): system-change on a basis of realism. This rejects fantasies of pivoting the entire system on a dime overnight and thereby totally avoiding lasting climate damage. Transformative adaptation seeks to change our society in the direction it needs to change in anyway (e.g. relocalizing), *and* trying to 'mitigate' (reducing emissions) in everything we do, *and* at the same time trying to adapt to (and become more resilient to) the worsening climatic and ecological situation that is coming. It does all three at once.

Let me give a quick example. Rather than building ever higher sea walls and conventional flood defences to try to enable us to perpetuate our current society, transformative adaptation invites us to accept that there will be some rise in sea levels. We accept the need to work with, rather than against, nature. And so we cultivate wetlands. These are flood defences that can grow and move. We 'build' and restore wetlands, mangrove swamps, and so on. And those sequester carbon, acting as very real, very careful flood defences. By working with nature, we can begin to move in the direction of the kind of transformed society that we need. We can adopt a humbler, more co-operative attitude to the Earth.

I am not of course asserting that it is always wrong to build sea walls or flood defences, but simply pointing out that they make sense only if built within a broader framework of fundamentally rethinking, with humility, our mode of co-existing on a damaged planet. Otherwise they amount to more mere kicking of a can down a dead-end road. The broader framework must be one of *a transforming of normal*. And that transformation needs must be open-ended; for the likelihood is that for generations to come we will have to cope with changing conditions more than was the case during most of the Holocene. The climate genie we have shoved out of its bottle will not be getting back in again for a very long time to come, not least because of long processes of ice-melt that are probably unstoppable (Brennan 2020).

We have to turn more to these agendas of deep and of transformative adaptation. And that means we have to push for various kinds of changes in government policy. *And* it means we have to do stuff at the local level. Because government is failing us, and may well continue to do so; and because the future is going to be more local, whether we like it or not. It could come through an intelligent adaptation; wise, wide-ranging transformational modifications that we deliberately bring in. We could, for example, reduce the length of our supply lines, increase our resilience, cut carbon emissions, rebuild our communities and so on. It'll come in that way – *or* it will come as a result of catastrophic collapse, because in a catastrophic collapse, when everyone is just trying to survive, things are definitely more local . . .

Why has there been so little focus on adaptation in climate activism, climate politics, and climate science? Adaptation is creeping steadily up the international agenda, but is still not being taken anywhere near as seriously as mitigation/prevention.

Why is this, given that adaptation offers more 'selfish' and short- to medium-term benefits to those who undertake it, whereas 'mitigation' is largely an altruistic gesture? My hypothesis is that it is because once one starts talking about/doing adaptation, one can no longer deny how bad the situation is. One can no longer deny that it is real, that it is *here*. The failure to engage seriously with adaptation at all, let alone transformative adaptation, *let alone* deep adaptation, risks typically being tacit/soft climate denial in action.

So merely the act of talking about adequate adaptation (not to mention resourcing this properly) is a kind of revolutionary act. It breaks through the fantasy that everything is going to be fine, that harm can be avoided, that somehow this epochal 'wicked' problem or tragedy is just going to go away/be solved.

To summarize this section, climate and ecological collapse are *the* determinative issues of our times. And unless we get our response to them right, all questions about how to create a fairer and more just world will become completely moot.[28] Unless we are willing to face up to the sobering facts about the systemic and holistic nature of the threat that faces us, then we will have absolutely no chance of rising to meet it. And unless we are willing to recognize that any adequate response requires a profound shift in how we structure our economy, our politics and our relationship with material consumption *and* much of technological innovation, then our efforts will be in vain. A central thrust of this book, then, is that an appraisal of the climate and ecological crises that ignores the entire panoply of their causes, as well as their horrifying extent, simply will not be able to respond to them with the urgency that they demand.

The will to face the truth confronting us

Conventional wisdom in mainstream climate activism has until recently – until the game-changing advent of the likes of Greta Thunberg and Extinction Rebellion – said that if we direct people's attention to the scale and severity of present and impending ecological collapse, then they will abandon all hope in the face of it and will fail to act against it. The consensus has largely been that messages of hope and progress motivate, while those of impending catastrophe and failure demotivate and alienate otherwise receptive audiences. In short, put on a happy face.

Consequently, the green movement has, in its worst moments and for different reasons, largely in practice toed the same line as those seeking to preserve the status quo.[29] We have failed to articulate the extent of the threat to our civilization and planet. This approach to messaging partly explains large sections of the green movement's inability to grapple with the seismic changes necessary to achieve climate and ecological stability. They have come to believe their own Polyanna-ish communication strategy over the scientific literature and ecological reality.

But the idea that the truth of our predicament is too scary and off-putting to communicate in full and honest terms has not been my experience at all. In fact, in my experience, especially in the time of Extinction Rebellion (Read 2020d), people often feel profoundly reenergized and motivated once they realize that it is OK to give voice to the holistic nature of the threat that we face. Often people are left unconvinced by the cosmetic and tokenistic policies that successive governments have adopted in the face of this emergency. They can feel deeply alone and isolated in fearing for their future in a society on the verge of a collapse that it appears others fail to see. There is often a sense of deep uneasiness with much of modern living and an anxiety that stems from observing – *noticing* – the clear and escalating erosion of much of nature. Dropping the cognitive dissonance that comes from pretending our ecology – and our society – is fundamentally fine, when it is clearly *not*, can be fundamentally liberating.[30]

On – and beyond – scientism and technophilia

One particularly galling aspect of our predicament, and a particularly troubling obstacle standing in the way of our being willing to face and tell the truth, is, ironically, our civilization's excessive attachment to the scientific-technological-industrial complex. Which is to say that a key propeller of naive optimism and soft denialism comes from our pretty deep-set cultural inability to envisage any alternative to the system that is destroying our planet. This collective failure of imagination has led to the proposal of increasingly absurd 'solutions' to ecological collapse. These 'solutions' often rely on a quasi-religious faith in 'progress' with a messianic role reserved for new technologies to redeem our ecological destruction and economic system. At its most extreme, this involves dystopian cli-fi fantasies of global geo-engineering: attempts to engineer the entire planet, to treat it as if we can truly be its overlords.[31] At a less extreme, though still unhelpful and potentially ruinous level, are proposals for the multiplication of the genetic modification of organisms (Taleb et al. 2015) and of nuclear power to allegedly ameliorate this crisis while leaving the existing social and economic order intact. (The love of nuclear power is particularly worrisome from a deep adaptation perspective; picture multiple meltdowns as societal collapse unfolds; these would hardly help the situation! (Chapter 7)). This ethic of insufficiently critical faith in technology is sometimes helpfully labelled 'scientism', because it places a faith in science and technology as panaceas for what are fundamentally social and political problems, and problems of how we ought to live.

Why speak of 'scientism', though? Why not just focus upon the problems fomented by technophilia/technocentrism? Isn't science our essential basis and ally? Surely the real problem is misguided, excessive faith in techno-fixes? Remember: scientism is not science (which is indeed an essential basis); it is a dogmatic ideology of science alone – in effect, 'science-worship'. And now we can see a key connection with the argument of this Introduction thus far: for this [32] ideology involves treating everything as if it were a problem to be modelled and solved via analysis, rather than a whole to be contemplated, a condition (perhaps a tragic one[33]) to be inhabited, or a way of life to be changed.

Applying scientistic procedures to the ecological crisis is a grave cognitive error that leads to an abject failure to recognize the seriousness of the predicament that we face. Scientism is actually a profoundly unscientific philosophy precisely because it places faith in science to deliver solutions to all the world's ills, thereby overegging the scientific pudding.[34] As I will show in Chapter 3, the fact is that our current way of life will not continue. Either escalating climate chaos will put a stop to it, or we will manage to make the decision to transition our society into something else. These options exist on a spectrum themselves; it may be that limited collapses jolt public consciousness enough to make the required changes before a terminal collapse presents itself.

As for the present, our being is on balance ever more *not*-being-in-the-world.[35] Being human has come to be dissociated from being an Earthling (Latour 2018). And that is, of course, why life is getting worse: less meaningful, less wild, less connected, less present. We need, in the face of this, to affirm life, and to overcome the great temptation to withdraw completely (rather than just tactically or temporarily). The temptation to give up. And there is a connected temptation, voiced by Nietzsche, to nausea at our fellow humans. We need to love life – knowing that, because of the self-undermining industrial-growth juggernaut, we don't know how long we've got.[36] (That can, of course, make the sense of each moment more piquant).

The situation is directly akin to the one explored in Kazuo Ishiguro's superb, haunting 2005 work *Never Let Me Go*, which imagines our health being dependent on the sacrifice of that of 'others' (and those others, non-coincidentally, are children). Will we actually be willing to do the right thing? Or are we too selfish? Here is what the authority figure Miss Emily says, close to the end of that devastating work: 'There was no way to reverse the process. How can you ask a world that has come to regard cancer as curable, how can you ask such a world to put away that cure, to go back to the dark days? *There was no going back*' (my emphasis). The analogue is precise: how can you ask a world that has come to regard many diseases as curable, given high-tech interventions, to go back to the 'dark' days? Will we willingly give up our high-tech life-prolonging devices, *even when these crush the futures of our own descendants*? The society that sustains our health into an ever older old age makes it impossible for civilization to be sustained long term. There will, one fears, be no going back – even if the cost (as is virtually certain) is, in time, to crash the entire system. (I develop this dilemma toward the end of Chapter 1).

In this context, 'humanism' is the problem, not the solution. The trail of the human serpent is increasingly over everything, and the solution is not ever more of us. We have held ourselves – or at least, some of ourselves – 'above' our animal kin and above our only home, in a way that literally can no longer be sustained. Humanism, which of course has in some respects a philosophically impressive pedigree and a noble history, has morphed all too smoothly into growthism, 'development', technophilia and (at the extreme) new influential trends, such as transhumanism. All of these are profoundly destructive ideologies. Any or all of them will be enough to perhaps terminally trash our Earth and certainly to crash (our) civilization.

Perhaps you think that increasing automation is our friend here, and presents a way out, a genuine tech-fix? To those who envisage robots increasing the efficiency of our use of energy, a simple question suffices: will your robots be additional to existing human beings (in which case they will without doubt add to net energy- and resource- consumption) or will they replace existing human beings?[37] Not (just) existing jobs – existing *human beings*. In which case, we ought to be told exactly who will be replaced, and how. One fears that some among the far-seeing rich and powerful are likely already to have plans that would make Huxley's nightmare-vision look benign.[38]

What hope is there for this civilization, when it shows so little sign of having truly absorbed any real understanding of any of this, let alone of having anything even remotely resembling a plan with which to address it? Despite our supposed rationality, despite the very clear warnings we have been given over and over, we continue moving on balance in the wrong direction. If this civilization were going to plan on saving itself, the last twenty to thirty years or so would already have seen strong, radical, mass-backed Green and Green-friendly governments taking power all over the planet,[39] turning back the 'free trade treaties' that institutionalize our peril, putting high finance and 'globalization' itself on a leash, and relocalizing on a global basis,[40] starting to move us collectively in the right direction. Nothing even remotely like this, of course, has happened. Above all, we would have seen an effective and just global climate agreement, not the unenforceable sticking plaster – which quietly commits us to the utter recklessness of geo-engineering – of Paris (and now Glasgow) (Tanuro 2016). It is a mark of how far we are from living in truth with regard to climate reality that Paris is, absurdly, widely regarded as simply having been a success.

We live *in absurd times*.[41]

It is this deeply desperate situation that has seen the emergence of forms of climate activism which stare courageously into the abyss, and seek to abjure all denialism.

The key first demand of Extinction Rebellion, probably the most striking example to date of emerging collective climate-consciousness-in-action, is for governments to tell the truth about the severity of climate breakdown and ecological collapse. But this demand will not be effective if *citizens* do not face up to climate reality either. So this book is my attempt to help you do just that. To stare honestly at the oppressive, nightmarish scale of the conditions that we face, and to help illuminate the sorts of changes that are necessary if we want to continue to exist . . . and how the very severity of those problems, if we dare to lean into them, might even yet contain within them the seeds of our changing the world. You have had the courage and patience to have followed me this far through my Introduction, so let me entirely blunt and direct now about where I think we are at as a civilization.

I think we are likely to face widespread social and ecological collapse within the next few decades. I hope that I am wrong, but like Bendell and others, I have come to believe that the science is very clearly pointing in a different direction to our political trajectory and that we have perilously little time to change course and perilously little full-blooded intention of doing so.

Besides still trying to do so (which we absolutely should do), what we can also do that is new and which still hardly anyone is even talking openly about doing (though I think that in the privacy of their homes and so forth, many are increasingly muttering it)[42] is to prepare for such a (likely) collapse in such a way that minimizes harm and allows us to birth something new and more resilient in the place of this civilization.[43] We can learn and internalize the values that would have been necessary to have prevented climate and ecological breakdown, and interrogate and banish the values that have tended to facilitate it. And we can teach others and our children those values, and seek to practise them.

Focusing on these live options, in the chapters that follow, I examine what sort of future we can expect to co-create, and bequeath (or, depending on your age, reader, inherit).

What is in this book

Having introduced you to the subject matter of this book, I round out this Introduction by briefly summarizing in turn each of the chapters to follow.

Chapter 1 continues what has been begun in this Introduction by addressing the question inherent in this book's title in a direct and philosophical way. I consider what it is about preserving the planet that makes it so central to our values and to our flourishing. I address my argument to the sceptical reader who may not intuitively or deeply grasp why climate breakdown matters. I argue that our relationship to our descendants, and in particular our love for our children, is the bond that links us inexorably to the future. My conception of love is that it involves caring for the well-being of the person loved. Central to our conception of well-being is our ability to love and care for our own children. Therefore, if we deprive our own children of the ability to be able to care for their own children, then we have inflicted a great harm upon them. This is something that I believe almost everyone will want to avoid.

And yet, even the obviousness of the logical and moving line of thought I crystallize in Chapter 1 doesn't seem to be enough by itself to actually turn the supertanker around. We are virtually devouring our own children, as lizards do. So I – we – need to go deeper.

Chapter 2 builds on this Introduction by seeking to inject some unadulterated reality into the discourse around climate breakdown. I address the 'sceptics' about the science, who argue that remaining uncertainty in the science means that we ought not to regulate in response to possible climate breakdown. Far from uncertainty providing a reason for cautious regulation, I show that remaining uncertainties serve only as a reason to regulate and move more aggressively. For while the changes predicted by our best available climate models could be less extreme than feared, they could also be far worse than we imagine. With the stakes this high, the precautionary principle dictates that we must throw ourselves into minimizing our chances of potentially-terminal ecological decline. I then consider how despite a large degree of consensus in the scientific community that full-scale climate breakdown (such as a 'hothouse Earth') is a real possibility, we have nevertheless collectively continued unabated on the path of ecological destruction. This reveals something profoundly wrong about our society and our value-set.

Chapter 3 responds to these conclusions with the honesty that they demand. I argue that we shouldn't shy away from the conclusion that our current trajectory very likely means that we will face civilizational collapse. Even if we can avoid such an outcome, then we will only have done so by changing our civilization so radically that it scarcely resembles what we know currently. Consequently, it appears certain that *this* civilization is finished. I consider what this means in this chapter and how we can navigate this time of upheaval.

(At this moment in the text, the axis of my analysis shifts. For in the next three chapters, while venturing yet deeper into our contemporary heart of darkness I show that that very venturing is what can show us the light, and even *make us* the light).

Chapter 4 examines climate disasters. I focus on the question of what sorts of social responses we can expect to emerge as the intensity and frequency of disasters is amplified – as it will be. I draw on the work of disaster studies scholars that shows that the popular narrative of these events as a catalyst for the worst elements of our nature is (thankfully) hugely inaccurate. Instead, thoughtful and attentive empirical research suggests that disasters are often the scene of intense community building. This shatters an important cultural myth about human nature. More importantly, it is also a source of real hope for fast changes in our attitudes to climate breakdown. It may be that from the aftermath of disasters we can seize renewed vigour for creating a better and more resilient world.

Chapter 5 examines the ever-growing phenomenon of climate grief. I open by exploring grief of the 'ordinary' kind. This serves as a springboard for considering the distinct dimensions of climate grief. My conception of grief is that it embodies a psychological paradox. This paradox emerges when we come to have beliefs that are fundamentally incompatible with our lived world and sense of identity: beliefs such as that who (or that) we hold most dear, is dead (or dying). These are often true beliefs. The process of grieving involves a profound rupturing of our lived experience as we seek to come to terms with the loss of something (or someone) that we cannot help but feel remains ever-present. This brings me onto the topic of climate grief. While 'ordinary' grief involves the rupturing of one's own personal lived world, climate grief is a response to the rupturing of *the Earth itself*, of 'Gaia'. Moreover, unlike 'ordinary' cases of grief, there is no end to the cause for climate and ecological grief. Rather than a rupturing of our personal world that can be adapted to over time, climate grief is something tied to a constant, reiterating rupturing of our world. Any adaptation to it needs therefore to be in process, permanently transformative. As climate disasters increase, there will be an amplification of this type of 'irrecoverable' grief in the decades that come. We will only stop producing such grief once these rupturings cease. Meanwhile, such grief is the most vivid manifestation there is of love for what (who) we are losing. Climate grief can therefore serve as a formidable catalyst for sufficient climate action.

Chapter 6 investigates our interconnectedness with others through an investigation of some of the other more overtly pro-social animals. I frame my critique of the liberal individualist ideology that captivates 'Western' (and increasingly, global) society through a contrast with the way that cetacean societies are organized. I argue that the pseudo-freedom that our dominant ideological paradigm offers is corrosive of a sense of interconnectedness that is fundamental to our flourishing. While different human societies are in most cases to different extents enmeshed within a system of exploitation of nature and each other, whales and dolphins are quite decisively far removed from the trappings of liberal individualism. For this reason, I argue that there is wisdom to be gleaned from careful observation of their social structures and cultures. Of course there are limits to the extent to which we can embody or adopt the psychology and values of non-human animals. Nevertheless, the process of attempting to do so may well shed some light on what has gone so terribly wrong within our societies – and on how, through moving to very different beings of comparison[44] for ourselves, we might profoundly change this.

Chapter 7, the book's conclusion, ties together the different strands of this book and brings into focus a set of pretty concrete proposals for us. I have resisted the common temptation to round things off with unconvincing naive optimism. Instead, I argue that our actions need to be sensitive to the very real possibility of collapse. This means that our actions must be directed towards transformatively (and deeply) adapting to a more hostile climate; a programme that of course will simultaneously reduce that hostility. Once we recognize that an ongoing climate breakdown is a likely outcome, then our climate activism will look very different. That is not to distract from the need, more urgent than ever, to reduce the likelihood of collapse. It is simply to point out that it would be a mistake to bet the farm on 'mitigation' (i.e., on prevention of collapse) alone. In this seventh chapter I outline seven proposals that we ought to integrate into our lives if we are to take climate breakdown as seriously as it demands.

To return finally to this chapter's epigraph, and to summarize the arc of the whole book very succinctly:

Chapter 1 lays out a logically decisive argument that should focus us resolutely on the ecological emergency. The argument is so simple and powerful that it should already have been widely spotted, felt – and acted upon. But somehow this has not been the case, which suggests that something more is needed. Chapters 2 and 3 take us deeper into our predicament, such that there is less space to mentally avoid the white swan of climate and civilizational breakdown heading our way. Chapters 4, 5 and 6 take us yet *further* down: into the coming climate disasters, into our grief, and into contemplation of collective para-suicide . . . *but* they constitute simultaneously perhaps the book's greatest offerings. The greatest chance we have of coming through the incipient breakdown of our life-support system is through entering fully into its impact upon us, in collective emotional reflection (and then action). Passion, not just logic, is what is needed.

The way down *is* the way up, it turns out. I conclude by setting out how we can take advantage of this and make climate breakdown matter even more.

I hope this book can go some way towards dispelling some of the common myths often sold as 'solutions' to the desperate global predicament that we face. As will become abundantly clear throughout the course of the present work, any genuine attempt at addressing the climate and ecological crises require a holistic transformation of much of our politics, our economics, our society, and ultimately our philosophy. I say 'addressing' rather than 'solving' these crises because, through our collective and systemic inaction, we have already committed to a certain amount of irreversible more or less catastrophic change in the future. What is now locked-in and unavoidable, we must seek to adapt to as resiliently as we can. It is our actions now that will determine just how terminal our past inaction was – or was not.

1

Just How Much do you Care About the Future of Humanity?[1]

[B]ecause of its continuity, a collectivity is already moving forward into the future. It contains food, not only for the souls of the living, but also for the souls of beings yet unborn which are to come into the world during the immediately succeeding centuries.

Simone Weil, *The Need for Roots* (1952)

Our most fundamental care

The climate crisis is here. The ecological emergency is here. It is not something remote that will affect us in 2100, or 2050, or even 2025. It is here, now. Global weirding has become an everyday reality for many of us in the last few years: consider for instance the out-of-control fires that have raged in California, across Australia, around the Mediterranean, in the Amazon, in South American *wetlands*, in western Canada, and indeed in the Arctic.

The matter of this book is not one that concerns only future generations or the non-human world. Increasingly, it concerns every one of us, personally, in the present. Some of us are already dead because of it. Some of us can no longer read these words, or any words, because the crass exploitation of our world has killed them.

A structural feature of climate breakdown is that it will kill far more in the future than it has done yet. It will affect the young and unborn future generations far worse than it has already affected those in my generation (at time of writing, I'm fifty-five) or my parents' generation.

To say it succinctly: climate breakdown threatens most those who are our most fundamental care. Our descendants.

There are few things worse for a human than being unable to look after their loved ones. Being unable to actualize the love and care that are so fundamental to our character and most meaningful connections is a cruel fate. However, at least one outcome eclipses that malady. Because no matter how abject our inability to protect our loved ones might be, active complicity in their destruction is a far greater state of wretchedness. It is a state of the most profound *ill-being*. And yet, dear reader, this is the quandary that we have collectively stumbled into.

Now, as promised earlier, there is space in this book for what I've already begun, an examination of the genesis of our predicament. The way in which a potent cocktail of ineffectual and unresponsive political structures combined with the laissez-faire economic consensus has been turbocharged by our bankrupt liberal-individualist,[2] growthist[3] and technophilic[4] philosophies. The way in which the nature and magnitude of the existential threat that we face has been obfuscated by the worst aspects of our psychology, under the magnifying effect of those philosophies. And how those facets of our psychology that might galvanize us, for example the climate grief and eco-anxiety that some of us are already experiencing a good deal of, are not enough collectively explored or processed (Chapter 5). And the way in which these factors have combined with others to prevent us from facing up to climate reality. However, I want to begin by first addressing that most fundamental of questions: why should this even matter to us?

Sure, our steady, blinkered march into climate breakdown may not reflect very well on our powers of collective decision-making. And sure, it looks likely that unprecedented human misery will accompany our descent into a world beset by climate disasters. But why should this concern us on a personal level any more than other causes that do not affect our day-to-day safety? Is there anything unique about climate breakdown that warrants uprooting it from the periphery of our concerns and centering it in our everyday decision-making?

Now, for some readers, especially those of you who picked up this book because you feel in sympathy already with its implied 'vibe', this question is likely not to arise at all. It may be that the facts as you understand them already generate enough of a reason to motivate and mobilize you to throw yourself tooth and nail into minimizing the incalculable harm of climate breakdown. But for many, perhaps the vast bulk of us, climate breakdown does not appear to personally affect us on a day-to-day basis. At least not yet. And so the question naturally arises as to why we ought to treat this cause as different in type rather than simply different in scale to the other ills of the world?

In this chapter, I argue that climate breakdown matters to our most fundamental of interests. Not simply because it may disrupt, blight or even end the lives of some readers of this book, although it almost certainly will do that. But because impending climate breakdown severs our ability to look after *our own* children through their lifetimes, *and* compromises their children yet further (and so on, indefinitely), in a way that I shall explain the full importance of. With each passing year, it grows in threat. It is bearing down upon our children: we need to find ways to look up from the more immediate issues that (in many cases understandably) preoccupy us (especially the poor), to focus upon it, or it will sweep them aside.

Failure to act on climate breakdown reveals a disturbingly shallow aspect of our love towards our own children – and thus calls for that love to be realized and deepened in its expression. Indeed, because we are almost all, albeit to very different extents, enmeshed within the systemic destruction that is driving climate breakdown, we are doing worse than simply failing to protect our own children. As I've said, we risk being actively complicit in their ruin.

Most humans are, at present, co-destroying the lives and undermining the central interests of those that we love most. Yet I believe that if we truly profess a deep love for our own children, as almost everyone with children does, and if we come to understand what that love entails, then this love will inextricably, determinedly drive us towards genuinely doing what we can to protect future generations. That is a key basis of my enduring hope against hope, reader. And I think this is the basis of perhaps the greatest hope that together we can still have.

How could the future matter as much as the present?

This may at first appear to be an overly bold claim. While most people agree that future people matter, the notion that the present matters more is woven into the very fabric of our civilization. There have been civilizations whose guiding values have futurity woven into them. Consider, for instance, the Iroquois' 'Seventh Generation Principle'. This mandates that important decisions should explicitly posit the interests of those living seven generations from now.[5] Imagine if a politician were to say, in an election address, 'What will those living 150 years from now think of this policy?' The fact that this never happens is an important and sad fact.

The idea that the distant future matters less still appears largely uncontested outside of certain corners of academia and the green movement. Elected politicians, until recently, were under no significant pressure to defer benefits in the present to protect our collective future.[6] Economists regularly discount benefits in the future as somehow less valuable than equivalent benefits in the present for no reason beyond the fact that they occur later.[7] While climate anxiety is growing fast, especially among the young (Rao & Powell 2021), most psychologists deal with far more everyday and often relatively self-generated concerns and maladies.[8] Meanwhile the forces of climate delay, shamefully, call out the symptom (climate anxiety, and those suffering from it, and those seeking to make plain the *reasons* for anxiety) rather than addressing the cause (in particular, the very climate delay that they seek to foster!).

The weight that we give to future people through our institutions, our everyday decision-making, and the time we spend thinking about them, appears to reveal that their protection is *in practice* often relatively low on our list of concerns. Opinion polling shows self-reported concern with climate breakdown dramatically and stably increased since the advent of Extinction Rebellion and the School Strikes for Climate movement (Barasi 2019; McGrath 2021), which is a tremendous fact that may be able to be leveraged into more concrete commitment (especially, from 'policy-makers'). However, for now there remains a gap between reported concern and actual on-the-ground willingness to prioritize and act on it meaningfully.[9]

The empirical evidence is relatively clear cut: people, on aggregate, simply don't care enough (yet) about climate breakdown to motivate the sorts of changes that we would need to avert it (Read & Eastoe 2021; Read & Knorr 2022). A cynic might take this to be definitive evidence that our strongest values are in irreconcilable tension with humanity's continued survival. There is some truth to this diagnosis. That we prioritize the present to the extent that we undermine the possibility of having a future is a profound indictment of the ideologies that have driven the world's fixation with material consumption, economic growth and 'progress'. This includes the philosophies of Social Darwinism and of the 'invisible hand', but more broadly encompasses all mainstream dogmas of 'Right' and 'Left' (Read 2013).[10] The extent to which we have allowed these values to infiltrate our societies is a weighty obstacle to our continued survival, let alone to the advent of the kind of conditions needed to for us to truly flourish. Our civilization contrasts with some historical forebears whose concern was for (their) futurity, or for the glory of God, rather than for short-term gratification.

Nevertheless, despite the existence of these values pushing us toward terminal decline, the picture is not as clear cut as those truly convinced of the inevitability of climate collapse sometimes suggest.[11] Because while we do hold some values incompatible with averting collapse, we have other profoundly strong, indeed stronger, values that militate in the opposite direction. In fact, our strongest values are intimately connected with and premised upon the continuation of a viable future.

Our love for our children is the starkest and strongest example of this type of value.[12] If we truly examine what is required of that love, then I think we have a chance at changing course before breakdown occurs, or at least a chance at softening our landing when it does. At the very least (and this already, rightly, demands a lot) we will be able to look our children in the eye and tell them that we did all that we could.

Sometimes the question is framed among environmentalists as, 'How do we make people care about the future?'. Put like this, it can seem like a hopelessly daunting task. As if we need to find a quick way to germinate new values within masses of people currently unconcerned with posterity. Such a Herculean task seems hopelessly doomed on the short timeframe that we have left to change our trajectory (Read & Alexander 2019; Read 2020a). Fortunately, the problem is not so stark. Our task is not to instill new values in people, but rather to illuminate that their own values, once properly understood and taken seriously, already reveal that they do care about the future. Coming to understand this can change everything.

Of course, all this works only if there is something within most people's values that connects with posterity (Scheffler 2013; Johnston 2011). And although at first appearance the evidence may seem stacked against such a claim, there are nevertheless good reasons to think that the love that we profess for our children can ground it. To galvanize action against our predicament, we do not need to create a new type of person. All we need to do is better understand the type of people we are: mammals; and human beings. *People*: who deeply love their ('our') children.

Our loving care iterates down the generations

What then is the 'mechanism' by which our love for our children necessitates and enables the protection of future generations? Most obviously, loving our children means not undermining the conditions necessary for their survival or flourishing. These will be undermined if our civilization collapses, particularly if it collapses terminally, and no successor-civilization is birthed.

Most people do not consider that such scenarios are 'live options'. Outside of disaster movies and fiction, society does not often contemplate seriously that collapse is what we are *likely* heading for if present trends continue. This remains true even if things are reformed mildly for the better (International Scholars Warning on Societal Disruption and Collapse 2020; Ophuls 2012). But even if you are unconvinced of this, even if you admit only that there is only a small chance, for example a 5 percent chance, of climate-induced civilizational collapse this century, then such a chance should still be taken profoundly seriously. Not doing so amounts to playing a perverse game of Russian roulette with the people we love most.

Our decision-making must be sensitive to risk and uncertainty. This is especially true when the threat we are considering is catastrophic or even existential. And it is doubly true when there is uncertainty about the magnitude of the risk that we are taking and the likelihood of it materializing

(Read 2018b; Chapter 2). This appears to be the case with the existential threat posed by climate breakdown.[13] We can be confident that climate breakdown is unlikely to result in our species' complete extinction, but it seems absurd to try and put a number on exactly how unlikely that is to happen. There are simply too many unknowns for such an endeavour to generate precise answers. In such cases, leaning on the side of caution is the most prudential course of action. After all, what benefit could possibly be worth staking the survival of humanity for (Read & Craven 2017)? Even significant costs are worth incurring to eradicate what could be relatively 'minor' risks of extinction. Humanity's relatively large investment in the (in relative terms straightforward and one-dimensional) monitoring of the trajectories of meteors and asteroids is an example where we seem to have taken this reasoning seriously[14]. Our treatment of the existential risks inherent in climate breakdown is one where we have failed the same test (Taleb et al. 2014).

In response, maybe you agree that impending climate harms will impact our children's lives, while still disagreeing that we ought to throw ourselves wholeheartedly into preventing such eventualities arising. Indeed, you/we may even think that the best way to protect our children is to invest our time and resources into better preparing them on an individual level to weather the incoming climate storms. Perhaps this is a more effective expression of our love for our children than attempting to collectively minimize such storms?

This reasoning has some obvious appeal. For instance, you may be able to invest large amounts of time and money into collectively tackling climate breakdown, or to give that same time and money directly to your own children. The latter course may provide them with more financial and educational (and perhaps psychological and practical survival) resources to live as well as possible within an increasingly broken world. It is not necessarily obvious why the former approach demonstrates superior love for them.

When faced with this type of reasoning, we need hardheadedly to explain why making space for collective action is in the final analysis more loving (not to mention much fairer than) than solely focusing on individual/family 'prepping' for collapse.

One way of doing so is to point out that if your children have basic survival skills but the society around them is collapsing fast, those skills are unlikely to buy them more than a few days. Another is to point out the psychological and ethical awfulness, or even intolerability, of surviving or seeking to do so through privilege while others are falling by the wayside.

More fundamentally, focusing solely on individual prepping rests on an impoverished notion of what our children's interests are. Unless we can stave off the worst of climate breakdown, then their lives will be irrevocably blighted in such a way that impedes their ability to live fully flourishing lives. *This is true regardless of how many resources we bestow upon them.* To see this, consider recent events such as the unprecedented, deadly 'heat dome' that settled over western North America in summer 2021, or the German floods that swept away both rich and poor the following week. It is a widespread illusion that only the latter are vulnerable to the festering, permanent climate emergency.

Rich countries are not immune to what will be a rising tide of unprecedented disasters. And if that tide rises high enough, then even great wealth will not shield the descendants of the rich from it. *The only way we get to actually protect our children now is collectively.* We get through this together or not at all.

I am not suggesting that we don't 'prep', or that you don't teach your children to do so. I think trying to prep is a good thing that we should all do. However, in my experience, one of its key benefits is that it brings home the reality of how thoroughly hopeless an endeavour it is to seek to prep at an individual or family-only level.

Protecting our children collectively

Of course, one may still hold out some hope that investing significant resources into individually shielding one's children may still alleviate some of their suffering. And to a certain or superficial extent this is true. But as I've already started to bring out, it overlooks the extent to which a world blighted by terminal climate breakdown is one where our children's interests simply cannot be protected. This becomes clear when we turn to consider what exactly the contents of their interests are likely to contain.

When considering what it means to love our children, we need to take a sufficiently wide lens to understand what that love entails. Surely, it's self-evident that a large part of love means caring for the interests and well-being of those that we love,[15] for it is not simply the survival of our children that matters to us, but (more importantly) their *flourishing*. Few would be content to sit with the knowledge that their actions contributed to an environment whereby their children were able to survive but missed out on all or most of what makes living worthwhile. There is no point in providing our children with the resources necessary for survival but depriving them of the resources needed to flourish. If we fail to collectively act on climate breakdown, however, we are condemning our children to just such a fate.

I began this chapter by observing that few things are worse for humans than being unable to actualize the care and love that are so fundamental to our character and our most meaningful connections with each other. This is such an evident harm that it is recognized by all plausible definitions of flourishing, happiness or well-being.[16] From this it follows that if our children are unable to look after their own children, then this constitutes a harm to them. This may well be considered a decent definition of the failure of the idea that was in the minds of those who first envisaged the concept of 'sustainability'. If we fail to take meaningful collective action on climate breakdown, then our children will find themselves unable to provide for their children, and *they* in turn for *their* children, and so on, into a declining future. Loving our children means that this devoted care necessarily must iterate down the generations. The only non-reckless attitude to have toward the future of the human race is thus to care for it profoundly: because over time your descendants will, for all you know, be spread anywhere or everywhere in the world. What's more, there will, over time, if we don't f**k things up too badly, cumulatively be many more of them than there are of us. They will sum up to much more than the present-time of humanity. That too deserves not inconsiderable weight.

This is why it is inadequate to simply respond to impending climate breakdown by preparing your children for living with a more hostile ecology. Because at some point, probably within a couple of generations at most, including in rich countries, that ecology is going to move from hostile to almost unbearable. And at that point, no amount of wealth or education will be able to insulate our future kin from climate chaos. The only way to protect our future relatives, our children's own 'interests' in them, and ultimately our own 'interests' in protecting our children's interests, is to avert climate nemesis. And that cannot be done by individual action or preparations alone. It must be primarily a collective effort. Therefore, investing time and money – investing *your life* – into supporting collective action is what is required by loving your children. (We'll return later in this book to look at what forms – and there are many – such action might take).

Objections

In this chapter I have tried to show that, starting from even the most uncontestable of premises, our genuine love for our children, we can derive a reason to act strongly against climate breakdown. However, I want to turn briefly to examining a few objections to my argument.

First, a reader would be right to point out the obvious truth that not everyone has children.[17] Consequently, the argument that I have been making seems not to universally apply. This is a prima facie valid concern. Throughout this chapter I have been using the word 'children' in both a literal and metaphorical sense. 'Children' is clearly not limited to biology, as the love of adoptive parents for their children shows. It also need not be limited to the nuclear family model. Quite often the love of godparents, uncles (as I myself am) and aunts, and even close family friends, for the children of others is comparably strong to that of parents. Really all that is required to motivate my argument is love for someone in the next generation (or indeed, love for someone in your generation who has love for someone in the next generation). I use the framing of our love for our children simply because it is more evocative and directly relevant for most people. Nevertheless, the argument I am making is not confined to the parent–child relationship and this *stands in* for the other relationships I have discussed.

Second, readers may be concerned that some parents simply do not love their children in the way that most people profess to do so. Clearly, this is true of a very small minority of people who openly admit not giving a damn about their kin. It may be true of a slightly larger group of people who do profess to genuinely love their children, but perhaps their love is somewhat shallow. These people may over-inflate their description of their love simply to avoid the disdain that accompanies admitting that one has only a passing concern for one's own children. For this group, it may be fair to say that my argument holds less force. If these people lack genuine love for anyone in the next generation, or anyone with love for the next generation, then they may be unmoved by my argument. Nevertheless, I believe that such people are fairly few and far between, and will be unlikely to be proud of themselves, a telling point. Observing people's interactions with those that they profess to love serves as experiential evidence for believing that their love by and large is deep and genuine. Rather, the biggest problem for most people is (not) making the conceptual connection between their love and the need for action on climate breakdown. It is that gap that I am (let's hope) remedying.

Third, one could question my claim that a large part of love concerns protecting the interests of the beloved. Alternative definitions of love might ground love purely in our feelings rather than any expressions of care or obligation. However, such definitions do significant violence to our intuitions, not to mention (in their implications) for our planetary home and its inhabitants. I have not put forward a definition of love in this chapter. Rather, I claim that any plausible view of love will self-evidently involve concern with protecting loved ones' interests and flourishing. I take this to be, on reflection, non-controversial. Merely egoistic 'love' is not love; neither is love simply a feeling devoid of implications for action. Love is something you *do* (Solomon 2006). And doing it correctly means care for the beloved's interests and flourishing.

Finally, it might be thought that my idea – that one's love for our children iterates down the generations – won't work, because you can't love, value or care about something (someone) that doesn't exist yet. That this view is mistaken is already shown by the care for unborn future generations that we personalize by way of caring for the unborn as soon as they are in the womb, and that is expressed by our outrage against industries that recklessly and care-less-ly poison pregnant women and the life that grows within them (Westra 2006). Parents, perhaps especially mothers, have a (literally!) umbilical relation to their emerging children, who they do not know at all, yet. For, especially in the early stages, there is little to know. The more helpless the being, the more utterly it depends upon us and our proactive care, the more the need for unconditional love. Future generations are in this position of absolute dependence upon us to an even greater extent. That we don't know yet who they will be, that their very identity (indeed, their very existence) will depend upon the choices we make, only underscores the point.

Even if one doesn't buy this argument, it still stands that the love for our own children requires the protection of their flourishing and interests. This alone means protecting and preserving their future children, even if we cannot love them in quite the same way. Thus we might put things this way: I've set out in this chapter how we do, can and must care for our descendants, *whoever exactly they will turn out to be.*[18]

An obstacle to 'enoughism': human health as, paradoxically, a 'limit' to limits to growth[19]

I take this chapter to have outlined an ineluctable logic. I am seeking to spread awareness of this logic of love; I invite you to do the same, as well as to feel it for yourself and follow through on the implications.[20]

But we need to be honest enough to recognize that the very forcibleness of those implications will invite pushback. I explore in this section one way in which such pushback is likely to occur.[21] This will demonstrate the challenging nature of the task before us, and thus the need for the journey deep into our shared heart of darkness that we'll take together in the rest of this book. I believe this journey will result in an expanded, stronger, more connected heart – but it won't be easy.

Healthcare costs seem to rise continually around the world, both as a percentage of GDP and in absolute terms. In many cases, this is partly because of privatization, which makes healthcare more expensive to provide. That could be reversed. In virtually all cases, it is partly also however because many of the drivers of ill health are being exacerbated: forms of pollution, unhealthy diets, inequality that leads to worsening mental (and physical) health, isolation, insecurity, a destruction of community resulting in (and indeed constituting) a loss of meaning as well as a loss of informal and familial support networks and safety nets, and so forth (Wilkinson & Pickett 2010 & 2017). A healthy society organized for the common good, and living within ecological limits, would reduce or eliminate these causes of poor health and spiralling attendant costs. But would such a society be able to *eliminate* rising healthcare costs completely?

I will now give one reason for thinking it might well not. If it does not, then this constitutes a major obstacle to the prospects for a needful philosophy of 'enoughism', the kind of necessary alternative to hegemonic ideologies of liberal individualism, of no limits, that are (as sketched already in the Introduction above) destroying our prospects for long-term existence on this planet, or at least our prospects for long-term civilization.

The reason is essentially this: while it can perhaps be imagined that we come to curb our desire for unnecessary fripperies, for consumer trinkets, for endless novelty, it is harder to imagine that we may be able successfully to curb our desire for improved/good health. It can perhaps be imagined that we put corporations and new technologies on a leash, and forbid them from exceeding ecological limits; it is harder to imagine that such a leash could prevent us from continuing to push for new technologies and treatments that could enable us to live longer and healthier lives.

Perhaps we can win through to a new awareness that in the affluent world (and among more and more, at least in absolute numbers, in the Majority World) we have more than enough – of material things. But can we ever have enough of good healthcare?

Imagine a 'steady-state' economy: a society that looks to develop itself only qualitatively, not quantitatively, and that is determined to inhabit the 'safe operating space' for humankind (Attenborough & Rockström 2021; Raworth 2018). Such qualitative improvement surely includes living healthier lives. Doing so can reduce demands on healthcare. Perhaps this might compensate for the additional expenditure incurred from making feasible the improved health (e.g. expenditure incurred on working for ever more effective personal treatments). But if we imagine this not leading to longer lives, and to an expectation of ever longer lives, we have ultimately to imagine some kind of sense of *enough life*. This might involve something like a maximum desirable lifespan (with liberal availability of voluntary euthanasia). This is difficult to imagine. Not impossible, but a demanding requirement; it pulls against the fantasy of immortality that lies behind the seemingly growing appeal of 'transhumanism' (and of cryogenesis, etc). To live in a steady state, we might need to limit our lifespans. For we need to be willing to let go of the endless effort to prolong life (often, at the end, life of very low quality) if we are serious about accepting a limit to our resources, which is what a steady state implies.

Even imagining this would not be enough. For if the percentage of our spending devoted to improving our health increases permanently (if people continue to demand more and more effective and resource-intensive treatment of remaining ailments, for the sake of quality of their lives), eventually it drives down to unsustainable levels the percentage of our spending devoted to . . . everything else.

So even with something like a sense of a maximum lifespan, a willingness to see life that has not been even marginally prolonged as enough (already a very demanding requirement), eventually we have to say 'enough' to the demand for improved health, too.

In other words, at some point we have to say to some ill people: we cannot justify treating you as much as you may wish.[22] This is very challenging to imagine, particularly given the innate human urge to survive. It will require a real devotion to (and obedience to) the community, to future generations, to our non-human kin, etc. For it is ultimately for their sake that we would be saying this.

Some of what we will have to say to ill/old people won't be so hard: a lot of the medical expenditure currently devoted to keeping people alive at the end of their life would be better not spent at all, from everyone's point of view. Voluntary euthanasia/dignity in dying will ease the problem.

But some level of problem will remain: there will be potentially endless further treatments to reduce morbidity. And potentially endless further research to reverse life-threatening diseases, from COVID-19 to cancer.

The dilemma can be put starkly and generalized in the following fashion: the desire for diminished morbidity (and/or for delaying mortality) is a driver for permanent economic expansion, and/or for permanent technological improvement. Ultimately, this is surely closer to an 'and' than an 'or', for it is likely to be possible or at least imaginable, permanently, that – with additional economic resources (with additional materials, energy, work, etc.) – we can go on endlessly improving our individual health, if only to a marginal extent. If we are ever to live within ecological limits, then we have either to lose or to restrain that desire. This, once again, is very challenging. A serious obstacle to our achieving the sense of 'enough' that I am suggesting is needed if we are to do . . . enough to ensure as best we can the potential well-being of our descendants and of unborn future generations. Ultimately, I would suggest, this is likely to be a harder obstacle to overcome even than our consumerism, our desire for 'choice'.

The point I have been making here is of course related to a slightly more familiar (and very important) point: that the desire for immortality is, in the final analysis, incompatible with love/care for one's children/for future generations. For a world populated by immortal or would-be immortal humans is a world that will not devote sufficient care for (or will literally not have room for!) one's (and others') descendants.

The desire for health is much harder to argue against or even for the restraint of than desires for (say) exotic holidays and fast fashion. It raises the question of whether the search for an ecologically viable future is constrained by the human 'need' to be ever healthier?

I think that what I examined here is a worry that such a constraint does exist. I think that there is a serious obstacle to shared sanity here: a society cannot in the end be judged sane if it is not able to fulfil its first virtue, of providing for, rather than undermining, those who come after it. But thankfully I think the obstacle can potentially be overcome. Perhaps human beings set themselves only such problems as they (we) can solve. Even if some of those problems are wickedly difficult . . .

To overcome this deep problem requires the spirit of community, of post-individualism, and of enough time, that we need *anyway*, if we are to survive (let alone flourish), in the age of incipient climate breakdown. (I use the word 'spirit' not unadvisedly. It might be that a spiritual or religious dimension is an unavoidable part of the mix here, if we are to get past the obstacle discussed in this section[23]).

We do indeed need to foster a sense that quantitative extension of life, and even *qualitative* extension of health, is not an unalloyed good. If I improve my health very marginally, at the cost of significantly diminishing the prospects of my descendants, is that really a good trade?

There comes a point where further technological 'progress' is no longer real progress (Read 2016a). Eventually, in an ecologically sane society, we will understand the need to limit our own hunger for ever longer and healthier lives. And this means that technological improvement in such a society *may even eventually come to an end altogether*. We will need to voluntarily self-limit even the most welcome kinds of technological improvement,[24] of which improving human health surely is one. Human ingenuity and creativity may well be endless, and it is not that hard to imagine (say) a society that endlessly continues to create better art, and that endlessly improves at learning from its own history. But medical improvement may eventually come to an end – when it is recognized that it is not truly healthy to demand further increments of individual health, given their cost to other areas of life, to our descendants and the planet. Medical technology that requires more than a certain level of material inputs will not be viable. If the economic pre-conditions for medical improvements (in terms of resource-allocation, technological risks, etc.) push us beyond planetary boundaries (Rockström & Gaffney 2021), they are a trade not worth making.

And indeed it may well eventually come to be found that the level at which those material inputs are durably viable is not some way off distant level. We might indeed even have already exceeded it. Recall that, in a country like the UK, we are living as if we have about three planets, according to extremely limited and conservative ecological footprint assumptions.[25] To get that down to one, and to allow plenty of space for safety and for non-human animals, will require the most enormous adjustments and reductions.[26] Are we confident that the long-term viable steady state will involve us spending as much as we currently do on medicine? Or even as much as would be necessary if we were to reduce obesity, mental ill health, and other maladies at source? Are we confident that even our current level of medical technology, with its dependence upon radiation and significant amounts of cheap steel, plastic and energy, will be able to be maintained in a lasting, viable economic/ ecologic structure?

It will be a long time, I'm sure, until human ingenuity is exhausted in terms of improving our health within a fixed 'resource' base. However, ecological limits require that our ingenuity be largely devoted to finding low-consumption 'work-arounds' to try to maintain the level of healthcare provision we already have, rather than to discover endless 'new frontiers' of medical technology.

So, the demands of a future in which we and our descendants will have enough are, as I have said, clearly challenging. I have outlined briefly how they can be met. But actually meeting them will require daunting adjustments in our expectations, our structures, our values, perhaps some of our 'freedoms'.

It may turn out that ending consumerism is comparatively 'easy', when set alongside the daunting and tragic task of developing a culture of 'enough' *vis-à-vis* human health.

Looking forward …

I take this first chapter to have shown that if we love and protect our kids, we must make it feasible for them to love and protect theirs. The great chain of love must remain unbroken.

But will it? The previous section put a potential spanner in the works. The obstacle to 'enoughism' that I have just described is a key example of how we may be tempted to violate that logic. And so not care enough about the future of humanity. Not even perhaps if we see that future through the eye of our own familial heritage, as so many humans do.

This is in part why Chapters 2 and 3 are needed: to turn a clear-eyed spotlight on our inaction on climate and ecology. They showcase uncompromisingly that the realities of climate and ecological breakdown, and the realities of our inaction to date, put us firmly on a trajectory towards societal collapse. This is now the most likely path.

Chapters 4, 5, 6 and 7 think through impending collapse and consider our new possibilities for community, authenticity and connection. I argue that despite the horror of our predicament, climate breakdown gives us the opportunity to be more authentic and real and alive than we ever have been before. Whether or not that enables us to actually succeed in averting collapse.

This book seeks for wisdom about the unpresent, the as-yet non-existent. Yet it embodies an ultra-practical philosophy, put to a purpose of gentle yet firm persuasion: to persuade you about what your love for your kids actually *means*. To persuade you then to help persuade everyone else to change the system, to transform our society so as to stop climate breakdown. To date, philosophers have intended mostly only to *interpret* the world. This philosopher is determined to change it. And right now, that change starts with *you*.

Are you willing to accept this invitation?

2

Is Climate Breakdown a *White* Swan?

At the advent of danger there are always two voices that speak with equal force in the human heart: one very reasonably invites a man to consider the nature of the peril and the means of escaping it; the other, with a still greater show of reason, argues that it is too depressing and painful to think of the danger since it is not in man's power to foresee everything and avert the general march of events, and it is better therefore to shut one's eyes to the disagreeable until it actually comes, and to think instead of what is pleasant. When a man is alone he generally listens to the first voice; in the company of his fellow-men, to the second.

Leo Tolstoy, *War and Peace* (1904)

The spectre haunting our world

There is a spectre haunting our society, our world, our common future: the spectre of a 'slow' anthropogenically induced climate cataclysm. Why do I call it a 'spectre'? Because it typically doesn't quite seem real to us.

I speak even for myself here. Not infrequently I get an uncanny feeling, when I am writing a book like this, or when I am standing in the dock charged with having broken the law for non-violent direct action on climate. I can't help feeling, 'Is this really happening? Perhaps I am over-reacting, as the denialists claim?' I look out the window, or in my fridge, and (except when occasional novel 'biblical' downpours are occurring) things seem so ... normal. Can we really be off the cliff?

A vague and peculiar air of unreality hangs pervasively over our whole situation. If anthropogenic climate change were as very bad as all that, then surely collectively we'd already really be doing something about it ... right? How can it conceivably be that we are on the verge of committing human civilization to oblivion? Surely it would take a truly unpredictable 'black-swan' event to accomplish that? Surely intelligent governments and elites couldn't be plane stupid enough to knowingly drive us all, including themselves,[1] off the cliff?

We can already take a step toward understanding how all this is conceivable if we build upon the thinking I began in the Introduction to this book: on the very credible threat of mutual annihilation from nuclear weapons. I believe that we have probably been extremely lucky to escape this,[2] and we are by no means out of the woods. It remains not implausible that civilization will be brought to an end through nuclear war this century.[3]

So in at least one way, governments have for several decades already been keeping humanity in a permanent state of near-oblivion. Nukes have been on hair-trigger alert virtually continually for much longer than my lifetime. This existential threat ought to attract more attention than it does; it has faded overly from our attention since 1989. I leave that task to others (Schlegelmilch 2020; Caldicott 2017).

My appointed primary task is to consider the existential threat consequent upon our triggering of dangerous climate change. Let's consider, then, what climate breakdown would need to look like to conveniently explain our collective inertia in tackling it. Well, it would need to be what is sometimes referred to as a 'black swan' event. These are largely unpredictable events of an enormously greater scale than similar events of their type. I say they are 'largely' unpredictable because, while we cannot determine the probability of their occurrence, or numericize the extent of their impact, nevertheless we are often able to roughly predict when there is high exposure to possible black swan events. If we are smart, then such an awareness can influence how we prepare for them and inform us about steps we can take to minimize our exposure to them.

Take, for example, the now tragically topical case of viruses.[4] Most viruses have a relatively limited human impact. The harm is thus to an extent usually manageable because it is broadly predictable on a year-to-year basis. Yet, occasionally a plague of a great magnitude will emerge as a 'black swan' more or less.[5] In cases such as these, the outlier event (the plague) has a far greater impact on human health than the common viruses that we encounter. Indeed, the impact in terms of casualties can be hundreds of times greater than the seasonal flus that we regularly experience. As was the case with the 'Spanish flu' or 'Great Influenza', which infected over a quarter of the world's population exactly a century ago, and killed far more than died in the entire First World War. The knock-on effects of a pandemic can be even larger, perhaps far larger, than the direct casualties, if, for instance, the health service of the afflicted country is overwhelmed (or even collapses). This is pretty much what happened for a short while in northern Italy in early 2020 in the coronavirus pandemic, and something similar happened in parts of India in 2021.

Of course, we can predict that plagues will sometimes occur, given only certain basic parameters of there existing significant concentrated human populations, which are in inevitable interaction with other animals, and so forth. However, we cannot pinpoint with any precision when, where and to what extent they will affect us. We are highly limited in our ability to assign probabilities to them and to adjust our preparation in accordance to those probabilities. Viruses are a good illustration of a domain where more or fewer black swans occur.

This means that we need to exercise precaution, and not remain tied only to evidence-based approaches. By the time all the evidence is in, *it will be too late.*

Some readers might be alarmed by the suggestion that an evidence-based approach is not sufficient for dealing with threats to human and ecological health. Are we not for instance constantly pleading with governments to follow the evidence about climate science? Isn't being evidence based a self-evidently good thing?

Indeed, I am not rejecting the idea that there is force in calling for governments to follow the science. And if they were to do so, then that would be a good start. However, calls to simply 'follow the science' can obscure the inherent ambiguity that exists in real world predictions and modelling (Read 2015a; O'Riordan & Read 2017). In such cases, values play a role alongside evidence in determining how we respond to uncertainty. The value of precaution is one that is perilously absent in our society and one that calls to follow the science alone overlooks. So yes, we should be evidence based, but we should apply the complementary value of precaution in guiding our decision-making under conditions of uncertainty.

When we are in 'domains' where black swans may be present, it makes little sense to rely upon previous experience to predict future consequences. In these domains, it is largely unpredictable outlier events that have by far the biggest and most consequential effects. This is especially so when there are novel factors attending them: as for instance, the fact that COVID-19 is the first ever truly global pandemic in the age of rapid globalized travel.[6] The Spanish flu travelled at the speed of steamships. COVID-19 travelled at the speed of jet planes (unless we were willing to take bold precautionary action to stop them travelling). This made it predictably desperately difficult to deal with and unpredictably deadly in the totality and specificity of its spread and effects.

Taking the existence of black swans seriously is an antidote to the scientism of our times that seeks to conceptualize all human impacts on the world as analysable, modellable, predictable and controllable. Instead, thinking about black swans encourages us to pay attention to how unpredictable events can vastly shape the world, and it challenges us to build structures that are more robust to these uncertainties. The hubristic idea that we can intervene in complex global systems without unforeseen consequences is instead replaced by an ethic of precaution. We accept that we are living in a world that we will never fully understand or control.[7]

Much of my work in recent years has concerned the impact of such events that can be 'determinative', wiping out the effects of decades or millennia of normality or 'progress'. For instance, in my work alongside Nassim Taleb, we have argued this case *vis-à-vis* financial crises and genetic modification (Taleb et al. 2015). We have argued the same case with regard to climate (Norman et al. 2015). In these examples, we claim that there are reasons to believe that we are operating in domains where catastrophic black swan events may be present.

Black swans are particularly worrisome in complex interdependent systems such as financial markets, international trade systems, and ecosystems. In these cases, the threat is greatly amplified because harm cannot be localized to a part of the system. When a catastrophic black swan emerges, it threatens to bring down the whole system. We saw this in 2008 with the US subprime mortgage crisis, which reverberated across the whole international economy and led ultimately to a global economic recession. We also saw it in 2020 with the coronavirus crisis (Sinclair & Read 2021).

Nassim Taleb and I use the term 'ruin' in our work to describe determinative system-ending events that can be the most severe consequences of black swans. In cases where the possibility of ruin may be present, we argue that the precautionary principle ought to be applied. This principle judges that in the absence of near-certainty of safety, we ought to avoid interferences that may magnify the occurrence of ruinous black swan events. In short, better safe than sorry.

The ultimate example of a ruin-risk is widespread ecological collapse. As such, we ought to be particularly cautious with any interference with global ecology. And yet this is precisely what we are doing on a gigantic scale. We are interfering in multiple dangerous ways (Attenborough & Rockström 2021; Rockström & Gaffney 2021), and in particular with the delicate membrane that surrounds us, our very atmosphere. This thin shell protects us from space (and from the dangerous radiations that soak space) and co-constitutes our climate.

This is how applied philosophy can add a vital tool to the arsenal provided us all by climate science. As well as scientific evidence, precautionary thinking can position us where we need to be in relation to global threats such as climate breakdown: out in front. Ahead of the threat, ahead of the data. In a space of ethics and care. Fore-care.

From this perspective, we can see that even if we didn't have overwhelming evidence of risk of climate ruin from scientific modelling, our current behaviour would still be monumentally unwise (Norman et al. 2015).

Precautionary thinking is crucial if we are to avoid ruin. Technological innovation increasingly subjects us to such risk by enabling us to interfere at scale more effectively with the global ecology. The precautionary principle can help us curb the worst excesses of our 'Promethian' instinct to act as if we could predict all consequences.[8] At a time when new technologies are unwisely being developed faster than ethics, implementing the precautionary principle can inoculate us to many black swan risks.

Climate science is to geo-engineering as genetics is to GM food

Some will still doubt what I have just said. They will want to lean more heavily on the credentials of science. They will try to insist that scientific evidence and modelling alone should be enough.

Why will they do this? The main answer, as I pointed out in the Introduction, is: because of scientism. Because, that is, of the ideology of science-worship that is widespread in our civilization (and that, in its excesses, leads to its even worse reactive polar opposite, science-hatred).

So we need to take a moment to further consider such thinking, now in specific connection with the availability of a precautionary alternative to it. I will do so via a brace of linked examples that are salient: Genetically Modified Organisms (GMOs) and (even more directly on topic for this book) climate engineering.

Advocates of GM lean heavily on the claim that GM is science. But this is itself a highly dubious assumption. GM is essentially a technology; it is more like engineering than pure science. And, of course, this is actually tacitly (well, in fact, explicitly) acknowledged in the very concept/framing of 'genetic engineering'.

Now, I have of course nothing against engineering per se; on the contrary. But whether a form of engineering/technology should be adopted or not ought always to be prima facie an open question. A question to be settled through public debate and wide-ranging interdisciplinary and political discussion, not through mere appeal to the alleged epistemic authority of geneticists.

There is nothing remotely anti-scientific about questioning GM technology. Nor does such questioning in any way spill over into questioning genuine sciences. For example, I do not for a moment question climate-science's scientific status. Sciences are sciences, and forms of engineering are forms of engineering/technologies. The effort of some genetic engineers to inherit the mantle of authority restricted to science is a rhetorical trick that needs exposing.

'Genetic engineering is to genetics as climate engineering is to climate-science'. *That* is the requisite parallel. Now: do GM-apologists think it 'anti-scientific' to question climate engineering/geo-engineering? That would be a crazy stance to take up; that is to say, it would be crazy to think that questioning whether we ought (for instance) to put mirrors in space to reflect the sun's rays back so as to 'counter-balance' GHG-driven over-heating is 'unscientific'.

They ought to draw the requisite conclusion: that it would be crazy to think that *only* genetic engineers are legitimately allowed to raise questions about and arguments against GMOs. The conclusion is clear: there is absolutely nothing 'anti-scientific' in the raising of such questions about GM food, any more than there is in the raising of parallel questions about geo-engineering.

Tacitly, some GM-apologists think that actually there ought to be a default assumption not just in favour of (genuine) science but also in favour of the adoption of any new technology. This is a presumption that I find hubristic and dangerous. This default assumption has been exposed by Heidegger in 'The question concerning technology' (1954). Our society operates on the basis of a problematic default assumption in favour of (technological) 'progress' (Read 2016a).

Overcoming this myth of progress involves overcoming the extreme Prometheanism and the lack of precaution endemic to our current technocracy. We are held captive by a myth of progress, so long as we do not step outside the assumption that there ought to be a default assumption in favour of the adoption of (for instance) new forms of engineering.

In terms of genetic engineering, I have a concern that it operates in a manner very different from nature. This is different in consequential ways even from how selective breeding operates (Taleb et al. 2016). Selective breeding is 'artificial selection': the contrast-class against which Darwin defined 'natural selection'. Genetic engineering by contrast involves neither natural selection nor a human tweaking thereof; it involves a top-down imposed manipulation of genetic material that is then imparted/imported on a large scale into the environment.

It is crucial not to be misled by popular images of science into thinking that even genetics, considered as a science, is a fully stable body of knowledge. A science which, like any other genuine science (as opposed to certain forms of engineering and certain contexts; and also of course as opposed to pseudo-sciences), I am of course fully behind and do not question. On the contrary, as Thomas Kuhn explains, a science (such as optics, for example) that stabilizes into a fully stable body of knowledge becomes engineering (Sharrock & Read 2002, Part I). It becomes something which no longer has a research frontier, but 'merely' involves questions of applicability. Any genuine science has a research frontier, and that means, by definition, that no scientist can know where their discipline is going next. It means for instance, and contra the idiocies of 'climate scepticism', it is inevitable that there will be questions the answers to which are uncertain in (say) climate science. If that weren't the case, it wouldn't be science.

Moreover, no scientist can be entirely confident that their discipline will not soon experience a 'scientific revolution' which will overturn the received wisdom. This means that, in any actual science, there cannot ever be full confidence even in fundamental/paradigmatic results. So, even if genetic engineering were a science, this would hardly help in establishing its alleged certainty against external doubters. For, at its research frontiers, there is by definition no such certainty. And again, the research frontier might at any moment circle back to include fundamental exemplary assumptions in the discipline: what we don't know is always liable to trump what we know. So in any case, even if the GM apologists could succeed in redefining genetic engineering as itself a genuine science, this would not help them in achieving their aim: an allegedly justified complacency in their own knowledge concerning their subject-matter, immune to potential criticism or political questioning.

There are already calls for increasing investment in GM (for example, to breed more drought-resistant plants) as an allegedly sensible and harmless way of adapting to our climate-damaged world. There will be similar increasing calls for climate engineering, as climate breakdown escalates this decade. What I have explained in this section is therefore of some importance. It underscores why precautionary thinking is needed in relation to GMOs and 'climate engineering'. Especially given that the latter is, obviously, worse off even than genetic engineering. In that it has never been tried (thankfully); and it is even more hubristic. The very idea of being able to 'engineer' the climate of the whole planet is in fact about the most extreme hubris that humanity has ever indulged in.

In an emergency, nothing can be ruled out ahead of being discussed. But just because we have been reckless so far, there is no reason to be even more reckless now.[9]

Does 'climate-attribution science' remove the need for the precautionary principle?

Let's assume you accept the relevance of the precautionary principle hereabouts; such that climate engineering doesn't look like a great option if there is a reasonably safe alternative (and of course there is: by tackling the problem at source through rapid reduction of greenhouse gas emissions). But don't we know enough, by way of climate science, not to need the precautionary principle? After all, there is a cast-iron case for attributing growing climate chaos to human action, and thus for undergirding the obvious way to stop escalating that chaos by reducing emissions to zero.

A potential affirmative answer to that question has been provided in recent years by the exciting emergence of climate-attribution science, or 'extreme event attribution' (Carbon Brief 2021). This has emerged as a natural response to scepticism around how solidly we can pin the blame for (say) the German flooding of July 2020 onto human-caused climate decline. Climate-attribution science makes it no longer possible to claim that such events are perhaps natural variations.

A cheer for climate-attribution science, then. But not three cheers. Because the danger is that this new development keeps us playing the same game that has been played for many years now – on the terms favoured by climate-delayers, those who are trying to slow down serious action to save our souls/ civilization. A primary emphasis on climate-attribution science means we are always playing catch-up, looking back at disasters that have happened, always trying to prove that something was human-caused, rather than moving onto the front foot: moving pre-emptively to head off potential danger before it manifests. Emphasis on the precautionary principle works by analogy with 'doping' in sport: you don't try to prove on an individual basis that every one of Lance Armstrong's victories was caused by his use of illegal drugs, you simply accept that the drugs gave him an unfair advantage. And you move proactively to stop the use of such drugs across the board. Similarly, if you look at our atmosphere now . . . well, this is our atmosphere on drugs.

Our times are no longer normal, so it's no longer a time for normal science. It's a time for what is called post-normal science; science which aims pro-actively to protect humanity, not science that aims to cover its own behind, as scientists are doing when they say always only what they can definitively prove. The precautionary principle should be our guide, practising proactive precaution for the common good, not selfish 'precaution' against one's saying anything that might be proved wrong![10] The precautionary principle is the only way we can move ahead of the danger, taking the risk of the occasional false positive along the way but raising the alarm swiftly and strongly enough.

And so climate-attribution science should be reserved only for refuting those wayward souls who are so stuck in their ways that they are still saying things like 'Maybe it's all just natural variation'.

Human-triggered climate breakdown is a white swan

Thinking precautionarily about black swans – about the untold potential downsides of interventions in complex systems which can have 'epidemic' knock-on consequences, as is the case for genetic engineering and for geoengineering – is wise. It is also the best way to do a successful 'end run' around the tedious obstructionism of climate denialists (and delayers). The precautionary principle shows that one does not need to prove with certainty or even beyond reasonable doubt that human action is causing dangerous climate change in order to have a watertight case for radical action to rein in climate destabilization. Because the worst-case scenarios presented by climate breakdown are ruinous, we have reason to pre-emptively act to minimize the chance of their occurrence. This is true even if we have doubts about the science predicting ecological collapse.

However, my argument in the previous sections notwithstanding, there's also a basic way in which the case of climate is very different from that of finance, or of GMOs (or of 'the singularity', and so on). For it has been shown beyond reasonable doubt that anything remotely like a business-as-usual path puts us on course for climate nemesis. There is a plethora of ways in which anthropogenically induced over-heating of the planet promises to devastate human civilization. The basic science is settled; the prognosis for the planetary 'patient' is clear, without a rapid course-change.

Ever-worsening anthropogenic climate breakdown is not a potential 'black swan' event. It's a *white* swan, an *expected* event. It is, quite simply, completely what anyone with a basic understanding of the situation should now expect. It is what our scientists have been telling us for decades. And it is what is unfolding before our very eyes today on a global scale.[11]

It is beyond reasonable doubt that we are driving ourselves towards what is almost certainly a cliff edge. Yet it may be one with a fatally larger drop below it even than our best current science suggests.

Catastrophic climate change is a white *swan*. (And even the odd grey or black feather only underscores how badly we are exposed to it. To catastrophe. For we don't know how bad the downsides of climate-related unknowns may be).

Climate denial: Our common failure?

This question raises many significant questions.

Are we, as Aristotle claimed, rational animals?

Possibly not, given that virtually all of us, and not just a fringe minority who the rest of us love to hate, are – in practice, most of the time – in some form of dangerous climate change denial.[12] Yet this is a 'softer' climate change denial. One that expresses itself every time that we allow ourselves to speak of the future as if it won't be blighted by climate nemesis. A 'soft' denial that clouds our imaginative prowess to stop us from raising the deep political, social, economic and ultimately philosophical questions that impending climate nemesis should be provoking.

How, then, can we be woken up?[13]

The uncomfortable truth about seeing dangerous anthropogenic climate change as a white swan is that it means we almost certainly actually have much more in common with the increasingly small minority of outright climate-denialists than we like to think. The sad fact is that most years, global carbon emissions are increasing (Woods 2019). Even now.[14]

But yet, perhaps there are still grounds for hope in the very fact that we who take ourselves to be genuinely determined to see reality have more in common with climate-denialists than we tend to suppose.[15] Perhaps by recognizing our (to some extent) common failure to acknowledge the 'white swan' proceeding smoothly toward us, we might come together to confess our joint failings, and then at last be in this together?

True, perhaps full-on climate-criminals such as certain international oil and gas companies are beyond the pale; but perhaps the vast majority of us at least can seek to share our common fears (and failings, to date), and then start to rise to the occasion?

Facing up to climate reality collectively

Over the past several years, I have been making a habit of periodically asking people directly what they think the future will be like. I find most are somewhere between fairly and incredibly scared about it, so much so that they are overwhelmingly 'primed' to go into 'denial'.

What if we joined together, and admitted this publicly? In fact, isn't one of the reasons why Extinction Rebellion shot to prominence in 2018 precisely because it allowed people the space to do that? To feel the fear together – and then to do something meaningful about it.

Millions upon millions of us are (mostly) quietly desperate about the future and mostly feeling fairly lonely in this desperation (Bendell 2021). But what if we were all actually to risk talking to one another about it? What if we were then to find that we have more in common with each other than we'd realized? In particular in our terror, and the desire to do something with it rather than just suffer it. I think one of the things that we have to do now is to find more and more spaces where people can voice their suppressed anxiety about what we are doing to our planetary home, and thus to ourselves. This can be the first step, perhaps, toward a new shared sanity.[16] Returning to this chapter's epigraph, can we yet prove wrong the final sentence of this wonderful remark of Tolstoy's? Can we change up such that when we are (most truly) *us*, we will dare to wake up to the nature of our peril and the means of escaping it?

We need to ponder. We need to reflect on the extraordinary fact that the most likely future for humanity strongly appears to be not a steady progress – nor an unexpected destruction – but a steady, *expected* self-destruction.

The incipient climate breakdown threatening our world is a white swan. It would be the ultimate marker of sheer stupidity, as well as of shame and short-termist selfishness, if humanity succumbs to it. We ought to have the foresight not to.

Returning finally then once more to the case of COVID-19. The timescales with COVID-19 were weeks and months. In relation to climate, they are years and decades. This means that we are less urgently prompted to change; *but also* that we have more time in which to do so, more time to get things right. (In the end then, once one knows, there really is no excuse therefore for not doing so, save for laziness, procrastination or simply not caring).

Tragically, much of that time has already gone. Just thinking about this with honesty, I feel a deep sadness arising. I must tell you: societal collapse because of climatic and ecosystemic collapse is so close now to being probably inevitable that it's heartbreaking. Terrible to force oneself to contemplate, especially when one contemplates what it will mean for our children (let alone their children, if any).

But if you are reading this, then you are signed up to being willing at least to start to contemplate it and what it means.

As I started this chapter by acknowledging, this spectre is hard to contemplate. Both in that it is a horrible thing to have to face. And in that it is hard to make real, unspectral, to oneself. Can it really be that we will drive our kids over this cliff? To someone sitting in a state like the United Kingdom right now, it jars with everyday reality. As I write, the birds are singing, the sun is coming out, my larder is still pretty full; is this last fact really at serious risk of changing? It feels as if it can't be believed.[17]

Climate breakdown is a white swan, and the fact that somehow we still mostly don't see it as such is a key part of the reason why the situation is so desperate. We will examine in the next chapter whether or not societal breakdown – eco-driven civilizational collapse – is a white swan too, as a consequence.

3

Is This Civilization Finished?[1]

There is nothing more difficult to carry out, nor more doubtful of success, nor more dangerous to handle, than to initiate a new order of things. For the reformer has enemies in all those who profit by the old order, and only lukewarm defenders in all those who would profit by the new order, this lukewarmness arising ... from the incredulity of mankind, who do not truly believe in anything new until they have had actual experience of it.

Machiavelli, *The Prince and the Discourses* (1950)

The elephants in the room, charging towards us

In the previous chapter, we saw that climate breakdown is not a 'black swan'. It's not something uncertain or unexpected. It is exactly what one should expect, given that we have been pumping the atmosphere full of greenhouse gases and interfering with the biosphere on a global scale. That's why I call it a white swan event. Or, if you want a more 'colourful' image, think of a herd of elephants charging straight towards us. They are in plain view. The trumpeting is loud. It's an emergency of a very different kind to those we are used to: it's an emergency without end. The elephants will keep charging, even if and as we move to reduce the speed of the charge or to get out of the way. The main reason, I suggest, that it doesn't feel like an emergency to most of us most of the time is only that they are charging in slow motion. But this should give us no reassurance whatsoever. Because it will take us years to get out of their way.

And yet: despite the overwhelming evidence that we are hurtling towards ecological collapse, including climate collapse, we have seen little more from our governments than warm words on the national and international stage.

Some within 'the green movement' are keen to highlight that we still have time to turn things around and keep the global climate within relatively minor degrees of warming. Hopefully they might, conceivably, be right. Yet every year that passes brings us closer to / takes us over precipices of systematic ecological breakdown. Worse yet, the time lags built into the global climate system mean that the effects of ecological destruction today are often not felt for years; carbon that is emitted damages our climate (and our oceans) for decades, even centuries, its effects building up over time. This means that we may unknowingly have already passed some tipping points (Singh 2021).[2]

The science in its essentials has been settled for decades. If we had been going to get a grip on this, then we would surely have done so a generation or more ago, at the latest in the 1990s, perhaps following on from the 1992 Rio Earth Summit where the UN Framework Convention on Climate Change was signed. We would have elected governments that prioritized ecology over economy. We would have enacted 'unpopular' policies to preserve our civilization for our descendants; the Conferences of the Parties (the climate and biodiversity 'COPs') would have overseen the implementation of these. Cars, flights and meat consumption would be far less common than they are today, and the signalling of social status through material consumption would be vilified rather than glorified. But absolutely nothing like this has happened. Instead, every other year sets records for both global emissions output and global temperature increase. Business as usual continues,[3] virtually unabated and out of control, morphing into climate nemesis.

There is a stark injustice to this. Those calling loudest for action will bear the brunt of our inaction. This applies drastically to the global South, but it is perhaps most terrible of all when we think about the young worldwide who are mobilizing to fight for climate justice and eco-wisdom. The school strikes for climate are organized and composed almost entirely of young people. Since Greta Thunberg began them in August 2018, students from around the world have walked out of lessons on Fridays to protest inaction on climate breakdown. We are inflicting a grave indignity on our young. Through our inaction, we force them to sacrifice their education to beg for their lives and futures (Thunberg 2019). The fact that they have been reduced to this should deeply shame us all.[4]

Young people have been let down by previous generations of leaders and governments who have failed to initiate emergency green measures. But more tragically, they have often been let down by their parents and teachers, who have failed to raise the alarm over climate breakdown (Read 2017). Almost all of us are culpable to an extent, however. We have allowed the reality of this emergency to be obscured in the popular imagination, sometimes with warm words and misplaced optimism but all too often simply with an eerie silence. Our common discourse around climate and biodiversity loss are woefully impoverished.[5] We seem unable to collectively process it, to grieve it and to be motivated by it. Instead, we raise our children largely in ignorance of the looming threat that stalks their futures. We prefer to shield their eyes rather than fight full-bloodedly for their future.

This obfuscation is partly a psychological coping mechanism. I argued in Chapter 1 of this book that there is nothing worse for human beings than not being able to take adequate care of the next generation, but that is what we have done by not acting sooner. And it is what we continue to do by not acting now. On top of this, we have the audacity to soothe our children's anxieties about their poisoned ecological inheritance with messianic fairy tales of new technologies that 'promise' panaceas.

Our inability to look younger generations in the eye over climate breakdown is telling. But to truly face up to climate reality we must be willing to think through our current trajectory. We must be willing to consider the idea that it is increasingly likely that we may fail to act in time to prevent climate breakdown. And we must be willing to consider what happens next if we do fail. *Do we still have time to save (our) civilization? Can we turn things around, or is this civilization finished?*

To answer these questions, we need to consider the progress made on halting climate breakdown.

The failure of the Paris Agreement

Consider the 2015 Paris Agreement, which was supposed to ignite international action on climate breakdown. It was heralded as being, and indeed is, the best-placed existent international treaty-basis on which to do so. If the Paris goals are achieved, then we are supposed to be able to breathe easy again.

Paris was a remarkable diplomatic and political achievement. It remains hard to expect anything better. Almost every country in the world had to agree; and, incredibly, they did. They even came up with reasonably bold proposals for reining in climate dangerous emissions, at least when compared to what had been done previously.

Paris committed 'developed' countries to *aim* for vast multi-billion-dollar annual spending on emissions reduction for the developing world. The goal is to peak at collectively spending at least $100 billion a year until 2025.[6] Paris also reaffirmed aid commitments for poorer countries to facilitate higher environmental standards while 'developing'. It aimed to keep global overheating at no more than 2°C above pre-industrial times; and calls upon countries to make ambitious emissions reductions strategies.

But despite all this, the reality of the extraordinary achievement that was Paris is that it does not even give us a good chance at averting climate breakdown. The extent to which Paris falls short is stunning.[7] But the fact that we could not reasonably expect anything better should concern us, if anything, even more. It is testament to the way in which climate has been consigned to just one issue among many. We have sought to fit action on climate around our other policy priorities.

At time of writing, soon after the Glasgow COP summit, the Paris Agreement is seven years old. Since then things have of course deteriorated. True, they might well have become even worse, without Paris. But the niggling worry is that Paris' very existence may have lulled us into a false sense of security, that 'they' (always someone else, usually those 'in charge') are doing something. So it's OK ...

It's not OK. The world's weather systems continue to spin out of control (McKie 2019). The increasing intensity of Australia's annual bushfires is a stark example of this. Every year now leads to the devastation of vast swathes of Australia's fragile ecology (Ward et al. 2020).

Moreover, there have been new and worrying developments. Evidence has continued to emerge about excess heat stored in the oceans (IPCC 2019). This is a ticking time bomb lurking within the wider global overheating problem. That heat is there for the long haul, poised to raise surface and air temperatures. Even if we somehow stopped emissions tomorrow, it would continue to gradually warm the planet for some considerable time to come. Of course, we are not going to stop emissions tomorrow, or anytime soon for that matter. Far, far from it.

Evidence is also emerging about how desperate the situation of life in (and thus oxygen from) the oceans may be becoming (Dryden & Duncan 2021) as a result mainly of ocean acidification and pollution from plastics and chemicals (not to mention over-fishing). The oceans themselves may be enough to sink us.

Things are not much better on land. Consider the vital case of Brazil. Its president, Jair Bolsonaro, has turned a blind eye towards – or worse, effectively condoned or encouraged – the destruction of the world's greatest green lung, the Amazon rainforest (Scott Cato & Read 2019). His stance has encouraged the illegal setting of fires to clear more territory for pasture and the production of crops. At time of writing, in a deeply worrying legal battle, indigenous forest-defenders are in the course of being deprived of their rights to their home territory by a Bolsonaro-influenced Supreme Court (Harris & Da Silva 2021).

Although most of Amazonia lies on Brazilian land, it is of global importance. Bolsonaro claims that attempts to preserve the rainforest by Europeans are neo-colonialist. There is an irony to the fact that he has pursued this policy agenda while claiming that Brazil will remain in the Paris Agreement. This makes a mockery of the agreement and underlines its toothlessness. Never forget that while Paris is an international agreement that therefore has legal status, and thus, wonderfully, it can be used by 'activist' lawyers to challenge and overturn Government decisions,[8] it is at the same time (as inter-governmental agreements go) merely a voluntary agreement that *lacks enforcement mechanisms.*

It gets worse. Consider the 2°C 'realistic' target of Paris. (Never mind 1.5, which is more like what we would really need, but which is utterly eye-watering for the actual world we inhabit. 1.5 was essentially killed by the chronic inaction at Glasgow (Read 2021e)). Most scientists agree that even if all the commitments that are supposed to be made for the treaty to work were acted on, then the actual resulting dangerous climate change may well still raise global temperatures by a lot more than 2°C (UN 2019). In other words, the science on which Paris is based is itself overly conservative, overly optimistic, unsafe and unprecautious (Howard 2016; Knorr 2020). It was a start, but not a start that one could ever realistically have hoped would lead towards a happy ending.

Hasn't this situation been changed or improved, by Glasgow, I hear you ask? Well, very little, at best. A realistic estimate of the hot new world we are headed towards now is probably upwards of 2.7°C (Climate Action Tracker 2021). Tellingly, and in line with my anecdotal experience of what scientists will say off the record, a recent *Nature* survey of IPCC scientists suggested that most actually expect 3°C or more of global overheat (Kahn 2021).

The fact that the IPCC itself has tended if anything to underestimate the likely gravity of the situation all becomes less surprising when you consider that the IPCC is not actually a properly scientific process. It's a scientific process that has built into it a political process. Like Paris itself, it typically achieves only a kind of lowest common denominator (Spratt & Dunlop 2018; Knorr 2020). And it lags behind reality, because each report takes years to assemble. These points form a key reason why the Paris targets themselves probably wouldn't keep us safe from climate cataclysm, *even if they were achieved.*

But it's worse than that – because they *won't* be achieved, barring a miraculous transformation.[9] The actual concrete commitments that countries have made towards those Paris targets are well short of what would be required to meet those targets. Countries voluntarily commit under Paris to say what are they going to do to meet their obligations. Even if you add up all those commitments, then they come to considerably less than what Paris requires to work even on its own terms (let alone in terms of what would actually be needed to limit us to 2°C of over-heat; let alone 1.5°C!).

But it's worse than that; because the commitments that countries have made to reach those targets, are in stark contrast to what virtually every single one of those countries – with, possibly, the exception of Bhutan – are planning to do over the next ten years or so. Almost every country in the world has plans to encourage further economic growth. Plans to encourage the building of infrastructure: agro-industrial infrastructure (including for more intensively reared, climate-damaging meat), transport infrastructure (including for expanded air travel, which cannot be effectively greened), industrial infrastructure (including for high-carbon products such as cement), and energy infrastructure (including for climate-damaging fracking). These decisions have long 'half-lives'. They commit us to ongoing high-carbon pathways at the very time when those pathways need to be radically transformed (Rockström et al. 2017).

Most of those plans stand in stark opposition to the possibility of achieving the Paris commitments. Consider then which side is likely to win. It is a classic dilemma: if you have the business ministry against the environment ministry, or the Chancellor against the climate change minister, which one wins the fight? The answer is sadly often all too obvious.

But things are worse even than *that*. Because probably the worst thing about the IPCC process is that, because of the way it has in effect played down possibilities in which scientists are not highly *confident*, it tends to underestimate the possibility of feedbacks which could spiral the climate system completely out of control, and which may already be kicking in, potentially explaining the emerging disastrous weather chaos of the last few years (Harvey 2018; Knorr 2020). Such feedbacks occur when global temperature increase triggers damage to the biosphere, which in turn further causes temperature increase. They are a serious obstacle to our attempts to stabilize global temperature (Lenton, Rockström & Gaffney 2019; O'Neill et al. 2017). Applying the precautionary principle would lead us to take such feedbacks more seriously.

Among those feedbacks is the loss of 'albedo' reflection, the process by which our planet's ice reflects warming rays back out into space rather than absorbing them. This is under threat due to the loss of surface ice on the planet, most notably in the Arctic. The less ice we have, the less warming light gets reflected out into space, and the more that gets absorbed by the dark oceans. A warming planet, which melts ice, in turn fails to reflect as much warming light back, which in turn leads to more warming, and thus more melting ice … You get the picture. The reduction of albedo reflection is one of the many 'feedback loops' that threaten to lead to severe overheating. There are scientists who suspect that the albedo-loss situation could be a lot worse than the IPCC have taken into account (Pistone, Eisenman & Ramanathan 2019; Knorr 2020).

More scary still perhaps is the situation around methane, which we have reason to believe is starting to be released in significant quantities from melting permafrost, primarily in the Arctic (Phys.org 2018). If methane release starts to accelerate, which might already be happening and may well happen in a big way over the next five to thirty years, then that locks us into catastrophic climate change; possibly runaway climate change, because you then start getting a further vicious circle of more ice being melted, and so more methane being released. Long term, methane is over twenty-two-times more powerful a greenhouse gas than carbon dioxide (Wallace-Wells 2017) (and more in the short to medium term (Vaidyanathan 2015)). If the vast reserves that are stored in the Arctic are released in significant part, then we are in very serious trouble indeed.

We don't know that this is going to happen nor to what extent. And one of the few genuinely positive moments from 2021's Glasgow COP was the welcome announcement of an international agreement to cut methane emissions. But we might already be basically too late here. As noted, some of the feared methane feedback appears to be starting to happen, including in surprising ways (Kindy 2021), and we know that it is a possible existential threat. It would be utterly reckless to allow it potentially to fire up. As we have seen in Chapter 2, the remaining uncertainty in the science only serves as more of a reason for us to act swiftly and decisively to minimize our risk. Precaution demands of us a radical change of direction.[10]

The final thing to know about the Paris Agreement is that in practice it depends on 'climate-engineering' technologies, also known as geoengineering, to achieve its targets (Paul & Read 2019; Anderson 2015), the idea being that you can purportedly engineer the climate of the entire earth to stave off climate breakdown. We discussed this idea at some length in conceptual terms in the previous Chapter; now, we turn to discuss its proposed implementation.

There are only two problems with this proposed dependence on geoengineering. The first is that the technologies do not exist – and I mean that pretty much literally; most of them are simply fantasies that scientists, technologists and engineers have. The ones that do exist have not been tried at scale and we do not know if they will work at scale. The second problem is that even if they did exist, it would in most cases be profoundly reckless to bring them in at scale – an experiment with the entire globe as its subject. The possible and actual side-effects, and the existential risks that come with catastrophic failure, would be unprecedented. Indeed, I argued in Chapter 2 that such interference with the globe's ecology is a prime example of a terminal ruin-risk.

The geoengineering technology that receives the most attention is 'bioenergy with carbon capture and storage' (BECCS for short). This involves growing huge amounts of crops, and then burning them. The carbon from burning is sequestered, and then needs to be kept safe for hundreds (preferably thousands) of years under the surface of the earth.

There is serious reason to doubt whether this can all be done safely and economically at scale. Yet even if this process works, and even if we were able to figure out how to do it at scale, then doing so would devastate the Earth's ecosystems. We would need to destroy rich biodiverse ecosystems to make room for vast monocultures. This is the only way we would be able to produce biomass on the scale needed for BECCS to work, but these ecosystems need restoring rather than replacing. The biodiversity crisis is often overlooked, but it comes with its own unique set of harms.

Geoengineering is built into virtually all the Paris scenarios. We have no reason to believe BECCS works at any useful scale and even if it does work, it probably still shouldn't be used.

Why is the Paris process, the COP process, so dependent on such a shot in the dark? The answer is simple: because the concept of climate engineering provides an excuse for not acting with sufficient speed and seriousness *now*.

It seems to me that the conclusion one is bound to draw from all this is that, to put it in a slightly crude way: Paris is toast. Barring an unheard-of transformation, the aims of Paris will not be achieved; and we have seen proof of that in the way that, on balance, Glasgow, the 'COP' that was meant to make Paris real, has failed us. The Paris aims will almost certainly continue to be missed by a long way (Anderson et al. 2020). That means that unprecedently dangerous climate breakdown is coming and it is going to get a lot worse for a long time to come.

It seems me there's only one possibility for avoiding this awful conclusion. There's only one possibility for how what I've just said could conceivably prove to be wrong. Which is if people came to realize the kind of points that I've been making and just how desperate our situation is. Then we might collectively decide to do something completely unprecedented to change it. But it really would have to be almost completely unprecedented. You get a sense of the scale of what I'm talking about, if you take those words quite literally.

We're talking about turning around the entire supertanker of the world's economy, the entire supertanker of the world's hegemonic civilization, almost on a dime. It's a pretty overwhelming prospect.

And so we come to Glasgow. Does serious reflection on the Glasgow COP encourage us to think that the situation is genuinely less grim than I have been laying out? I was at COP26 for the whole time, and it was a very sobering experience. COP26, the supposed successor to Paris, was a disastrous failure. It did hardly anything – beyond coughing up a bit more money (though still less than had been long promised), and creating a leaky carbon market – except for kicking the can down the road to COP27. At the very time when we needed a dramatic course-correction, we got a damp squib.

As a result, our situation is almost unimaginably bad. And it is made worse by the still fairly widespread unwillingness to recognize that fact. Call this the 'meta-emergency': that the true, desperate nature of the emergency is unrecognized doubles the sense in which we are in emergency.

Until we are willing to face the fact that we are nowhere, and that we can have no confidence in the processes designed allegedly to keep us safe, then we are doubly nowhere. To have any chance of being able to turn things around, we need to come to terms with a painful reality, and admit that it's five past midnight. We have left it so late to do anything, and are still doing hardly anything, that it's too late now to avoid massive pain and destruction.

I hardly have the heart to write these words. We're flying off the cliff in real time. The turning we need to undertake is great indeed; and we show collectively almost no sign as yet of actually even beginning it.

On those who deny planetary boundaries – on the 'Left' as well as the 'Right'[11]

A key part of the essential shift in perspective required if we are to be able to any degree to accomplish this 'great turning' is a recognition that there are ecological limits to economic activity on this finite planet. This more or less common-sensical starting point looks controversial only against the backdrop of a weird hegemonic ideology of constant economic growth as an overarching goal for society, 'growthism', which first entered the wider public consciousness explicitly through the publicity generated by the Club of Rome's seminal book, *Limits to Growth* (Meadows et al. 1972). A few years ago now, an All Party Parliamentary Group that I helped set up in the UK published a follow-up report to the book analysing some of its key claims and predictions – and finding that the authors' general thrust remains true today. The leading economist Tim Jackson has also gone some way towards popularizing these ideas with his influential books, *Prosperity without Growth* (2017) and *Post-growth* (2021). Information and understanding about the conflict between ecological stability and growthist economics is beginning to be disseminated more widely into the public consciousness. Tragically, this is happening much slower than needed for it to become a new hegemony. The desperate extent to which humanity is behind the clock with regard to moving beyond an obsession with growth is one of the key indicators that our chances of finding a path to ecological salvation seem slim to vanishing.

Limits to growth thinking means that we should be deeply cautious about ambiguous concepts such as Green Keynesianism, the Green Industrial Revolution and the oft-discussed Green New Deal, which at their heart typically also demand increasing economic activity. If you look at the renewable sector alone, then green growth appears real. But that of course is not the way we need to look at things; it is an artificial slicing out of a good part of the economy, ignoring the rest. We need to look at the whole economy, in the round. When we do, we typically find that net green growth is an illusion (Blewitt & Cunningham 2014; Read 2015c; Jackson 2017 & 2021).[12] Net 'green' growth sounds great but under the surface is about as convincing as the fantasy of 'clean coal'. It is the rebrand of a failed policy, not a change of policy.

There are, of course, some sections of the economy that *do* need to grow for a while (especially in the global South), and if a Green New Deal can facilitate that, then all power to it. We would be foolish not to make full (though judicious) use of renewable energy technologies like low-impact solar panels, passive solar and wind power to meet our genuine energy needs (Read & Rughani 2020). But while we grow these sections of the economy, we must be just as eager to radically shrink many other sections of the economy. If, as appears tragically likely, the Green New Deal comes to mean simply the pursuit of 'green growth', then it will inevitably fail to ameliorate the climate and ecological emergencies. If, improbably, it comes to mean growth in some sectors with net degrowth over the economy as a whole, then it is a concept that we desperately need. Learning about and popularizing the limits to growth argument will help us shape the implementation of projects such as the Green New Deal to make sure they are (and remain) firmly grounded in ecological wisdom. It will enable us to spot more effectively the political sleight-of-hand that parliamentarians often now use to promise voters the conflicting priorities of strong economic growth *and* a stable environment.

But this is a big, hard ask.

While our political class are keen to position themselves as 'green' by making positive noises about ecological protection, they are also engaged in a race-to-the-bottom competition on who can grow their economy the fastest. Indeed, even many Leftists (including such recent green-tinged luminaries of the Left as Bernie Sanders or Jeremy Corbyn) are bewitched by the ideal of continuous economic growth. They draw on the Keynesian insight that redistribution can stimulate economic activity and facilitate strong economic growth. From this they argue that Left-wing politics can therefore beat capitalism at its own game and grow the economy faster. This leads to the absurd situation of left-wing politicians competing with capitalists over which economic theory is best equipped to grow the economy, while failing to recognize that it is the promise of economic growth that is the capitalist's best excuse for failing to redistribute wealth in the first place (Read 2011b). Because, after all, if the economy can grow endlessly, then capitalists can appeal to ('Rawlsian') liberal-individualist principles and argue that inequality benefits everyone by being the surest route to growing the economy. Without economic growth, those who wish to defend capitalism must rely on other principles – hard indeed to find – to justify the gross wealth and income inequalities that the economic model facilitates. So this is the dirty secret of growthism: it veils the ugly reality of gross economic inequality. It provides an 'excuse' for it.

By accepting the 'growthist' framing of Left vs capitalist politics as partly about who can best meet the growth demand, many would-be green Leftists are shooting themselves in the foot. We have been seeing this Leftist growthist philosophy taken to more extreme limits by those who combine extreme techno-optimism with radical Leftist politics. I recently reviewed a book, *Fully Automated Luxury Communism,* which, while paying lip-service to our plight, in practice largely ignores the ecological emergency while claiming the growth potential of new technologies is what will liberate workers from oppression (Mariqueo-Russell & Read 2019). In my view, this technophilic fantasy fails in any way to challenge the growthist ideology that capitalism uses to justify itself while sowing seeds of catastrophe for our planet.

'Soft' climate denial is therefore patently not a straightforwardly Left vs Right issue. After all, trade unions also have a lot invested in continuing the industrial growth economy. To address the climate and ecological emergencies, we must extricate ourselves from the 'growthist' framing of economic issues. We must cease to perceive these crises as exogenous problems faced by our civilization and instead see them as *integral products of our political economic system.* Yet to truly acknowledge the planetary and social limits to economic activity, and to understand why they have been so wilfully ignored, we must also interrogate the capitalist system that has driven us to the edge of civilization collapse, and call instead for a genuinely just transition. We must tackle the way in which capitalism's insidious ideals and dynamics have blinded us to the ecological reality before our eyes *and* to grave economic inequality.

In the end, this goes deeper even than simply challenging the ideal of an economy premised on infinite economic growth. That dangerous pursuit is simply one of the more egregious examples of a cultural ideology premised on (a bastardised idea of) 'progress'. The need for systematic reorganization of our society and the values that shape it is one of the key strands that tie the chapters in this book together. That is why I explore how some of our values and ideological precepts, particularly those centred around 'growth', 'progress' (Wright 2012), technology and liberal individualism, are driving ecological collapse.

We appear to be so thoroughly caught up in the ideology of 'progress' that even the most intelligent of us don't quite notice that life is getting worse on balance. I stress: on balance. We shouldn't forget that – mainly (frankly) because of the sterling efforts of activists and public-spirited citizens – some things have (of course) got better, and some things continue to get better.[13]

But we should not accept the widespread propaganda (found, for example, in Steven Pinker's well-known work (2018)) that claims that on balance things are getting better in general in the world today. How could they possibly be, when wild nature has been cut in half in just the last forty years, and domesticated animals are suffering terribly in ever vaster numbers the world over? How could they possibly be, when we have constantly to fight off the knowledge that we may well be on the verge of committing our children to an ever-declining world, and indeed continued human existence is in doubt? How could they possibly be, when we are substituting for rich and robust traditional cultures goals of material enrichment that will never be met, and which bring with them escalating deeply harmful inequalities?

Pinker and his fellow travellers (who write similar extensively researched and often compellingly argued books) have two particularly outstanding blind spots: 1) their work is typically about percentages not about absolute numbers (e.g. the percentage of the world's population having no secure access to clean water might have declined, while the *absolute number* of people without such access may well have increased at the same time; this is the same kind of baleful mistake as is involved in jumping for joy over relative decoupling without noticing that absolute decoupling has not been achieved); 2) it was blind luck, unlikely sets of circumstances, that have prevented nuclear devastation in the last sixty years or so: so it is not enough to try to calculate war deaths, in absolute numbers or as percentages of the world's population, when it is just luck that potentially billions were not killed in a nuclear war and nuclear winter did not then potentially destroy the human and many other species (Christopher 2019).

Let us turn explicitly then to considering how the prejudice in favour of a narrative of progress (a prejudice writ particularly large in Pinker, but he is merely a symptom of a hegemonic phenomenon that normally passes without note) plays out in political thinking:

On the Right, venerable traditions of true conservatism (conservation, caution, looking to preserve the past for the future) have almost entirely collapsed in favour of an embrace of neoliberalism, right-wing libertarianism and ethnic nationalism, profoundly destructive schools of thought.

On the 'Left', there is often either a sell-out embrace of the same gods (of neoliberalism and growthism), and/or an endless journey into what I call identity-consumerism, a form of liberal-individualism that now masquerades as the essence of 'progressive' and 'Left' thinking.

The latter is a particularly worrying trend. Consider these famous words, from the founding statement of the Combahee River Collective. This was the first-ever coining of the term 'identity politics'. In it, the seeds of our contemporary disaster of some so-called 'intersectionalist' divisive identity politics are already clear:

> We believe that the most profound and potentially most radical politics come directly out of our own identity, as opposed to working to end somebody else's oppression.

This thought may well have been fine, even perhaps entirely necessary, for that group of black women at that time, who were trying, understandably and rightly, to make feminism more representative. But it is a dangerous idea in terms of the way it can block projects of assembling majorities for socio-political transformation, because its trajectory encourages (endless more specific) division, rather than unity;[14] and it is a cataclysmic idea for animal rights, for environmentalism, and for activism on behalf of future people. The latter movements are by definition concerned with working to end 'somebody else's' oppression.

This danger and this cataclysm are now writ large, in this age of narcissism of ours: in our politics and in the world slipping away from our grasp. One now encounters regularly an obsession, obsessively policed, with being 'obliged' to focus on 'your own' oppression[15] – and being prohibited from discussing/remedying anyone else's oppression.

While we gaze at our navels, most animals that enter into our orbit suffer an eternal genocide, and the living Earth itself and all its countless future humans tremble on the edge of the sixth mass extinction. But still, the insistence escalates: concentrate only on 'your own' identity: do not seek to end anyone else's oppression.

The narcissism of extreme identity politics involves a systematic retreat into the present, and into the self. It motivates statements like 'We don't know what future generations will need, and it is presumptuous to speak for them. Therefore we should focus on the present. We should focus on liberating ourselves'. This kind of sentiment – anthropocentrism as short-termist identity politics – is in my experience now surprisingly and worryingly widespread.

So much for contemporary identity politics.[16] As I already hinted above, we see everywhere, including on the 'Left', a complementary, vast, *pseudo-religious* idolatry of technology, a faith in machines to free us from work and even to send us to new 'space-colonies', or to 'free us' from our bodies altogether. So-called 'post-humanism' is nothing more than humanism combined with techno-fantasy. This pseudo-Promethean human-centredness (aka self-centredness) involves a vast industry of denial, whether that be the 'full-on' climate-denial which still, pathetically, exists and indeed flourishes, or the 'softer' denial of most of our lives and of our professed hopes for 'progress', today. A kind of kinder, gentler stamping of our footprint into the very faces of our descendants[17] ...

Most people, even most of the 'right-on', are stuck deep into ways of thinking, into assumptions and habits, into dependence on technologies and practices, that, madly, commit us to mutually assured destruction. How many 'environmentally minded' citizens are (going to be) willing to give up their cheap flights, even post-corona? How many of the rich will embrace voluntary simplicity (Read, Alexander & Garrett 2018)? How many of the poor will forebear to seek to 'rise up' to join the rich? How many of us are willing truly to throw our lives into the common cause of stopping the juggernaut? How many of us are even willing to put our money (by which I mean many thousands of pounds, if you have it) into this struggle for life's survival?[18] How many of us are actually wiling to say 'Enough!' to the growth of the juggernaut, symbolized effectively by the road-building and airport-expansion that virtually all political parties and governments endlessly undertake? Or 'Enough!' To the ever-seductive siren call of endless possibilities of healthcare, that I discussed the challenge of towards the close of Chapter 1?

As yet, relatively few, it would seem. I salute the exceptions to the rule. But our 'rulers', sadly, exhibit the rule, not the exception. Our ruling ideas, as well as our ruling class, are just not up to the task which now imposes itself on us. Denial in effect saturates our civilization. It manifests in the continuing habit of nearly all of us of going on having children, at a time when overpopulation looms, a time when there is a huge premium on being able to devote one's life to taming the nemesis confronting our children – and a time which threatens an awful life for those children we are bearing. Of course, this last is not necessarily about denial. It can also be about a commitment to the survival of life (Chapter 1), a commitment to the future, which is a very healthy instinct. But wouldn't the better way to manifest that commitment, for most of us who haven't yet rolled that dice, and who are open-minded enough to be able to have the conversation with ourselves at all, be to choose to parent the future by way of seeking to make it less bad for all, rather than focussing ourselves mainly on one or two beings who we choose to bring into the world?

Civilization and 'civilization'

Lewis Mumford, in his wonderful speculative critique of our rampant technophilia, *The Myth of the Machine* (1971), makes a wonderful distinction between civilization and what he calls 'civilization'. The single quote-marks are an essential part of the latter term (Mumford 1971, 186–7). By the former, he means civilization as opposed to savagery and barbarism; by the latter, he means civilization in its most historically dominant form, as vested in more or less aggressive kingship or empire. This is in effect a *form* of organized barbarism. But it seems to me that we have to accept that civilization has always come with positives as well as negatives (the negatives being what Mumford largely, and understandably, emphasizes), in greater and lesser quantities. It is only because of the positives, in terms of standards of behaviour as well as in terms of cultural achievement, that it was possible for Gandhi to even make his brilliant quip about Western civilization: that it sounds like a good idea. 'Civilization' is a normatively freighted term: it involves a commitment to being *civil*. This commitment in much of history has been honoured more in the breach than in the observance, *but the breaches are always implicitly condemned by the term itself.* 'Civilization' is all things considered something to aspire to, as well as something to critique, and almost necessarily so.

We can very roughly date civilization to the final period of 'pre-history', for it was civilization that seems to have created writing to record its capital (Mumford 1971, 192). Past civilizations have risen and fallen across different parts of the globe. By '*this* civilization', I mean the vast majority now of human life on Earth. For we increasingly do live in one large world civilization. As Tim Flannery, Jared Diamond and others have observed, the problem of this civilization is that, if it falls, then virtually everything else falls because of the inter-connectedness of the world we have made.

Now, it would be defeatist to write as if the present civilization had already achieved total global hegemony. Little outposts of alternatives to this global system still exist. They include obviously most of the remaining indigenous societies (Diamond 2012), as well as any undestroyed fragments of (say) mid- to late-twentieth century Ladakh (Norberg-Hodge 2000), one of those inspiring peasant cultures with much in common with indigenous cultures. These outposts badly need to be preserved and cherished. They are like seedbanks in this respect. The great question of our time, arguably, is whether we can preserve and learn from these fragments. Whether we can learn indigenous and 'uncivilized' wisdom, and synthesize it with what is still to be aspired to in civilization. To do that, we need to not only look outward but also to interrogate what is worth preserving from our civilization, while abandoning those misguided and dangerous ideologies that underpin so much of it (Read 2016a).

Three possible futures

Given the enormity of the task that befalls us, the inertia we have displayed in rising to it, and the bleak picture painted by the science, which becomes only bleaker still once we adequately consider worst-case scenarios (Harrabin 2021; Bendell & Read 2021, ch. 1), it seems that there are in total then three possibilities before us:

Possibility number one is that we manage to **transform civilization**. To do that, we would need to alter the entire basis of pretty much everything that we do. The kind of transformation we are talking about is a *lot* bigger than for example just a large-scale like-for-like conversion to renewable energy; that is in fact a fantasy of preserving the present (growthist, industrialist, consumerist) civilization. We also need to be (talking about and then actually!) radically reducing the amount of transportation of goods and people around the world. Radically relocalizing (Scott Cato 2013). Changing our farming practices profoundly and the entire nature of our agriculture, radically reducing the amount of meat that we eat. And much more. It would be a total transformation the likes of which we have arguably never known, at least as large as (and considerably faster than) the Industrial Revolution, perhaps as large as the prehistoric 'human revolution' that saw us transitioning from being fixedly hierarchical to being potentially egalitarian (Hockett & Ascher 1964; Power n.d.). It would be a paradigm shift, the move to a transformed normal. Call it Butterfly, for short.

I hope that that happens and – probably like (many of) you – I'm actively working to make it happen. But it would be a bold person who was prepared to commit to the thought that this will *definitely* happen, that we are going to make it happen, and that we are going to make it happen quickly enough to avert collapse. It would be reckless to bet everything upon us overcoming the vast vested interests, ignorances, stupidities and lazinesses which obstruct that unprecedented transformation. For such a bet would occlude the attention and resources starting to be devoted to taking seriously the question, 'What if we fail? How then could we make things less bad for whoever follows us?'

And even if this transformation were to happen, it will not do so in the way being dreamt of among some in California, for instance, who think that technological-connectedness will enable it to occur with a completeness and neatness that carries all before it. There will not be what Daniel Schmachtenberger calls a 'phase-shift' into a new civilization. It will instead at best be a much messier process, replete with much continued opposition from vested interests, much inertia, many mistakes and false starts. Human affairs are political. Politics just doesn't include such neat ways of accomplishing full-spectrum system-change. The very best we can hope for will be un-neat. And it is unwise to put all your eggs in the basket of the very best; because usually the very best is not what we get.

That is why it would be deeply irresponsible not to consider further possibilities.[19]

Possibility number two is **a successor civilization** after some kind of collapse, and that, it seems to me now, is what we have to start to think is very likely to happen. Or put it this way: actually, some versions of this possibility are now increasingly likely to become the *best* scenario we can realistically hope for or plan towards (because possibility number one is going to be so very hard to carry off). If the sketch that I gave you about Paris earlier in this chapter is even broadly right, then unless we are incredibly lucky or incredibly determined or incredibly brilliant (or almost certainly all three) then we are facing, almost certainly, changes around the world which are going to bring an end to this civilization more or less involuntarily. And if we are lucky and determined (and brilliant), then we will change it in ways that amount to ending it (possibility number one again). Either way, we need to think about what comes after it. We need to think about it now, and we need to start to work toward it; because there are many sub-possibilities within possibility two; and some of them are very ugly. The successor-civilization could for instance be largely a matter of warlordism. We must try to do what we can to prepare our descendants for survival and for a new civilization which will be worth the paper it is written on.

A partial model here may be found in how Christianity was passed on from Rome to become the basis of the European Middle Ages. Christianity, despite the deformations it had suffered in becoming a state religion, had enough vitality to offer a compass to a civilization undergoing the massive challenges inevitable upon the decline and fall of Empire.

Call this possibility as it now shapes itself for us, of a new civilization emerging from collapse, Phoenix.

Possibility number three of course is simply **total collapse**. And in a way there is not much that needs to be said about that. It is obviously highly undesirable! I'll limit myself to saying a tiny bit about it. There are various different forms that it could take. It could mean simply there is no more civilization, but that there are a few people hanging on here and there. James Lovelock in *The Revenge of Gaia* (2007) speculates about a few thousand pairs in the Antarctic. Or it could be worse even than that; one cannot rule out complete human extinction and extinction of most or all other mammalian life on Earth, if a 'hothouse earth' scenario unleashes further feedbacks that are as yet unknown or unencountered (Steffen et al. 2018). It is obvious that total collapse has to be avoided[20] and in a way therefore it doesn't hugely matter, when you drill down into it, which version of it you have. But it still does matter quite a bit. For instance, it would (for more than one reason) be much worse for us to exterminate all cetaceans as well as ourselves, than it would be for us just to exterminate ourselves. This is because, above all, doing the former would render it less likely that a new species would be able to come along after we were gone and do a better job of creating a culture that can last. I discuss this further in Chapters 6 and 7 of this book.

I won't dwell further here on possibility three (Call it Dodo) and its variants. I'm more interested in talking about some kind of successor civilization after collapse. Primarily because I think that that is where we are most likely to be headed.

It seems to me that what we've done mostly up to the present day is assume that we can transform our civilization (without collapse). More accurately, we've assumed that tinkering and reforming the way we live will be enough to stave off climate nemesis. We've put all our eggs in the basket of mitigation. The most we've tended to assume is that we need a civilizational transformation. But it's no longer enough to 'just' aim at that; we must take seriously the possibility that – given how bad things are, how much we've let them get out of hand – this civilizational transformation is now going to be very hard to attain even if we aim toward it with determination.

Any way you look at these three possibilities – Butterfly, Phoenix and Dodo – they justify the conclusion that this civilization is finished. *This* civilization is finished because the best outcome that could happen, if we are lucky and very courageous, is that we transform this civilization out of all recognition. If we do that, then afterward it will not look the same at all; it will be in no meaningful sense the same civilization. For what is needed will be a transformation more radical, I'd suggest (and as noted above), than the change that took place in the Industrial Revolution. It will be as radical, arguably, as the Agricultural Revolution (and of course far, far faster).[21] I would suggest it would necessarily be a truly great transformation.

This civilization as we know it is finished. It has a sell-by date; we just don't know how far past that date we're going to be able to keep the show on the road. It will either collapse utterly, collapse and give birth to a new civilization (which could be wonderful or horrible or anywhere in between) from its wreckage, or it will be transformed out of all recognition. There is no chance of it simply continuing in modified form – the brutal logic of how the Paris Agreement will fail ensures that.

The chance of complete catastrophe is thus very high. But the logic of the precautionary principle applies all the more. Just as one must take every effort to avoid catastrophe even if the chances of it happening are low/non-calculable, so one must take every effort to avoid catastrophe even if the chances of it happening are very high (and the chances of averting it very low) . . . as they now are.

Making any progress with this great task, this great work that we are called to, depends on first being able truly to face climate reality and to accept something like the diagnosis found herein. We need to talk to each other about this (Chapter 7). My experience thus far, encouragingly, is that, when we dare to do so, we find some community; because it turns out that there are more of us who share the thoughts expressed in this chapter than we had realized beforehand. There aren't as few of us as we had feared!

Towards a 'successor civilization'

Some hopes are gone. Some things are no longer possible. For example, we have left it way too late to have a smooth, gentle transition with gradual reductions in fossil-fuel emissions. Either we have an emergency programme of emissions-reduction, or we face an escalation in the age of consequences.

But when we are honest about these matters, then we have greater chances of change than before. Of transformative adaptation.

So it is a total misunderstanding, a blatant reversal of the truth, to describe my work as in any meaningful sense 'doomerist' (Read 2021d). The whole point of this chapter is that in facing up to climate reality, we achieve our maximum feasible agency.

This is the central reason why we need, if at all possible, to break the silence around all this before we have to live through it. It's time to truly to face the future.

Ideally, this would be preceded by facing the (present and the) past – the destruction, the suffering, the passivity, the way that many people especially in 'the West' – including probably most of the readers of this book – have been complicit in a global system of exploitation, have profited from it, have largely stood by passively while one generation of children after another have led miserable lives and died prematurely. Some kind of truth and reconciliation process could be imagined for this. We are undergoing fragments of that process by way of undertaking processes of 'decolonization' actively within (for instance) universities, as well as within broader society (for example, though debates around statues).

But my grave concern is this: that these fractious debates and (understandably) angry attempts to achieve backward-looking justice may, on balance, distract us more than they provide a healthy backdrop for the desperately urgent task of facing the future. If our energy is diverted *primarily* into seeking redress for past wrongs, then we lose the capacity for seeking unity in the project of saving our posterity. It is better to focus on building an inclusive movement across classes and political affiliations, and to be confident that there will be massive class-justice implicit in genuine schemes to cope humanely with climate breakdown.[22] *There just is no way of tackling climate breakdown without reducing the insane levels of economic inequality within our countries and across the world.* An economic levelling will disproportionately uplift those unjustly marginalized on the basis of their identity by the current economic order as well. In this way, we get to join together in the marvellous common project of providing our children with a future, which has as a logical consequence a massive rebalancing of society (Harrabin 2020; Read 2019b; Beuret 2018; Howard 2016). This is how it could be conceivable that we square the circle: that we achieve a massive reduction in inequality relatively consensually. If we can bring enough ordinary people (including the moderately rich and business people) to comprehend that there is no way through this without an extreme convulsion along the lines of that which occurred in and after the Second World War equalizing our society to a considerable extent, for the sake of tackling the emergency we are and will be undergoing.

In the meantime, we need to find a way (and this is very hard) of talking to our children about all this, and in particular about their future 'options'. They don't deserve to be brought up in ignorance of where their world is headed. They deserve to be taught for instance how to grow food, how to practise self-defence, how to build resilient communities, and how in the past humans have best survived grave civilizational shocks. And if everyone had to tell their kids what was coming, and that we are desperately afraid for them (and if this were manifested, for instance, in the part-changed curriculum of education that I've just intimated), then we might yet, together, even head it off: for it is an outrage to have to say to your children that their birthright is probably premature death (and certainly abominable loss), and outrages are motivating. Or, if we were to tell the truth to our kids and still not act, then perhaps they would say to us, 'If you don't act, knowing what you know, knowing what you have told us, then you don't love us'. That painful truth-telling might be the spur we need. If even that didn't get us to transform our civilization, then it would not be worth 'saving'.

One could go further. The remarkable, deeply moving 2018 film *Capernaum* imagines a Lebanese slum-child suing his parents for bringing him into the world. If people hear the truth about the foreseeable future, and about the need for many of us (especially those of us in the global North) to have fewer or no children, but did not act on this truth, then their children might one day reasonably ask them: why did you bring me into this world, where I am forced to be complicit in all kinds of destruction because the way our society is organized does not allow me any other way, and also where I am almost certain to suffer horrendously from the results of all this destruction – how could you do this?

Those with children seem to find it, in a way understandably, even harder to face these desolate truths than those of us without. Is it possible to face climate reality, to face the likely end-times of our civilization, while choosing to have children? Our children are our greatest hope, partly for the reason given in the previous paragraph. But their very presence may cocoon us from being able to face the awful reality we are setting up for them. They are our greatest joy and meaning, and they can also be, tragically, the planet's greatest burden. I write with the aim of provoking a difficult, but beautiful potential, awakening that aligns parents with taking true care of the fate of those they love so dearly. As some, such as Extinction Rebellion Families and Mothers Rise Up, are strikingly already doing.

We need to start to create a 'plural' (no longer 'Too Big To Fail') civilization that will succeed this one.[23] A civilization able, like those indigenous cultures that have survived previous overshoots, to harmonize, and stay within limits. A civilization that will be determined to sustain and renew itself and to learn from our civilization's failure. A civilization that will actually be civil. A civilization entirely worth saving.

A civilization that, unlike this one, can last.

People are looking for what Jean-Paul Sartre called a 'reprieve' from this. They are secretly hoping for something which can absolve them from having to dare to keep hoping. And from having to act.

Most people really don't want to hear what I'm saying. They remain, in Machiavelli's word, 'incredulous', and may not believe the terrible truth until it is utterly upon them or has overwhelmed them.

What I want to do is to reach those who are not looking only for a reprieve, but, rather, are looking for community. Who do not equate giving up realistic hope for the 'sustainability' of the present civilization with: giving up hope full stop. (The quote marks around the word 'sustainability' are essential. For we need always to ask: sustainability of what? 'Sustainability' without qualification is no longer a viable objective, in the sense that this civilization cannot be kept going. Our viable objective now is one form or another radical world-*renewal*. Transformation is coming. Our task is to assist in midwifing a transformation that isn't ugly or depraved).

With this chapter, I want to reach those who have not given up in complete nausea at humanity, those who still have some hope – *but* who are becoming desperate for honesty.[24]

Luckily, we have some unexpected things on our side in this grave task. From here, this book will pivots. Chapters 1 to 3 have sought to answer questions that take us deep into the crisis. The next three chapters concern ways in which, *through* our very travail, we can be helped. Where the danger lies, there presences the saving power.

To assert that the way we ought to take must be one that is only 'positive' is to lie. The truth of danger, of despair and heartbreak, the truth of the 'bad', is that it contains the seeds of the good, if we have eyes to see with and hearts still to feel with.

Specifically, in the next chapter, I will discuss the saving power of (climate-related) disasters, which, while being disasters, can also change everything for the better. And following that, I will turn to the saving power of our suffering from (all) this; the way in which our very painful emotions about the world situation can be precisely what we need in order to create a common future. In order, that is, to survive and go on. And then, before the conclusion, there will be a consideration of ourselves alongside certain other animals who may be able to teach us something about how to act *in extremis*. How their spirit of sticking together even if it may lead to death may, paradoxically, lead us back to life.

4

The Great Gift of Community that (Climate) Disasters Can Give Us[1]

The concept of progress must be grounded in the idea of catastrophe. That things are 'status quo' is the catastrophe.

Walter Benjamin, *The Arcades Project* (2002, 473)

Disasters and their discontents, from Hobbes to the Anthropocene

The world of 'natural' disasters is fast becoming history. The climate disasters of today are increasingly *unnatural* in frequency and intensity. Indeed, we are now firmly within the anthropogenic era of these.

And yet, due to the time-lags between the climate-deadly emissions that we create and their full effects on the global climatic and oceanic systems, not to mention our continued pumping of greenhouse gases, and to decimation of ecosystems, as well as the deadly climate feedbacks that we have started to set off (beginning with the scary ongoing reduction in the capacity of the world's forests to absorb the excess carbon still pumping into the atmosphere (Harvey 2020)), we know that there is much worse to come.[2]

In the first half of this book, I argued that we are heading toward some level of ecological breakdown. Terrible biodiversity loss coupled with, exacerbated by and exacerbating (CMCC Foundation 2020) climate breakdown, means that this judgement is now unavoidable. Indeed, such breakdown has already started occurring. The fact that we are increasingly able to perceive the damage that we are doing to our ecology, and are nevertheless mostly continuing unabated on this ruinous path, does not inspire hope that it will be averted. However, as we'll see, the actions that we take today can, even yet, prevent ecological collapse from becoming terminal and global. (I'll argue in this chapter that the very onset of the anthropogenic disasters we are now encountering offers one of our greatest chances of coming to (ourselves), and turning our path).

In the previous chapter, I argued that our trajectory points towards some level of civilizational collapse. Our failure to get to grips with the climate crisis now means that the sorts of policies we need to adopt to avoid 3°C or more of global over-heating would make the resultant civilization scarcely recognizable. We either transform deliberately and collectively, or we collapse. Such a shift, while by no means painless, is also the best possible outcome we can now dare to hope for.[3] (And in many ways it would be a consummation devoutly to be wished: for our present civilization is not satisfying our human needs. This is in a crucial way a hopeful thought: in the hard times to come, we can promise the possibility of what can nevertheless be on balance *a better life*).

So far, this book has discussed climate and societal breakdown mainly as an outcome. However, breakdown is as much a process as an outcome. I turn now to consider that process. I argue that the pain of that process may yield the very gift we need in order to come through the breakdown.

This then is the pivot-point of the book that you hold in your hands. Building on but going beyond the three chapters so far, this is the first of three chapters that together constitute the book's 'heart'. For the heart is what beats an ongoing message of life, through many trials. As the torch of life passes from one generation to the next, that inexorable power-rhythm comes through despite and even because of the suffering endured. Roughly as Nietzsche said: whatever does not kill us makes us stronger. And these three chapters are the heart of what I have to offer positively (and I hope somewhat originally) in terms of a way forward, through the coming disasters, through the elements of breakdown occurring or likely to occur.

And that's the key word: *through* (Read 2017c). Through letting our hearts rend as we turn to face what we have done to the other beings of this world (Chapter 6). Through letting them rend as we turn to face – and feel – our own emotions in this time of trial (Chapter 5). And precisely *through*, by way of, the coming climate disasters.

The process of climate breakdown as we experience it as human beings is a process that is largely composed of individuated disasters. It is climate chaos, not the slower, steadier effect of global over-heating (and of consequent sea-level rises etc.), that mostly strikes us. This brings me explicitly onto the subject of this chapter. How should we expect climate disasters to affect our communities. Only for ill, or not? Can breakdown lead to break*through*?

In this and the following chapters, I offer the hope I think we can now live. It is a hope founded in our travail. A radical hope that seeks to find (and face) the saving power exactly where the danger (and the trouble) is, rather than in any way turning away from it.

I begin by asking whether the experience of climate disasters might, rather than breaking us, make us. Disasters are here and are coming; that much, a Stoic truth-telling must own. Yet might these disasters be the very route to preventing catastrophe?

There is a widespread (if rarely explicated or interrogated) assumption among those who dare to consider the character of the future which climate chaos is likely to yield. The assumption is that, under pressure of unprecedented eco-induced stresses and strains, civility will give way and a Hobbesian war of all against all will be unleashed. According to this view, human nature is one where our natural tendencies, under threat, are towards violence and selfishness. Thomas Hobbes thought that government was necessary to create social arrangements that contained and regulated these aspects of our nature (Hobbes 1651). He is the unacknowledged grandfather of liberal individualist philosophy – the kind of philosophy, unfortunately hegemonic still today, found in Locke, Mill, Rawls and many more. This pessimistic atomistic position of his forms the basis of his defence of (limited) government, and by extension can be seen through a glass darkly in theirs. His is a picture that is frequently borne out in popular culture (think of the books *The Road*[4] or at best *The Hunger Games,* and their brilliant film versions). On the Hobbesian view,[5] disasters that undermine existing social arrangements weaken the constraints that keep in check the worst elements of our nature.

Yet, there is some genuinely good news in this otherwise bleak portrait. And it's this: this Hobbesian view was/is mostly wrong. Far from disasters dividing people and turning them against each other, they often have the reverse effect. They can be opportunities for levels of cooperation and altruism that are almost unheard of in everyday society. Rather than degrading us into selfish hyper-individualistic nihilists, terrible events often bring out the best of our pro-social behaviour and potentialities. In many ways, disasters encourage the inverse of what our economic system incentivizes. They give us an opportunity to be better people, provide mutual support, and form stronger communities.

We need a decisive transformation in the 'imaginary' by which we are now possessed. We are deeply caught up in an economistic, individualistic, selfish, short-termist, materialist way of life and by a concomitant image of humanity itself (a more or less Hobbesian idea of 'human nature'). We need, rather desperately, a new community spirit. We need a basis on which to feel part of each other.[6]

In this chapter I offer my personal experience of disaster-anticipation and disaster-aftermath. And I give an overview of some results in the field of Disaster Studies. The results scholars in that field bring to us seem to show that our fear of the Hobbesian nightmare is overblown. After that, I consider what prospects and precedents there are for positive community-building responses to climate disasters. Then I consider a possible objection to my approach in this chapter (and this book), based on the concern that it fails to pay enough attention to those living lives of quiet disaster already. In the final section I argue that the surprisingly silver-lined reading of disasters offered here certainly does not imply we can just leave it to 'history' to sort things out. Far from it. The whole thing is likely to rest on a fine pivot: from disasters running away with us to them being the making of us. Or back again. We need to learn from previous disasters to make sure our future responses are the best that they can be.[7]

However, first I want to briefly address the worry that my chapter title may already have raised, for some readers, perhaps putting them off. Is there something troubling about the very willingness to consider the benefits that can be conferred by disaster, the opportunities offered by crisis. How dare one speak of disaster as potentially the bringer of a *gift*?

Disaster as gift?

Dangerous anthropogenic climate change is not only a steady increase in world temperature. Such global overheat (euphemistically known as 'global warming') may well be the worst single element of dangerous anthropogenic climate change (too often still known by the even more bland moniker 'climate change'), at least in the long term. But the more immediately noticeable effect, for most people, for a long time to come is likely to be climate *chaos*. And the weather chaos that is the most immediate manifestation thereof. We are facing an increased incidence of ultra-powerful storms, floods, droughts; and more striking or surprising phenomena such as the possibility of the Gulf Stream temporarily or permanently 'switching off',[8] or of a permanent El Niño.

In other words, for a long time to come, the most noticeable and perhaps the most damaging impact of the heating that we have unleashed will be events that will manifest as disasters. We are going to see 'biblical' floods, hurricanes of unprecedented scale (Category 6, anyone?), '1,000-year' forest fires, overwhelming heat (including, increasingly, killer 'wet bulb' heat (Raymond et al. 2020)) and much more.

These will be disasters. I am absolutely not quarrelling with that verdict, that nomenclature. We can foresee right now the deaths of millions, perhaps of tens or even conceivably hundreds of millions, cumulatively, from these disasters. That is an unutterably terrible thing. However, these disasters, though terrible, will nevertheless not be unmitigated. In fact, they will provide us with an opportunity for something wonderful and necessary.

When disaster occurs, one can simply be defeated by it. Or indeed one can use it to make things even worse for others, as in *The Shock Doctrine*, famously named by Naomi Klein (2007). Or one can quite literally make the best of it. *I think that we should make absolutely no apology for choosing, if ever possible, the third of these three options.*

Disaster, when it comes, in its coming, is of course unwelcome – a dreadful thing. It would be a twisted theodicy which would try to reframe such disasters as nothing but a good thing. It is not the best of all possible times, if one has to endure disaster (still less, obviously, if that disaster wipes one and/ or one's loved ones out). But yet, disaster can yield an astonishing, direly needed gift. The worst of times can bring out our best, an *us* that we are yearning for.

Disaster experience, and Disaster Studies

I am not a Disaster Studies scholar. Let me now therefore speak personally. (Such speech, I've learnt, has an authentic power of its own). In doing so, I will try to break further through a wall of 'stealth denial' that I think we virtually all tend to build around us, today, even those of us who are well aware of the likelihood (on a business-as-usual pathway) of a potentially irrecoverable civilizational collapse within the next generation or three.

For nearly a generation now, I have been afraid of the nightmare that (I thought) would unfold, if true disaster comes to a place like England, where I live. I have engaged in some fragments of reasonably serious though seemingly hopeless 'prepping': that is the term used by those who are actively preparing for the contingency of such future disasters through trying to equip ourselves and our loved ones with some means to survive them. I have not infrequently been in a state of some, and sometimes pretty extreme (Chapter 5; The Poetry of Predicament 2021), anxiety about such possible futures. I believe, incidentally, that one of the main reasons why disaster movies and (especially) apocalypse movies (and it is notable that the latter have been increasing in number in recent years) are popular is that they provide a 'safe' environment for us to explore our conscious and unconscious fears about the coming of such disasters, in a fashion first, famously, outlined by Aristotle with his theory of *katharsis*.[9]

It is by coming to understand something of the field of Disaster Studies that I have finally reached a state of some peace and indeed optimism, in relation to all this.

And how did I become open to the ideas of this field, in the first place? Disaster Studies, as I understand them, yield conclusions that tend to fly wildly in the face of conventional wisdom about disasters and chaos. This has soothed somewhat my anxieties about how quickly things could collapse and how dire they could get in our fragile, long-supply-lined, overly complex globalized world. Perhaps it might soothe yours, too.

How does one even get to the point where one can contemplate an alternative to frantic 'prepping' and to rising eco-anxiety, or indeed to the more usual response of denial?

For me, what is in retrospect the key moment came early in 2002. I couldn't process it at the time – it pretty much bounced off the frame through which I saw the world. But it came back to me and motivated me, when, more recently, I happened across Rebecca Solnit's work.

It consisted in this: I was conversing, in January 2002, in New York, with an American friend, a New Yorker, about his having been present in the city during the 11 September 2001 attacks. I had recently wandered around the site of Ground Zero, formerly, the World Trade Center, and been concerned and downhearted by the often violent graffiti and messages left there expressing a desire for vengeance on those who had carried out the atrocity (and sometimes on anyone who looked like them or shared ancestry or religion with them). I said to my friend, whose politics were close to mine: 'It must have been just awful, being in New York in those days after the attacks. I mean: with all the death, the terrible smell, the deadly pollution, the chaos and worst of all the ferocious yells for vengeance'. His reply completely flummoxed me. He said:

> Actually, it was the one time in my life that I ever felt part of a community. It sounds strange to say it, but it was actually a happy time. People spoke to each other. Strangers helped each other – and this is New York, remember! Distinctions fell away.

And, after a pause, he said, again: 'it was truly the one time in my life when I have ever felt like I was really: part of a *community*'.

Years later, when I came into contact with Rebecca Solnit's *A Paradise Built in Hell* (2009), that New York memory came back to me powerfully. And instantly I saw how maybe this very surprising, very encouraging thing could be true. Perhaps, contrary to what, in our 'liberal' individualist culture we assume, people don't become degraded and reduced to nasty brutish selfish types, when they are put under extreme pressure: perhaps that isn't our actual 'state of nature'. Perhaps, more often, the reverse.

Once again: I am no scholar of Disaster Studies. So I will use here as my guides to the field three main sources that in different ways have formed or cover it: Solnit's book; Charles Fritz's classic of the field, tragically unpublished for thirty-five years after it was written, *Disasters and Mental Health: Therapeutic Principles Drawn from Disaster Studies* (1996); and Jeff Schlegelmilch's comprehensive recent work, *Rethinking Readiness: A Brief Guide to 21st Century Megadisasters* (2020).

What does their work appear to show?

Schlegelmilch's compendium of research on disasters sets out how our 'social capital', our connectedness as and in communities, is *the* most crucial factor for our ability to cope well with and recover well from disasters. This outweighs factors that one might have thought more important, such as wealth or even previous direct preparedness (Schlegelmilch 2020, ch. 6; libcom.org 2014). This suggests the importance of seeking to feed such social-connectedness, especially where it is weakest. This can be done in all sorts of ways, from one's friendship-network all the way up to carefully designed political programmes. It feeds directly into an important suggestion implicit in this chapter: that a systematic (ideally, global!) well-resourced 'programme' of *relocalization* is a key to resilience in the age of climate disasters (Read 2019a; Read & Steele 2019; Norberg-Hodge & Read 2016). For a key problem in our current way of life is how weak neighbourhood-connectivity is, in a 'globalized' world. Most of us know few people locally. If and when disaster hits, your Zoom network is of comparatively little use to you. You need to be present with those, including the vital community first-responders, who are actually *in your community*. That is: where you live.

The work of Solnit and of Fritz concentrates on something even more interesting. Drawing in detail on many examples, from the 1906 San Francisco earthquake to 11 September 2001, from the devastating explosion in Halifax, Nova Scotia, to Hiroshima, from the Blitz to Hurricane Katrina, Fritz and Solnit suggest to us that disaster tends *to enable new communities to be born* – instantly and often lastingly.

They relate how, against our expectations of chaos and panic, people in the immediate aftermath of a disaster are often remarkably calm. How they tend rapidly to develop mutual networks of support, based on need rather than on prior distinctions, whether of wealth, of ethnicity or so on. How looting, though often assumed to be inevitable, is actually rare (and how, in any case, some of what is described as looting would be much more reasonably described as the requisitioning of supplies; for remember, often we are talking here about people suddenly desperately short of life's necessities).[10] How, remarkably, it is at least as common for people to converge on the scene of a disaster in order to help as it is for people to flee.[11]

And how all of this – against a backdrop of fear, injury, death and loss, often affecting most of the survivors more or less directly – happens relatively spontaneously, rapidly, and even joyfully. How this festival of altruism is not even experienced primarily under that star: people don't think of themselves as engaging in self-sacrificial behaviour when they help and care for others, in the aftermath of disaster. It comes naturally to them, rather, and is experienced by them as something they want to do, even something they actually find helpful (Solnit 2009, 197).

Here is a contemporary account of the phenomenon from a survivor of the great San Francisco earthquake:

> Most of us since [the earthquake] have run the whole gamut of human emotions from glad to sad and back again, but underneath it all a new note is struck, a quiet bubbling joy is felt. It is that note that makes all our loss worth the while. It is the note of a millennial good fellowship ... In all the grand exodus [from the most devastated areas of San Francisco] ... everybody was your friend and you in turn everybody's friend. *The individual, the isolated self was dead. The social self was regnant.* Never even when the four walls of one's own room in a new city shall close around us again shall we sense the old lonesomeness shutting us off from our neighbours ... And that is the sweetness and the gladness of the earthquake and the fire ... // The joy is in the other fellow'.
>
> Solnit 2009, 32, emphasis added

This, I believe, is a key to the meaning of what happens in disasters: a possibility of joy, because of community, that was previously absent. Note how people in the United Kingdom often remark, and are sometimes vaguely surprised by, the nostalgia that so many have for the Second World War. This is how that feeling can be explained, in my view. The Blitz wasn't in the main experienced (only) as an awful, anxiety-making mortal threat; it was experienced (more) as the occasion for a new, genuine community. In this way, arguably, it served as the midwifing agent for the historic achievement of the post-war welfare state in the UK (Holman 2010).

We are living, nowadays, in ways that involve us in a virtually permanent and disastrous absence of community. Disasters enable this feeling of loss to be overcome.

It is important to note that for this overcoming to take place, typically there has to be a full-scale *disaster*, not merely a dreadful accident. Fritz emphasizes this point in particular. He writes that disasters need to be big enough to not leave 'an undisturbed, intact social system' (Fritz 1996, 21).[12] Only if that system is disrupted sufficiently can the new forms of community emerge. The ground has to change, so to speak. *Only then* can a new figure emerge.[13]

'Disaster provides an unstructured social situation that enables persons and groups to perceive the possibility of introducing desired innovations into the social system', Fritz goes on to argue (1996, 56). Moreover, in disaster (though not in lesser upheavals): 'Many pre-existing invidious social distinctions and constraints to social mobility are removed; there is a general democratization of the social structure' (1996, 66).

This latter feature in particular can have really helpful knock-on effects. Consider the way that, to almost everyone's surprise, the British electorate in 1945 ejected the 'war hero' Prime Minister Churchill from office and replaced him with the great reforming Labour government that began that year and went on to create the NHS and so much more. This amazing event starts to make more sense under the aspect that I have sought to make prominent here.

Or consider a fascinating lesser-known example that Solnit sets out at some length in Chapter 3 of her book: that of the 1985 Mexico City earthquake, which is widely credited by experts with creating the conditions of possibility for the ejection from power (after three generations in constant control) of the basically corrupt PRI Party in that country.

Perhaps you have figured out where I am going with all this. My hypothesis is that the rising tide of disasters that climate chaos will bring could be the (re-)making of us. These two wonderful works by Fritz and Solnit make evident that, when actually tested in the crucible of back-to-back disasters, it is *at least* as likely that humanity will rise to the challenge, and be transformed for the better in the process, as it is that we will shun the victims. What Fritz and others suggest, on my extrapolation of it, is that we will likely find ourselves manifesting a truer humanity than we currently think ourselves to have, in this climate-stressed future that we are now entering. We do not have to be gripped by the doomy thought that we are about to prove right Hobbes and his many contemporary followers (including the tedious throngs who endlessly assert that 'human nature' is selfish). Instead, we can be optimistic that we are about to prove them wrong, as they have in fact – if largely unnoticed – been proven wrong so many times before.

Thus the post-normal, climate-stressed world offers us a tremendous gift amidst the carnage, a gift we may well, remarkably, even (especially from the safety of retrospect) welcome and literally make the best of.

Making the best of disaster appears in simple fact (though the fact is remarkable and gives great hope) to be what comes naturally to human beings. It is what we do spontaneously unless we are stopped from doing so by cack-handed or malevolent intervention from the authorities. I would go as far as to say that human beings today – particularly in those (ever increasing) parts of the world where terrible strain has been put on any and all traditional embedding of life in communities that can be relied upon – are even yearning for such an opportunity. I don't for a moment mean, of course, that people are yearning for disaster to strike! But I would suggest that very many of us are living lives of quiet desperation, more or less inchoately awaiting *something* that can enable such communities to be . . . *recreated.*

Anti-Hobbes

I have argued that an escalating series of climate disasters will yet carry with them as an unexpected boon an opportunity for the development of community. A great chance for us to show our quality.

But how much and how well we actually realize this gift depends on our preparing the way for it, rather than probabilifying the other main realistic possibility – unrestrained destructive authoritarian elite panic in the face of disaster.

For something else that Fritz and Solnit alike make clear is that often things *do* go wrong in the wake of disaster. This is most often as a result of (a largely delusive, but nevertheless consequential) elite fear of selfish, 'Hobbesian' reactions on the part of ordinary people.[14] A striking example is New Orleans after Katrina, when African-American citizens desperate for help were painted as selfish villains, when baseless stories of savagery among the 'natives' fuelled a violent and repressive response by government, police and army, as well as by 'vigilantes'.

Moreover, one needs to be wary even of well-intentioned accounts that dwell on such elite Hobbesianism and disempower ordinary people in the process. Such is Naomi Klein's famous account in *The Shock Doctrine* (2007). She highlights the tendency of ruthless elite/rich elements in society to seek to exploit disasters and to reconstruct afterwards in a very different direction to the democratic, quasi-revolutionary spirit unleashed by the people's collective response to the Mexico City earthquake. This elite panic, I would say, is partly about stopping the upsurge of citizenship, fervour and hope that can arise in disaster. But where Klein goes wrong is in suggesting sometimes that this elite activity almost invariably succeeds in disempowering the victims of disaster, stripping them of their agency. Here is Solnit on this:

> [Klein's book] is a trenchant investigation of how economic policies benefitting elites are thrust upon people in times of crisis. But it describes those people in all the old unexamined terms and sees the aftermath of disaster as an opportunity for conquest from above rather than a contest of power whose outcome is sometimes populist or even revolutionary . . .

It's a surprisingly disempowering portrait from the Left and one that echoes the [unfounded, as the Blitz proved] fears of pre-war British authorities, the apparent product of assumptions rather than research . . .

2009, 107

She goes on to cite how Fritz himself shows a different path, a path whose remarkable outlines and consequences I sketched in the previous section:

Fritz's first radical premise is that everyday life is already a disaster of sorts, one from which actual disaster liberates us. He points out that people suffer and die daily, though in ordinary times, they do so privately, separately. And he writes, 'The traditional contrast between "normal" and "disaster" almost always ignores or minimises these recurrent stresses of everyday life and their personal and social effects. It also ignores a historically consistent and continually growing body of political and social analyses that points to the failure of modern societies to fulfil an individual's basic human needs for community identity'.

2009, 107

We should add to that last sentence, I believe, something implicit in this chapter's epigraph from Benjamin: that much of ordinary life under the rule of atomizatory neoliberalism *is* a kind of constant low-level disaster. And if unmitigated, disasters add up to a kind of catastrophe. Life is characterized for so many of us as low-grade loneliness and despair. We lack community; we live in our separate boxes, deprived of the kind of linkage that – by way of fire and food and dance and drums and chant, or shared worship, or shared work – arguably *forged* us, for millenia upon millenia (Yunkaporta 2019; Brody 2003).

Thus, extraordinarily, disasters can be felt as a release. The love, frankly, that people have (secretly) for endured disasters – including the actual love that was engendered in them and practised by them[15] – shows us the paucity of the 'normal' condition, in the contemporary world. It highlights dehumanized much 'normal' human life is; how our isolated, meaning-weak condition is thrown into stark relief by a situation that, though horrific, is nevertheless *preferable to that condition*. Because at last, for the first time perhaps, we experience real community, as my friend in New York explained to me so surprisingly in early 2002, proving wrong the Hobbesian script.[16]

We consistently underestimate how much other people care; but disasters show the extent to which they do.

The Hobbesian 'script' is, we should note here, among other things quite literally that, *a script*. An alarming number of books and films and TV shows suppose that disaster necessarily unleashes the worst in human beings. That said, interestingly, there are also many that at least posit some kind of heroic team-building as a means to community among the chaos. And then there are the standout cases, real art, where the whole faux-Hobbesian architecture gets *aufgehoben*.

I mentioned earlier *The Road* and *The Hunger Games* trilogy. These are, actually, clear cases of the latter.

The Road is, on the surface, a remarkably bleak book/film. It is set in a post-apocalyptic world peopled by Hobbesian monsters. The scenario in *The Road* is so grim because the author has manipulated the conditions in his fiction: some kind of ecological catastrophe has occurred to such an extreme[17] level that it appears the entire biosphere is dead, except for humans. As a result, the remaining few denizens of the world devour each other, often literally. And yet, what is often missed is the stunningly moving, redemptive ending of the story, as the dying protagonist refuses to give up on the life of his son, refuses to take him out of the world with him, refuses to give up on the future; and as the son is found, after his father's death, by a family who want to take him in, and whose dog – the blessing, added to human fellowship, of a non-human other, loved even more in the absence of other life-forms for us to love – evidently persuades him to say Yes.

The Hunger Games may well have put many off from watching/reading it by, once again, the extreme – the explicitly manipulative – horror of its premise. A climate-devastated, much-depleted future America is held together by a rabidly authoritarian regime of the 1 percent, lording it over the destitute rest in particular by means of subjecting them to ritual combat (as a 'reality TV' show) annually. The combat taking the form of randomly selected teen children from each of the poor districts having to seek to survive hunger and cold and fight it out to the death to the last survivor in an arena rigidly controlled for mass audience entertainment by their rulers. And yet, the actual story of *The Hunger Games* is of an emergent struggle against this utterly vicious system; a system that pretends to reveal, as Hobbes claimed to reveal, that only centrally administered violence and inequality can restrain the lower classes from tearing each other apart. (If one disliked the idea of (and perhaps avoided watching) *The Hunger Games* because one assumed that it was essentially a reality-show-style spectacle of mutual savagery unleashed, then there is a risk that one is in fact buying into the highly dubious elite assumption of what ordinary folk are 'really' like . . .) In the first part of the trilogy, that struggle begins, with the refusal of the two last survivors to kill each other, an extraordinary act of defiance. In the second part, that act of defiance, that spark, catches fire and in the end launches an outright rebellion, when many of the participants in the new Hunger Games, participants chosen by virtue of having been survivors of all the previous hunger games, tacitly refuse to kill one another and in particular strive to keep alive the girl who had initiated that defiant first act of refusal. The third part is the story of that rebellion as, with immense self-sacrifice, the districts rise up and finally overwhelm their oppressors. This story explores in gripping and moving detail how human beings can be transformed for the better 'even' by *an imposed disaster* – that is, by the Hunger Games themselves, which self-evidently are a take-off of the obsession in our contemporary sensationalist mass media with 'reality TV' shows. I would hypothesize that *The Hunger Games* is one of the most successful box-office films/series of all time *because* of the resonant quality of this exploration. Because deep down we sense the capacity of our transformation for the better by way of adversity, the kind of capacity writ large in phenomena such as 'the Blitz spirit'.

The Hunger Games dispels the illusion of Hobbesianism. The only Hobbesianism one finds in it is that that is created by the elite by the manipulation of conditions (both in the micro 'arena' of the Hunger Games themselves and in the macro situation of the districts) to try (and fail) to get the denizens of the world to act towards each other as if Hobbes had been right.

But there are clear echoes and anticipations of that in elite behaviours in our world today; not least, as Klein and Solnit alike show, in the way that elites, operating often on quasi-Hobbesian assumptions, make disasters worse. We need to sow the seeds instead for a healthy, broadly democratic response to disaster. How then do we do this?

My first suggestion is a simple one: we need to interpret and celebrate stories like *The Hunger Games*.[18]

And, more important still (for fact is harder to dismiss than fiction): we need to learn and disseminate the learning that Fritz and Solnit achieved,[19] overcoming deep-set Hobbesian prejudices about ourselves in the process. The remarkable stories of 1906, of 1940–5, of 1985, of 2001, so on, need to be told and re-told until we have started collectively to twig that we humans are not 'underneath it all' as rubbish as we are have been told we are. (The ideological claim that 'human nature' is Hobbesian is a false but dangerously potentially self-fulfilling one).

My next suggestion is that we heed the recommendations offered by Fritz. Consider in particular this remarkable culminatory portion of his text:

> The situational therapeutic features of disaster and the natural spontaneous techniques of group therapy developed in the community of sufferers might be translated into the following therapeutic action directives [for society/politics]:

(1) *Utilize the device of shock for disrupting dysfunctional habit patterns and for demonstrating their inapplicability* to present needs.

(2) Objectify the nature of the crisis and the threat which it poses to the integrity of the personal and social system. *Convert anxiety into fear.*

(3) Clearly specify the remedial needs as ones that require *social*, as well as individual, *adaptation* and physical manipulation of the external environment, as well as symbolic manipulation of the intrapsychic processes.

(4) *Slough off dysfunctional pre-existing interactional norms* and values and permit norms and values to emerge in response to present situational imperatives.

(5) Establish transcendent goals, which continually challenge individual effort and provide people with a sense of mission in life. Provide people with work roles that clearly and meaningfully relate to societal goals.

(6) Democratize social relationships by eliminating invidious social distinctions and material blocks to social mobility and achievement.

(7) *Change the reward structure of the group so that social recognition and reward are based on crisis-induced need and the achievement of social goals,* rather than on pre-existent ascriptive status.

(8) Eliminate formalized role relationships, free the channels for intimate communication, and *provide positive social sanctions for spontaneous, direct, informal, sentimental communication and the emotional sharing of experiences.*

(9) *Utilize a few extreme sufferers as a social reference point for enabling others to assess their pain and privation within a relative context.*

(10) *Dramatize the crisis or stress as an event, utilize it as a socially recognized juncture in life experience, and provide social absolution for guilt-ridden actions that preceded the event'.*

Fritz 1996, 79–80, emphasis mine

I think if we worked through that list systematically, and applied it in relation to actual climate-induced disasters, and were in readiness to apply it to the 'next generation' of worsening climate disasters, we would be in good shape. (Think for instance of how we could make a societal habit of points 9 and 10, here. Think, ultimately, how a healthy 'survivors' ethos[20] might be developed around moving beyond the narrative of blame for those (all of us, to a greater *or* lesser extent) whose actions have precipitated the crisis[21]). The climate crisis is going to provide us, for better and for worse, with a whole series of opportunities to work through 1–10 on Fritz's list. Let us help make it be for better: by being ready, and even, in our self-activation and our activisms, hopeful.

And my final suggestion is that we think deeply about how deeply things need to be overturned – including, about how only something like disaster will, it would seem, do the trick – if we are to turn our current path into something that will not nevertheless yield simply an ever-escalating sequence of disasters until there is no one left to tell any stories. In other words, what assumptions and paradigms do we need to lose and gain, if we are to be able not only to enter but to thrive in the paradises Solnit has suggested are potentially open to us? How do we make the most of disaster and even breakdown, ensuring that this does not become simply complete collapse? How do we turn silver linings into ways of living, of continuing to live, and even flourish?

As John Foster argued in *The Sustainability Mirage* (2008), 'sustainable development' and more-or-less Rawlsian[22] liberal conceptions of contract/ justice/fairness do not produce a solid enough basis to resist temptations towards denial and short-termism (temptations that will only underscore the momentum towards outright collapse), under such pressure. They are part of the paradigm which needs overcoming. Preparing our societies for the onslaught they are very likely to face requires instead the development of some true selflessness *and* of the healthy enlightened selfishness of taking care of oneself, one's family, one's 'village', one's neighbours: of charity beginning at home. I'll say slightly more about this, to round out the chapter: about how, as well as global consciousness, we need to make the very most of the kind of largely local action that is the most dramatic product of disasters. First though, let me tackle a possible objection to the line of thought I've offered here.

A potential objection: am I ignoring those already living everyday 'disaster'?

At this point, some may say to me, 'But you do not give enough attention to those whose lives are *already* disastrous. Your text is directed to an "us" that is thus exclusionary. You do not show the circumstances in which about a third of the UK population, and probably over 40 percent of the US population, live: in destitution, prejudice, family-trauma and poverty along with discrimination and a debilitating general sense of being left behind, that now tends to feed dangerous politics'.

To this charge, I plead 'guilty' – partly. It is indeed true that there are two simple senses in which these people are not the centre of my attention in this book. One sense is that there is already vast tranches of work being done to address their plight, which is obvious. Whereas the amount of thinking (let alone action) being devoted to considering our civilizational plight, and the prospect of collapse in the medium-long term, remains comparatively small.[23] Because it is less obvious; it is subtler, it is 'not here yet'. So I seek to redress the balance. A second sense is that I am under no illusion that many of the 'underclass' will be reading this book. They largely won't, precisely because of the immediacy of their predicament. Those of us who are able to raise our heads a little beyond our daily difficulties, to reflect and to act accordingly, owe it to them (and to everyone)[24] to do so.

I hope I am in fact very sensitive to the predicament of the 'left behind', just in a slightly different way from the usual 'direct' way. My work is directed toward a sense in which we really are all in this together, and thus I hope to leverage some greater buy-in to saving the future from those who right now think they are doing 'just fine'; that was a key point of the early chapters of this book (especially Chapter 1), and I think it very unlikely that the most vulnerable will get what they need unless there is a successful generating of a sense that we and what matters to us *are all vulnerable*, now.[25] Vulnerability is becoming a little more democratic across space, just as it becomes significantly more hierarchical across time — it is the young, including even the rich and privileged, who are now our most vulnerable.

Furthermore, if what I am saying in this book were taken seriously, the results would be enormously beneficial to the working class and the 'underclass'. For instance, a carbon-rationing scheme designed carefully in the cause of justice (Hillman 2008), if not a food-rationing scheme (Lang 2020), would be an enormous leveller. Citizens' assemblies would empower the voice of the worst off much better than our current democratic institutions (Read 2021a, ch. 4). These are the kinds of changes that would be seen if the actions suggested in this book found their way effectually into politics and actuality.

More fundamentally still, I aim of course at Chapter 3's 'Possibility 1' (aka 'Butterfly'), of transformation, and I assert that unless we aim to achieve this with far more resolution than we have yet managed, we will certainly end up in Possibility 2 ('Phoenix') or even Possibility 3 ('Dodo'). We will collapse. And in that kind of future, coming from too much societal unconsciousness, the 'left-behind' may well typically be the double- and triple- losers of the breakdowns I describe and will be far less prepared for them. *Unless we seek now to build community resilience, to initiate programmes of wide deep adaptation, as well as of wide transformative adaptation* (Bendell & Read 2021, ch. 11). 'Wide' in the sense of spanning society's different aspects, ideas and institutions. This is precisely the kind of thing I am arguing for in this chapter (and this book). *So* the focus on what will be needed to achieve Possibility 1 is vital for the sake of the left-behind. *And* the preparing for a likely Possibility 2 is also vital for their sake. In these regards, what I am offering in the present work clearly rebuts the objection framing this section.

Remember further: to those who say, 'But some are already living lives of constant disaster!', I say first that *I agree*, especially in the sense made present in my epigraph from Benjamin, and it is exactly for that reason that we need the kind of perspective afforded by and proposals implicit in the present chapter; and I say second that *I disagree*, because you ain't seen nothin' yet. It is short-sightedness of the worst kind to argue that *all* our effort and attention should be devoted to those living difficult or miserable lives in the present. It's temporal prejudice. It's a profound failure to raise our gaze to the much greater disasters coming down the pike at us and our descendants.[26]

It is the widespread myopia of our civilization that is keeping us fixated on the short term, to the long-term detriment especially – precisely – of the worst off. This book does not detail the forms of governance, democracy, economy and localism, including a direly needed massive redistribution of wealth, that might well yet head off collapse (and thus reduce the scale of the coming disasters), in the (unlikely) event that they could be swiftly and fully implemented; I and others have already done that or are doing it elsewhere (Norberg-Hodge 2000; Norberg-Hodge & Read 2016; Beuret 2018; Blewitt & Cunningham 2014; Read 2020f; Read 2021a; Rockström & Gaffney 2021; Read 2011b; Hickel 2020; Smaje 2020; Woodin & Lucas 2004; Coote & Percy 2020). I offer only a light outline of those things here. My focus here is rather on a detailed wake-up call, by way of a philosophical investigation, aiming at a sense of *what kinds of future we can now realistically aim at.*

Concluding remarks: The wake-up call(s)

William James famously suggested that we stand in need of a moral equivalent of war to give us meaning and bind us together, in times of (seeming) non-disaster, in times of peace. Without there being such a moral equivalent of war, James thought – rightly, in my view – that we would splinter into mutually indifferent pleasure centres. That scenario has, I fear, been realized much more than is prudent, in the modern North, under the rule of the political philosophy of liberal individualism. But it is on the point of being unrealized again.

And that may, for all its horrors, bring us a gift we badly need.

My hypothesis is that the moral equivalent of war is about to be 'forced' upon us; or, better, has *started* being forced upon us.

I have argued that the sadly likely litany of worsening (un-)natural disasters partly caused by climate chaos that we will experience need not, as many fear (and as I too feared, till recently), simply sap our morale and resources, debase our culture and hasten a descent into a Hobbesian condition, into collapse. What Rebecca Solnit and others have helped to show is that the Hobbesian assumption that people under severe strain become 'animals' is highly dubious. It is itself a piece of ideology that tends to be used to legitimate authoritarian, destructive behaviour by elites, behaviour that comes from fear (or sometimes venality) that is illicitly projected onto ordinary people.

What we need to do, therefore, I've suggested, is to seek to prepare for these disasters, in a positive spirit. The word needs to be spread. People need to understand that they can expect others, and themselves, to be resolute, in the face of disaster. Disaster-preparedness plans should not emphasize repression and authoritarian control; they should focus on how best to empower ordinary people to be amazing. As Disaster Studies appear to show, people usually spontaneously are, unless elite-panic gets in the way.[27]

We need to build for the resilience of immediate local practical action – and simultaneously grow that into a new collectivistic ethic of long-term global care (Chapter 1). We need more than cool justice; something more immediate (though, remarkably, such care iterates (Makoff & Read 2016)). We need to foster the kind of care that is unleashed in disaster. In the disasters that are coming.[28]

The worry remains, even here, that the field of Disaster Studies has focussed mostly on isolated disasters. The era of dangerous human-triggered climate change promises to some extent a new problematic: a ratcheting-up of connected, ramifying disasters (unless we manage to turn the supertanker of civilization around, and start to reduce our exposure to the whirlwind, and (after a time-lag) to reduce the whirlwind itself, rather than evermore reaping it). Life-as-disasters. Will we be able to maintain the kind of admirable spirit and humanity that Disaster Studies seemingly show us, under such long-term pressure? Or will we instead suffer disaster-fatigue, and attempt to withdraw from community and to retreat into bolt-holes that are too small to succeed, to survive for long?

Here is one reason for thinking that just possibly we will be able to make disasters make rather than break us. I have suggested that what our atomized, individualized society desperately needs is the means and occasions to rebuild community:[29] a great occasion for and drive for collective re-localization of our world (Read & Steele 2019, 62ff).

The horror, death and squalor of climate-caused disasters will not be unmitigated, not by any means. I have suggested that it will likely, as a 'silver lining' to those unprecedented storm clouds, facilitate just such a rebuilding of community. It is a way in which we can plausibly imagine what otherwise seems almost unimaginable: that we might embrace an agenda of transformative adaptation (rather than merely defensive, incremental, shallow adaptation) to the climate damage that is occurring and will escalate (Read 2021b).

Now, what if we were able to parlay that possibility into something still bigger? What if the spirit of community starts to reach more globally, and even across time? In Chapter 1, I suggested a concrete way in which one could start to imagine that happening. For I showed that one role that a philosophically informed deep reframing can play in the needful process of virtuous preparation for (and prevention of) disasters is in helping people to understand that, in order to care for their children, they need to care for *their* children in turn, and so on, *ad infinitum*. Philosophical thinking could start, in other words, to *multiply* the renewed sense of community that I postulated and recounted in the second section of this chapter. We are willing, at times of crisis and disaster, to act in ways that astonish us and make us proud to be alive. Won't we show that same compassion to our own children? What doing so means, as I've laid out here, is: planning now – starting now – to 'build down' the terrible threat which we are currently hanging over them and theirs. As Homer-Dixon's work, drawing on the respected scholarly work of Joe Painter and Buzz Holling (Homer-Dixon 2006),[30] suggests, and as my work alongside Nassim Taleb on the precautionary principle also strongly suggests (Taleb et al. 2015), we'll surely simplify and scale down our societies and reduce our impact on the natural world, at some point (Chapter 2). Will we do so in a way (and at a speed) that effectively prevents many otherwise-coming future disasters? Will we use the spirit of disaster-collectivism to be wise enough to prevent our descendants' lives becoming just one stream of disasters?[31]

Thus we can see clearly at last the outlines of the greatest gift that climate disasters can bring *if* we are ready to accept it. A gift that would stop us having to look for silver linings as we descend into collapse, and genuinely be able perhaps *to head off* that collapse. An *unleashing* of humanity, of decency, of care, that we could scale up.[32]

Because these disasters show the future on a business-as-usual scenario. They show it in its horror. But they also show us the riposte. Holderlin's great dictum holds true: exactly where the danger grows, so does the saving power.

For if I am right in thinking that climate disasters can bring a massively enhanced community consciousness in their wake, that means that they do after all have the capacity that many of us have been hoping that they might: to *wake us up*. Thus we really can still dare to hope that we may collectively wake up enough before we have committed our civilization to breakdown, let alone to terminal collapse.[33]

Ultimately the opportunity offered by disasters is to raise our consciousness, to come together to transformatively adapt, ahead of potential collapse. Transformative adaptation is so salient here precisely because it is something that we don't have to wait for states to initiate; we can move ahead of them, more nimbly, refusing to accept No for an answer. This has been seen powerfully when disasters strike, as was the case in Puerto Rico, following Hurricane Maria.[34]

Naomi Klein wrote of the danger posed to us by disaster-capitalism. What I have shown in this chapter is the very real silver lining available to us from climate disasters. It is the possibility of what we might call not just disaster-collectivism but *disaster-localism* – a genuinely adaptive, positive, transformative way through what nature, enraged by us, throws at us. This is good because such disasters are how we primarily experience climate breakdown.

When crisis hits full into consciousness, it is crucial, as Milton Friedman (of all people) said, that the right ideas are lying around ready to be picked up and utilized. I believe that the ideas present in the present chapter start to fit that bill.[35]

5

How Climate Grief May Yet be the Making of Us

Love is not a feeling. Love is put to the test; pain is not. One doesn't say "That wasn't true pain, or it wouldn't have ceased so quickly."
Ludwig Wittgenstein, *Zettel* (Translated by the author from the original 1945–1948 manuscript) (§504)

The personal is philosophical

In Chapter 4, we looked at the incredible, thrilling silver lining that the terrible dawning reality of climate disasters may have for us. In this chapter, we consider another example of how the apparently bad can be good. Aversive emotions such as melancholia, anxiety, rage and grief, *feel* bad. But what if they are sometimes necessary? What if they are sometimes healthy? Indeed, what if they are sometimes the only sane response to a situation where something is profoundly awry?

This chapter will focus primarily on grief. Specifically, on how the great pain of eco- and climate-grief, may, far from being something we should repress, avoid, or 'cure', be precisely the route to a greater sanity. The route I will take towards this conclusion is gradual. I start by examining grief of the 'ordinary' kind. And then consider how climate grief is a special case of this.

I'll start by making it personal. That is, by sharing the worst experience I've ever had with grief. At least, with grief of the 'ordinary', personal kind.[1] I think this kind of experiential approach is often the best way to create understanding. As one might put it: the personal is philosophical[2].

A philosophy of grief

I lost a young friend at sea, several years ago. His name was Matt Wootton. He was my best friend. The loss was a complete shock, a tragic accident. As I came to terms with losing Matt, I found that there was a sense in which I rejected coming to terms with it. Inextricably wrapped up in the process of accepting his death was a kind of denial.

The most natural way to express this state was that I found myself perplexedly but 'categorically' asserting or at least wanting to assert: 'Matt's dead, and/but I don't believe it'. To philosophers, such an assertion has the recognizable form of Moore's Paradox (Moore 1993). That is, that it might both be true that it is raining and true that I don't believe that it is raining (because, for instance, I'm inside and have been misinformed about the weather), but that it simply can't be the case that I can *assert* intelligibly that 'It's raining – and I don't believe it is'. Or at least; that it can't, in any even remotely normal circumstances. What I am describing, it turns out, is a situation that tests Moore's Paradox to the limit.

As a Wittgensteinian, my way with seeming nonsenses is to be charitable. That is: always to at least *seek* to find a context in which the form of words in question *can* be uttered (Read 2012a).[3]

I don't know whether a very interesting serious one can be dug up for 'It's raining and I don't believe it'; I haven't ever seen one offered. The closest candidate I've heard, put to me by my environmental philosopher colleague Liz McKinnell, would be the case of (say) a princess who had formed *her whole life* around the perfect wedding – which was being ruined by rain. In a case like this, her 'I don't believe it' would be somewhat relevantly similar to the case I am offering here. Her *lived world* – her very identity, her sense of what the world was all about – might be said to be incompatible with its raining on her wedding day. I don't know whether this case works. I am unconvinced that it does. If it does, if it did, this would be because of a 'break' in her lived world, a rupture in everything that she took life to hold and mean, constituted by its raining on this occasion. That's the clue, for what I will be wanting to say here.

For, in any case, the case that *I* have started to offer – the case of deep grief, and of 'denial' in the very midst of it - does seem to be relevantly interesting. When I said to myself, as I did in the months after his deadly sea voyage, things roughly along the lines of 'Matt's dead, he's *dead*; and (yet) I don't believe it', I meant that I both held that he was as a matter of fact dead and yet somehow found myself not (quite) believing that he was. I was not drawing from his being dead all the consequences – or, consequences on the right/ normal level, as it were – that one would (normally) draw from a fact. If a belief is[4] that upon which one acts, then mine (and I am suggesting that this is going to be found in deep grief more generally) was a case where the normal concept of belief started/starts *to break down,* and was substituted for by something deeply atypical.

For Matt's being dead, while a fact, was yet not compatible with my lived world. It as yet had no unproblematic manifestation in my 'belief-*system*'.[5] After a year or even two had passed, I still couldn't really quite believe that

Matt had gone (although it was, sadly, gradually becoming easier to). Now, several years on, I can. It took that long.

Moore's Paradox concerns the putting together of a fact (P) with what we can crudely term a mental state (I don't believe P), into one whole. In the normal case, for the first person, these two cannot contradict; or rather, it means nothing to have them contradict, and so there *is* no such whole. But there are cases which differ from the norm. One that seems strikingly relevant is 'Eroom's paradox': 'P and unconsciously I don't believe P'. For instance, P might be something one learnt about oneself from a psychoanalyst.

Perhaps that *is* roughly the kind of case we are dealing with here. Perhaps I could have rightly said about myself, while grieving, 'Matt's dead, and unconsciously I don't believe he is'. For the 'mental state' in this case is part of a lived world that, we might say, it is irrational simply instantaneously to abandon when it is factually-compromised. In the case of grieving, it is rational not (yet) to have adjusted your beliefs completely to what is true. If one just abandoned, as it were, one's dead friend, as soon as the basic facts were presented to one, that might even show something suspect about the friendship. There's something deep, in our difficulty in coming to terms with the loss of a loved one. That finds expression in grief.

These points have been missed in the philosophical literature on grief to date. Gustafson's famous analysis of grief holds that grief involves a belief in P (where P would be something like 'Matt is dead') and a desire that not-P (Gustafson 1989). But I've shown already that this is clearly too crude. It's not just that I didn't *want* Matt to be dead. It's that somehow he *wasn't* quite yet dead for me. Similarly, even Robert Solomon's subtle account doesn't grasp this point, for he insists that 'If the belief [that x is dead] is not secure, but still hovers in the realm of fear and uncertainty, the emotion is not yet grief' (Solomon 2004, 84–5)[6]. Solomon is here evading the *indeterminacy* and even perhaps contradictoriness of the world of the griever.

Someone who states, in the normal run of things, that 'P and I don't believe P' is, we can safely say, just confused. But grief is not a confusion, not at all! It makes perfect sense, in the case of a deep enough loss. But yet: there is something akin to confusion necessarily involved in grief. That thing is that one knows something to be so and yet cannot (quite) believe it. One is in a somewhat bewildering condition. One is in a state that does indeed involve what to others will inevitably seem downright confusing (inevitably – unless perhaps they themselves have had similar experiences, or unless perhaps they are capable of great empathy and wisdom).

Altered mental states are the most promising place to look for contexts in which Moore-style paradoxes are not simply utterly nonsensical, but are instead inevitable issuances of the state in which one finds oneself (Read

2012a, ch. 9).[7] Things one is inclined to say,[8] that one could not express adequately in any other way. And so it is with deep grieving. 'I know that Matt's dead; but yet I find that I can't quite *believe* that he is!'; this was the way in which I felt ineluctably inclined to express the state of grief in which I found myself. Any less paradoxical utterance would have failed to engage adequately with the phenomenology of my experience.[9]

The acceptance of Matt's death was necessarily partly expressed by denial. Moore's-Paradox-style remarks hereabouts express this. The process, over time, toward acceptance in more than a thinly asserted cognitive fashion seemingly ineluctably involves things like the assertion of apparent absurdities. What denial really means is the profound difficulty of marrying one's beliefs with the facts *even as one assents to them.*

The upshot, I think, is this: all of the 'five phases', Kübler-Ross-style (1969), of grieving will normally include cognitive acceptance. Most strikingly: denial (and the case is much the same for 'bargaining': as one bargains, one knows that what one is doing is completely, utterly hopeless, and yet it is very crude to call it necessarily irrational) includes acceptance. Denial, in such cases, is a form of (what Elizabeth Kübler-Ross helpfully calls) acceptance. It doesn't necessarily, as superficial observance would suggest, stand in the way of denial; indeed it should (and normally does) pave the way to it. Denial, properly understood, is a part of grieving in that it is far too crude to think that losing a person who was very close to one is simply a loss of one detachable element in the lifeworld. It rather threatens and *qualitatively alters* one's lifeworld.[10] Denial in such a case is the not-unreasonable resistance to this loss, this alteration; the motivated rebellion against it. It is not believable that one has lost the person; the world would have to be radically different, in order for one to have done so.

A great paradox that we live,[11] in grief, then, is that our very world has to change for us to emerge from it. Denial correctly understood is not an irrational or delusive belief, as some Cognitive Science advocates would assume; it is the form of (painful) transition from one lived world to another. Denial is an essential step on the part to complete acceptance. It is not the opposite of acceptance; *it is a transitional means to it.*[12]

Grief beyond liberal individualism

A powerful fantasy, an individualistic ideology connected I would suggest to the political philosophy of liberal individualism – the hegemonic philosophy of our time, the philosophy that, throughout this book, I am overtly or covertly challenging [13] – resists us acknowledging the truth of what I have been saying here. If liberal individualism were true of us, then we would be faced with a cleft stick. Either the loss of a close loved one wouldn't bother us that much (insofar as we conceived of ourselves as separate atomic elements lacking any co-constitution)[14] or the loss of a close loved one would *break* us (insofar as we cared deeply for the other, an other conceived of by liberalism as inviolable[15]). On the former 'economistic' interpretation (remarkably widespread, in practice, today), liberalism is fairly obviously an unattractive doctrine, and a false one. On the latter interpretation, it might seem very attractive: a kind of hymn to the sacredness and irreplaceability of the individual. The loss of individuals, on this reading of liberalism, would be impossible, literally unbearable.

But again, this is false. Sadly and wonderfully, the loss of a close loved one generally doesn't break us. Grief 'individualizes' and individuates us (Read 2018d); but through, I want to claim, our (and its) profoundly social nature.

What is it, to reconstitute our life-world, in the case of deep grief/loss? Well, as they say: time is the great healer. We can grieve and 'move on', because at a fundamental level un-understood by the hegemonic tradition of the liberal-individualist political philosophers – Hobbes, Locke, Mill and Rawls – *we are one*. We are a part of the main. We are one with others, such that loss hurts us and grief takes a toll on us in a way that 'objective thought' struggles to comprehend, but such also that it is recoverable from. For, while individuals die, together we go on.[16] The dead are present among us: for we are more than just a time-slice, and more than a slew of isolated individual atoms. When the bell tolls for someone, it tolls for us too, as part of them and them part of us; that is what makes death (the death of others) cope-able with. *Contra* liberal individualism, no human is an island. The idea that the bell tolled only for Matt when he died, such that either his death just wouldn't affect me very deeply, or that it would be a loss entirely intolerable because the loss of a unique individual the care for whom could not find any other purpose for, is, fortunately, a false idea.

This is how it is possible for someone to be irreplaceable, and yet for us to be able to recover from their loss.

This explains also how it is possible to be a fireman, a soldier, a nuclear-clean-up-worker, a revolutionary . . . How do we – and they – bear that some don't live to see the end of revolutions that they made possible? Consider for example the extraordinary heroism of Mehdi Mohammed Zeyo. He was a civilian who blew up the gates to a military base in Benghazi. This allowed the base to be seized by revolutionaries. He sacrificed his life for the success of the unlikely, unanticipated, and ultimately successful rebellion in Libya. This played a key role in the growth of the Arab Spring early in 2011, and in particular in the eventual toppling of the dictator Gaddafi.[17] To die for something greater than oneself is only possible if one is not an isolated atom – *and* if one is part of something bigger than oneself, rather than being completely incommensurable, a 'universe' unto oneself as it were.

To die for something greater than oneself requires that one *lives* for something greater than oneself. This is almost a definition of what it is to be a citizen of the Earth. To be an Earthling; someone who takes seriously their animal nature, their nature as a part of an ecosystem incomparably greater than themselves — rather than, as humans have too often done, finding this to be a matter of regret.

We can even (as a rule – there are exceptions) tolerate the murder of a loved one without it destroying us – and without being compelled to seek the execution of the perpetrator. Strange though it might sound, getting beyond insistence on the death penalty is a part of getting beyond the logic of the political philosophy of liberalism. We are a society. We can even accept murderers back into it. Liberal individualism as a political philosophy is an obstacle to realizing this. For liberal individualism pits the bereaved and the potentially vengeful, who have suffered an impossible loss, against the perpetrator. Rather than seeing us all[18] as tied together, inter-connected, inter-being.

All this adds grist to my mill: deep grief in its extremity is paradoxical;[19] and yet it is also something which, as beings who are not the isolated individuals that philosophy too often imagines, *can* nevertheless be encompassed, experienced, and emerged from.

Grief springs from the *depth* of our interconnectedness, which could be called our oneness. Grieving arises because we are not detached from one another; because genuinely human connections cannot be understood as 'external relations'.[20] If one of us takes a voyage at sea and perishes, their not being separate from the rest of us results in grief as an experience of an alteration of world. Yet this experience is not completely unworlding – not completely intolerable – because we are not separate. Because there is a body that goes on: our common humanity. This is what liberal individualism cannot understand in grief. Though the world is at present diminished for me, yet it remains: through and through more than just-mine.

And thus the delicate task of expounding the logic of grief comes down, in the end, to this: allowing the ineluctably personal dimension of it, while not illicitly bloating that into an individualist/liberal vision of what is a process (grieving) that expresses and re-achieves one's profound sociality.

Grief is living with a rip in the fabric of the lived world

In grief, the very world has changed because a condition for the world being itself - a particular presence as part of its ground, not just a figure within it - has ceased to exist. And so we come to the increasingly vital case of ecological grief. I want now to take my idea of grief being essentially about a rip in one's world, and apply it quite literally to the world. What happens when human-triggered climate change takes our winters (our snow, our heritage)? When it threatens to take our very futures? What happens when a loved species goes extinct? What happens in grief for Gaia?

Grief, I've argued, is how love survives loss. Grief is a reaction of pain and even outrage against the ripping of someone (or something) precious from out of one's lived world, the tearing of the very fabric of that world.

I've argued above that our very world has to change for us to accommodate the death of the loved and for us in due course to emerge from grief. Denial, correctly understood, is not necessarily an irrational or delusive belief here; it is rather the form of (painful) transition from one lived world to another. If there is to be complete acceptance, there must be some denial along the way; otherwise one has not been acknowledging the depth of the loss, the sense of loss.[21] Grief is how loss makes sense of the profound nature of the lost one as part of the deep ground of one's very world, rather than a substitutable element in it. Once more: *denial need not be the opposite of acceptance; it is a potent transitional means to it.*

Grief, as I've shown, radically differs in its logic from (ordinary) sadness over a loss. If an acquaintance dies, or if a loved object is lost, this does not imply the need for one to construct a new or renewed 'world' in response. Deep grief by contrast amounts to a deformation of the lifeworld. Metaphorically, one can describe it as having a hole punched into the lived world. That is why, unlike some small sadness, grief necessitates a transformed lifeworld, one in which that hold is somehow repaired or lived with.

As lived, grief then is not the removal of one object among others from the world; rather, the character of (that) world is altered. To put this in a 'gestalt' metaphor: it is a change not in figure but in ground. Sadness is a figure on a world with a secure taken-for-granted ground. Grief involves rather the reconfiguring *of the ground itself.* (This takes time).

Grief springs from the depth of our interconnectedness, which be called our internal relatedness with one another (Chapter 6), or (as I intimated in the previous section) our collective wholeness. Grieving arises because, contrary to the prevailing ideology of our liberal individualist society, we are not detached from one another.

In grieving, what one does is acknowledge the rip, the tear in that world that the passing of the loved subject made.

And now surely it is becoming plain how utterly appropriate the reaction of grieving is to the losses, the all-too-avoidable 'losses', that our species (and in particular a recent, privileged subset of it) has wreaked upon our shared world. For the wholeness, the interconnectedness, that I just sketched, does not end at the frontier of the human. Liberal-humanist and anthropocentric fantasies notwithstanding, it goes far beyond that frontier.

This can help us understand the less venal forms of climate-denial. That is, it helps us understand why some quite feeling, decent and intelligent people were for a long time tempted into its post-truth absurdities. For denial, properly understood, is a part of grieving; in that it is far too crude to think that losing a person who was very close to one is simply a loss of one substitutable element in the lifeworld. Such loss rather threatens and qualitatively alters one's lifeworld. Similarly, it is in a certain sense unimaginable, even absurd, to think of us destroying our very climate. That climate is not one substitutable element in the lifeworld. It is its very ground. No wonder people resist and deny. (This deepens the sense in which, as I argued in Chapter 2, climate-deniers are human too … and we have more in common with them than we might like to admit[22]).

To get beyond such denial requires you to remake your very world.

Denial is the not altogether unreasonable resistance to the devastating loss I've described. It is the motivated rebellion against it. After all, it is not entirely believable that one has lost (that we have lost) the person/the being/ the species/the sacred place. It is simply too awful to be (believed). This denial may at first take the form of a temptation toward out-and-out disbelief; then perhaps of ghostly or spectral presences (the lost loved one is present in their absence).[23] The 'lifeworld' one inhabits in such ways resists the absence of the non-substitutable one. Somewhat similarly: it is not surprising that so many people have been desperately hoping that the science must somehow be wrong, or acting as if we can still hope for the continuation of our same old world, while continuing to burn fossil fuels like there's no tomorrow. This willingness to disbelieve is something that those with vested interests in denying climate breakdown have willfully exploited.

It requires strength, and indeed grace, gradually to turn denial into acceptance and to build a new life.

To conclude this section: the integrity of the shared lifeworld is of course threatened by climate breakdown. The trust we have in life, in life going on, in/on this good Earth, is in my view a good example of what Knud Løgstrup calls (1997) a sovereign expression of life. It is something we have a sort of right to take for granted, as part of our frame. It is the ground of the lifeworld. Climate grief is an expression of that ground being, in-credibly, thrown into doubt. When I talk about the inception of climate breakdown, especially with young people, or with those I love the most (e.g. my mother), I find it hurts my heart. This is climate grief in action. I don't *want* to have to talk about it all honestly with them. That is what I have been talking about in this section, and will draw an inference from in the next: how our resistance to the terrible truth of our condition, which can easily take the form of soft climate-denial, is to be expected and is a big clue to what matters most to us, and, perhaps, to how to manifest that mattering more in our lives and acts.

Climate grief as living with an *ongoing* rip in the fabric of our shared world

How, though, do climate-grief and extinction-grief differ from grief at the loss of a loved one?

When we 'lose' a species or an ecosystem or some previously taken-for-granted part of our future, it's actually been murdered. 'Lost' is a euphemism.[24] Thus awakened eco-grief is typically angry as well as distraught. It resembles the grief of someone close to a murder-victim.

But there is a difference even from that case. Climate-grief and grief over the degradation of our beautiful natural world never lessens, let alone goes away. These emergencies will define our entire lifetime, and at present (and without doubt for a long time to come, because of the time-lags in the system) are still getting worse (Chapters 3 & 4).

Thus, while a healthy reaction to grief over a lost loved one is to grieve deeply and then gradually to recover, there is no 'recovery' from ecological grief. The only recovery from it that is possible at all is *for us to change the world such that it no longer keeps deteriorating.*[25]

This is how eco-grief, grief at the tearing from us of what we love and are not willing to do without, leads into radical eco-action (Chapter 7). When we finally allow ourselves to face the full terrible reality of what our species is doing to our home and our kin and our very future, then, to avoid getting stuck in depression or despair (which are understandable responses), there is no alternative but to struggle. And given how far gone we are now, because we allowed denial to rule for so long, that surely means: to rebel.

This is how grief expresses and powers the love that is the one thing that might yet save our future from being – once more to use a variation on Orwell – a boot stamping on the faces of all beings (humans included) forever. Until perhaps there are relatively few, or even no such beings left.

In grief, as in disasters (Chapter 4), the ground changes. It *gives way* temporarily. The ground beneath our feet is no longer there. This makes possible real change. Again: can breakdown be breakthrough?

The coming vast crisis of mental ill-health

There is a vast mental-health crisis coming. Those suffering from eco-grief are in the vanguard of it (Conroy 2019). Perhaps those of us in this position are the lucky ones. It doesn't feel like it, especially as we suffer, sometimes very badly (Bendell 2020). We feel like the unlucky ones; there's much we would sometimes give to be relieved of this power to see and feel. But I would argue that we are indeed we are the lucky ones; because it will be harder for those who follow, for those who experience their certainties being untimely ripped from them in more perilous circumstances than those which we are experiencing right now.

This crisis – a pandemic of grief, depression and worse that will rise in intensity as the world's citizens wake up to the slow death-march that their 'leaders' and the world's rich and powerful more generally are laying on for them – may yet, however, be a making of us. For what powers rebellion is facing the terrible truth of the decaying future we have manufactured. What enables us to face up to that truth, after and as we work through denial and depression, is our grief. Above all, grief is an expression of a profound love. It involves essentially a coming to terms with the loss of the loved (cf. Williston 2019, ch. 4). A truthful coming to terms which, I am suggesting, may well issue in a renewed determination for that loss not to be endlessly ongoing.

You might think that there is already a huge crisis of mental ill-health in our world. You'd be right. Levels of mental ill-health among teens for instance, in countries such as the US and the UK, are sky-high; generationally, average rates of anxiety are becoming typical of what was considered psychopathological, just a generation earlier (McCarthy 2019; American Psychological Association 2000). Much of this is due to social media; much to rising levels of inequality (Wilkinson & Pickett 2017); and *an increasing amount to climate* (Rao & Powell 2021), of which a striking exemplar is of course Greta Thunberg herself, who didn't speak for a year, so abject was her horror at the crisis. The coming mental health crisis, as climate decline sets in, may yet dwarf the rest.

This book has been hard to write. Harder than I anticipated. Chapters 2 and 3 were especially hard, but none of it has been easy. The present chapter has been hard, too. I'm writing about something that bruises my heart almost every day. And sometimes the writing processes the bruise, and other times it re-stimulates it. *Personal* collapse feels a possibility (Kingsnorth 2014), and sometimes a partial lived reality (The Poetry of Predicament 2021). When I came back from COP26 at Glasgow, for instance, even though I had been expecting virtually nothing there, I still found myself desolately disappointed by the brutal reality of the harrowing path that our 'leaders' have placed us on. It is utterly dire, to contemplate where we are headed unnecessarily. It yields despair, and it would be tempting to try to 'give up'; that would, however, mean giving up on what one loves, and on oneself, so is not actually an option.

I'm one of the lucky ones; to be going through this pain now, while things are tolerable (believe it or not, these are the good years) and while we can still make a difference. But please don't leave me alone in feeling this. As I have argued in this book already, we get through this together, or not at all. (And if we really get serious at getting through it together, then it could be great. A *transformation*).

The lack of sufficient admittance of the possibility/*probability* of climate/civilizational collapse makes such collapses more probable. To hold the difficulty of the reality we face, together, to support each other's nervous systems as we have trouble holding it: this is now true love. There is no alternative other than a collective downgoing. That's it in a nutshell. The coming mental health crisis is actually a coming back to life, to ourselves, to reality. It is a coming into a truer mental *health*.

Just as disasters may be the making of us, so may this rising tide of eco-pain. The onset of this pandemic of emotional pain is an inevitable consequence of life itself, health itself. It yields a hidden silver lining.

In this crisis, we need love – and (that means) grief

When I talk about the heart in this book, I mean it quite literally. I mean our beating hearts. And I mean the seat of our love. I mean the place that flutters and that can suffer palpitations. I mean the centre of us.

Love is at the root of all the aversive emotions. We feel eco-anxiety because we love life. We feel fear/terror for the fate of those who we love (including ourselves!). We feel rage at the state of things because of our passion for those weaker or more powerless than ourselves and because they are unnecessarily being put in jeopardy. And we feel heartbreak and grief for what is 'lost' and what more will be lost. For the ripping from us of what we love.

Or consider eco-anger. There has been much talk of eco-anxiety, and of climate-grief. What about eco-anger/climate-anger? Why has that concept not been wider spread?

Probably because we don't want to acknowledge it or accept it. Anger is a difficult emotion; it is risky, it can of course easily turn into hurt in others. But that doesn't mean we should turn away from it. Anger has an important role in drawing our attention to injustices (Nussbaum 2004, 67–70). And denying it isn't going to help resolve it. Anger, rage, are realities, and not infrequently they are motivated by love. They are an energy which cannot be ignored, and should instead be harnessed. Perhaps we have not much surfaced the concept of climate-anger because once we do, it is harder not to act . . .

Look for instance at how effectively Extinction Rebellion has sometimes managed to segue rage into effective consciousness-change.[26] Eco-rage is part of our ecopsychological response to what has been up until now.

I have argued in this chapter that the difference between climate- and eco-grief on one hand and individual grief on the other, is that the former doesn't stop. It can't heal. It's an open wound, continually re-damaged by the ever-growing frequency and magnitude of climate and ecological disasters. This is true of all the ecological aversive emotions.

And thus: climate grief is future-directed as well as past-directed. Unlike ordinary grief, it naturally morphs into anxiety too. We grieve for what is already gone and the more to follow that will go, as the climate declines further. Grief for what we haven't yet lost, anticipatory grief, is a rational anxiety too. A reasonable fear for what our world including our own lives will be like, if we get to be old.

The (only) consolation of and for all this: as I've said, it's that it powers us. It energizes.

And thus there is a way *through*. There is a route built on love. But it's now plain to see how that route is the very opposite of blind optimism, wishful thinking, or hoping it will just go away. As my witness here, I want to quote the provocative closing words of a wonderful essay by the literary climate scientist Kate Marvel:

> I have no hope that these changes can be reversed. We are inevitably sending our children to live on an unfamiliar planet. But the opposite of hope is not despair. It is grief. Even while resolving to limit the damage, we can mourn. And here, the sheer scale of the problem provides a perverse comfort: we are in this together. The swiftness of the change, its scale and inevitability, binds us into one, broken hearts trapped together under a warming atmosphere. // We need courage, not hope. Grief, after all, is the cost of being alive. We are all fated to live lives shot through with sadness, and are not worth less for it. Courage is the resolve to do well without the assurance of a happy ending. Little molecules, random in their movement, add together to a coherent whole. Little lives do not. But here we are, together on a planet radiating ever more into space where there is no darkness, only light we cannot see.
>
> Marvel 2018

This chapter has been an applied philosophical investigation of the field of 'eco-psychology', according to which we are not individual egos but rather indissolubly part of at the ecosphere. I spoke above in the conventional way of depression and anxiety as instances of mental ill-health. But when we understand ourselves aright, ecopscyhologically, then the aversive emotions that come to us from the climate crisis and the ecological emergency more generally shine in their true colours: as *healthy*. If you're not sometimes terrified and enraged, you are not paying attention. Despair, depression, anxiety, panic, grief: these are all rational responses to the emergency. It is mentally healthy to feel these things. (Just not, one hopes, to get stuck in them). It is thus healthy sometimes to have what conventional (un-)wisdom may call 'symptoms' of 'mental ill-health'. When we feel these aversive emotions, it is as if we are the consciousness of the Earth itself, manifesting the pain of what is happening to it.[27]

The final upshot of my argument, then, is: becoming clear on the role that grief etc. can play in motivating action in the face of climate breakdown. Conventional wisdom in climate campaigning until recently was that emotions like grief (and anxiety, and despair, and depression) fuel inertia. Indeed, part of the pushback towards some of my work and writings has been to accept that what I'm saying is broadly correct but to claim that it will simply scare or sadden people into inaction if it is conveyed so directly. So, allegedly, I shouldn't say it.

That was my fear too at first, and it stopped me from speaking out truthfully for some years. But, since I started speaking out without reservation in 2016, and proclaiming the bitter and brilliant truth that this civilization is finished, such has *not* been my experience. The extraordinary upsurge of brave willingness to face the truth and express one's fears and feelings has been manifested for instance in Extinction Rebellion, and (I hope and trust) in my small part in that upwelling. This chapter challenges the conventional failed wisdom around (the old, failed) climate campaigning and 'optimistic' messaging and argues instead in favour of directly and resolutely looking at – and *feeling* – the scale and trajectory of climate breakdown. It really is rational to feel grief in the fact of the destruction of our world. There would be something wrong with you if you didn't sometimes feel this. And that feeling can fuel the very movements that we need, which might conceivably even yet prevent collapse. And it can strengthen us for coping with whatever collapse does come, if and when it does, by enabling us to know ourselves, in our full wholeness.

At the start of this chapter I spoke in a 'natural' way about the 'worst' experience I've ever had with ordinary grief. But examine the situation, and you see that without grief, we're not human. The life without grief when grief is called for is not worth living. So the 'worst' is necessarily *part of the best.*

If you don't feel eco-grief yet, believe me you will. And it's better to let yourself feel it sooner rather than later. It is indissoluble from eco-anxiety. And ditto. And these two are an essential part of the human life at this time. We are not ourselves, not ourselves at our best, without such grief. These emotions may be aversive, but they are also utterly necessary. And even: beautiful.

That is why they may yet be the making of us. If our common future is to be saved, these emotions will be a central part in that process.

So let us embrace them. And thus, each other.

6

Can We Understand Cetacean Society?
Can We Change Ourselves?

There is no folly of the beasts of the earth which is not infinitely outdone by the madness of men.
                              – Herman Melville, Moby Dick, Chapter 87.

Individuals or in-dividual?

As in the previous chapter, this chapter opens with some thinking of a slightly more academic philosophical nature than has been present in most of the rest of the book (because ideally what I am claiming in this chapter needs some more academic philosophical placement and defence than was the case in Chapters 1–4). Reader, I'd earnestly suggest you give it a try, but, if you are finding it hard to compute the material in the first three sections, then you can always skip to begin with the section called 'The cultures of social whales and dolphins'. The guts of the chapter, its importance for the argument of the book as a whole, lie principally in its second half.

I undertake in this chapter to offer some reflections from animality on 'individualism', freedom and survival. This chapter suggests a rhetoric or philosophy of internal relatedness within greater wholes, that (I claim) we ought to be moved by, in the midst of the ecological emergency. By looking at a heart-rending part of our history, I seek to make available a way in which we could change history, starting now.

Today our world is largely possessed by possessive 'liberal individualism' (MacPherson 1962), the idea that who we are is essentially individuals who need to be allowed to be free of constraint. Despite its name, closer examination reveals this to be a pseudo-individualism. 'Individualism' as it actually exists typically doesn't encourage a liberatory independence of thought.[1]

Rather, 'liberal individualism' is largely a gigantic form of emulative conformism. When people all spout the same claim to be above all free unique individuals, they are unknowingly expressing this conformism. It is a telling tragic-comic feature of our time that the one thing in the realm of political philosophy that it seems that we are good at, namely individualism, we actually are no good at!

But at the level of explicit ideology at any rate, liberal individualism and narratives of freedom – versions of the world in which human beings can be considered initially as separate atoms[2] whose greatest fulfilment is in their own conceptions and in their own power rather than in essentially common projects – tend to predominate. And these have real consequences.

This position is utterly disastrous, at a moment in history when, more than ever before, we need to think *anti-conformistically*. We need to transform our societies, not conform to their failing trajectory. And we need to do so collectively, as a community. To address this crisis adequately, we need to think truly very radically, but the form of that thinking must, as set out in Chapters 3–5, be us thinking (and acting) as a civilization, not just as an aggregate of 'individuals'.

What would it be to really take seriously, contrary to the self-image of our time, our identity as a 'we', our belonging to each other and to our places, to our homes, and our planetary home? To be *us*, rather than just to be lots of 'mes'[3] To pull together, to be together, changing our destiny? What changes would it mean at the level of discourse and rhetoric? At the levels of reality, of vision, of policy? (And what changes would it require, philosophically?)

As I've argued elsewhere, a central such change is the overcoming of the prejudice of the very idea of 'the individual' (Read 2010a). It is not persons which are the fundamental units of social existence, **in-dividual**. It is embedded communities.[4]

We are born into community.[5] The fantasy of the individual-as-person resists this long temporality,[6] and gets caught up in 'presentism', in transience and often in despair/denial about mortality.

People die. The community lives. Unless it stupidly commits itself to death.

It might be objected that the community clearly *can* be divided without being destroyed – killed – whereas persons cannot be. But in the sense in which I mean to speak of division, it isn't obvious that that's true. If the internal relations within the community are riven, ruptured, so much that it is no longer a whole, then it cannot adequately function. And will commit itself to death, as most previous actually-existing civilizations have done – and as we at present quite clearly are doing.[7] Our rivenness today by 'culture wars' looks to me the sign of a culture in decline and fall, for this factionalism, moralism and general lack of civic behaviour makes it hard to raise our gaze to focus on the tidal wave slowly coming to engulf the lot of us, friends and foes alike.

Please note that I do not mean to pre-judge here who exactly 'us' includes, who is necessarily or actually present in or absent from such community. As I've just implied, it's sometimes clearly now necessary though will normally be rare (I suggest) for the community to be truly global.[8] However, I would also suggest that – against the liberal individualist fantasy of social contracting as the basis of society – past and future people should be included in virtually any meaningful community or '*demos*'; and some non-human animals in most.[9] We are not riven apart from them, any more than we are from each other. We exist over space, over species, *and* over time: as generations, even as a kind of 'infinity' (the community is potentially without end, as per Chapter 1), not as time-slices.

This 'anti-individualism' of mine is not, I hope, a speculative 'metaphysical' thesis. As will become clear, it is rather an attempted 'reminder' (of an utterly basic aspect of our existence, outlined above). It is a corrective to the propaganda in which we swim, the ideology by which we have been for centuries possessed. And in the end it is an invitational gesture: an ethical and political move that I am inviting you to join.

The enduring relevance of Peter Winch

I take as a lodestone in this chapter Wittgenstein's thinking on the nature of society, a thinking that has been focal for most of my books (Sharrock & Read 2002; Hutchinson, Read & Sharrock 2008; Read 2012b). But, as I've explored in those books, Wittgenstein's explicit writings on society (and 'social science') are not extensive. One needs to extrapolate – and it is helpful to have a proxy. I take my mentor, the late Peter Winch, as a rough proxy for Wittgenstein in these matters.

The thinking of Winch is deeply helpful, I believe, in orienting us toward these matters – and in orienting us from them onto what I now want to bring into focus. Namely, how we might see and inhabit what I have stipulated above better, if we were to cast our eyes wider than just to our fellow humans. I'll briefly outline it here, for those unfamiliar with it.

Consider first then the following important quotation:

Understanding is the goal of explanation and the end-product of successful explanation. But ... [u]nless there is a form of understanding that is not the result of explanation, no such thing as explanation would be possible. An explanation is called for only where there is, or is at least thought to be, a deficiency in understanding. But there has to be some standard against which such a deficiency is to be measured: and that standard can only be an understanding that we already have. Furthermore, the understanding we already have is expressed in the concepts which constitute that form of the subject matter we are concerned with. These concepts on the other hand also express certain aspects of the life characteristic of those who apply them.

Winch 1990, x

Certain aspects of the lives of cetaceans, and of what we can see of their concepts, shall be a central part of my topic, in this chapter. I shan't dwell at all on the not-insignificant problems I think there are with Winch specifically *on* non-human animals (Taylor 2020).[10] Rather than looking at what Winch wrote about animals, which was sometimes blinkered by an unthinking humanism, I hope to extrapolate some of his methods to thinking about animals and, thereby, to thinking about ourselves.

I want to suggest what is I think is an eminently reasonable proposal: that, by virtue of being thoroughly social mammals and by virtue of the concrete connections we have managed to forge with animals such as cetaceans, we already have some understanding of them[11] and can come to close our deficit in understanding. That is not to say that doing so will not be difficult and indeed painful in certain respects. So we may even resist doing it. But, by virtue of the nature of cetaceans' difference from us, the effect of closing that deficit may be much weightier than first appears.

I'm especially concerned here by the self-images academics often have as 'social scientists' or as philosophers or similar. That self-image tends to suggest a certain distance from one's subject-matter that I think is itself part of the problem. It can distance us as beings from one another. It is a spectatorial distance that we dignify with names like 'objectivity' and that we expand rather than close. (This kind of distance is, not by the way, already present in the use of deadening terms such as 'environment' to encompass the living world that co-constitutes us).

Consider the following helpful interpretive remark, aimed at highlighting the inappropriateness of such would-be spectatorship:

> The central message of Winch . . . – which has often been overlooked, or ignored – is the suggestion that in studying a so-called 'primitive society' we might, if we engage in the task sensitively and imaginatively, learn something important about our own taken-for-granted form of life. I . . . seek to follow Winch's advice that the very point of trying to learn about some apparently incoherent way of life is just as much to do with striving for an enhanced conception of one's own social conditions of existence, as it is with understanding that other way of life."

Pleasants 1999, 2, my emphasis

In support of this attribution by Pleasants to Winch, consider this remark from Winch: '[I]n clarifying his own mind about what he can and can't accept, a man is making important discoveries about himself: discoveries that may be barely distinguishable from decisions about what manner of man he wants to be' (Winch 1987, 138f). Consider also this following important remark of Winch's: 'seriously to study another way of life is necessarily to seek to extend our own' (Winch 1964, 32).

The activity of understanding them sets off a dialectic, in which we come to understand ourselves differently too. That dialectical activity or process is what I am talking about here. It is also what I am doing in this chapter.

I want to make here a certain comparison between so-called 'primitive society', as Winch seeks to avoid misunderstanding such society, and cetacean society. Clearly any such comparison is going to be a tricky enterprise. It goes entirely without saying, I hope, that I am obviously not seeking to say that primitive peoples are 'merely animals', in the quasi-derogatory way that conventionally the term 'animal' is understood! (In passing: we are all of course animals, biologically, and that is something of which we should remind ourselves more often than we do). On the contrary, implicit in this book is that those of us in the failing societies of the contemporary global North need badly to learn from indigenous peoples.

However, I will be seeking to say that it may turn out that sometimes, even when they are strange to us, some animal societies can sometimes ultimately in an important sense be easier for us to come to understand and appreciate than some human societies (including some respects even our own). If, that is, we are willing to do the surprising and difficult thing that it is to really take them seriously. Which means, as Pleasants and Winch stress, to allow ourselves to 'extend' our conceptions of who we really are, and thus potential our way of life.

So: what Winch is about, in the *key* part of his work indexed in the quote I offered from Pleasants, is not a hierarchical or spectatorial understanding of others. *The understander is always just as implicated in the process.* Understanding, we might usefully say, is always in one key sense a *second-person* process (or a process of developing a first-person *plural*), not a third-person would-be/ pseudo- objectivity. (The dubious thing about objectivity as a goal is that it seeks to remove the person doing the understanding from the situation altogether. The 'third person' is in this sense no person at all. Second-person understanding, by contrast, makes figural a relationship, and both sides of the relationship are permanently in play. Thus a 'new' first-person plural can be formed, in which we come to understand those who are as yet unborn, or those from other places or even other species, as part of who *we* are).

This means too that being understanding of others, being always in some sense reciprocal (because it makes no sense to seek to extricate oneself from it), is always *critical* (Pleasants 2010). I mean by this something quite specific: it involves potential re-assessment of society, which means of *ourselves*. It opens us to change. One is not merely coldly observing another. One is participating with them; and so the gaze can come back and envelope ourselves.[12]

Anthropology, sociology etc. are always inherently ethical enterprises (unless they fail to be, or obscure this, in which case they are *un*ethical). A trying to run away from that is precisely a crucial aspect of what gets obscured, in the attempt to categorize these subjects as sciences. The rhetorical move of classifying oneself as a scientist is in this regard a dangerous obfuscation.

Much of this emerges in Winch's late paper 'Can we understand ourselves?' (1997). In this he returns to the theme of his classic paper, 'Understanding a primitive society' (1964), where he critiques the anthropologist Evans-Pritchard's famous effort to understand the witchcraft practices of the Azande as a kind of wannabe technoscience.[13]

What Winch is crucially trying to do is to overcome the typical assumption of superiority on the part of anyone taking themselves to be a social scientist, a special case of the typical assumption of superiority felt by members of 'advanced' societies when comparing themselves with members of 'primitive' societies. The assumption of superiority inherent in the standard concept of 'progress'. Thus: understanding a 'primitive society' is, we might say, standing under it in a certain crucial sense. One has to stand under it, or at minimum not over it as usually we (pretend to) do,[14] in order to have a chance of getting it. And, when one really stands under it, when one really tries to see how/as they see, then one is changed, and there is a constitutive possibility of real transformation. The change is minimally in one's sense of what is humanly possible, and of what is contingent and what necessary. It may be much weightier than that. One may come to see a possibility of a whole different way of living.

Stupidity, irrationality or incoherence is always relative to certain framing assumptions. The way that Wittgenstein and Winch pursue this point is to ask: what 'language-game' is being played here? What is actually being done by and in these practices including of course linguistic aspects of the practices? Evans-Pritchard may have the obvious frames, but perhaps we need a non-obvious one, in order to effect a deeper, more real understanding. (That's what Winch provided, by suggesting for instance that the Azande practice might be better compared to a non-superstitiously understood Christian prayer than to a sort of ludic techno-science. This was the kind of way in which he thought it possible, though not easy, for us to find a route, less directly than we wished, towards understanding of a society much removed from our own).

Understanding a cetacean society

Winch famously wrote about 'Understanding a [so-called] primitive society'. In terms of intellectual history, his doing so, back in the early 1960s, should be considered an early move in the direction of a post-colonial, post-elitist reorientation of our understanding of others. As just outlined, it *pulls* that effort of understanding powerfully out of the trope of looking down on them, and instead into the zone of being with them, being changed by them; and it helps makes possible deep learning from them. The way it does this is in part by placing them at a greater distance from us in a key respect: Winch warns against reading their practices as a kind of failed effort at our technology or science (which is so integral to us, so much a ground we take for granted, that we unwisely tend to assume that it must be similarly integral to other societies too). What we do or could have in common with them can only be seen clearly once we effect such a shift. Connections emerge through clear vision of the reality of differences.

As I've already noted, at the present moment in history, we very badly need to learn from 'primitive' (i.e., indigenous) societies. We need to practise 'reverse anthropology'. We need to learn from them how to live lightly on the Earth, rather than (as those who Winch – and Wittgenstein (2020) – criticized did) seeing them as a 'primitive' stage on the way to our state of 'progress'.

I'll not try to add to the broad canvass of the way in which we in contemporary globalized failing civilization need to learn from indigeneity; others have done that job far better than I can. (Let me strongly recommend on this front Yunkaporta 2019, and Parry 2017). Such a task is entirely vital at this historical moment. One of the few good features of COP26 was growing recognition in the climate movement, and to some extent even in the official COP itself, that the world needs to listen to indigenous (and remaining independent (of globalization) peasant) peoples. Engaging more deeply with indigenous wisdoms would represent a real ray of hope in our desperate travail.

Can we go further still? I seek in this chapter to push the boat as far as is conceivable, in challenging liberal individualist philosophy. Indigenous peoples tend to be far removed from our atomistic tendencies, our separation from the natural world, our destructiveness,[15] but I think that *we may profit too from a new and less familiar 'object of comparison' that shakes us even more drastically out of our complacency.*

Thus I propose that we bring into focus another kind of society, another form of culture, one more distant in an obvious way from our own ... With my Winchian 'frame of reference' in place, then, let me turn explicitly to cetaceans.

The cultures of social whales and dolphins

I turn now specifically to the social species of whales and dolphins. For, as just noted, the present chapter does not primarily occupy itself with the important topic of letting ourselves be changed by those aspects of very different 'primitive' human societies we might come to find useful, if taken seriously (Read 2010b; Read 2018c, ch. 6). It looks yet 'further' afield. It aims at maximum philosophical boldness.

In roughly the kind of way indicated by cetologist Volker Deecke:

> To appreciate other people's cultures ... you have to shed your prejudices - strip yourself down to where you are just human and then build up your understanding. With killer whales, I feel we are moving one step beyond. You must strip all the way down to just being a mammal, then start from scratch trying to imagine how whales perceive and interpret the world. Imagine 'clicking' [focusing a sonar beam] on another member of your society.
>
> Chadwick 2006, 137

My key reference point henceforth is the well-regarded book *The Cultural Lives of Whales and Dolphins* by Hal Whitehead and Luke Rendell (2015). This book has an audacious title. The *cultural* lives of these creatures: really? Are they genuinely cultural?

I will not attempt here strictly speaking to define 'culture'. But a working idea of what it means might be something like this: there is culture if there are substantial specific traditions that are 'inherited'/transmitted *by way of teaching and learning and emulation* etc., rather than by way of genes.

If something roughly like this is what culture means, then it can be debated whether non-human primates are cultural beings. I think that there is a very good case indeed that some of them are, but there is still just about some possibility of debating the matter.

But what Whitehead and Rendell show us is that there is really no such possibility of debating the matter, when it comes to cetaceans. It is simply clear that it would be chauvinist speciesism not to grant the term to the social species of cetaceans.

And this is truly extraordinary, when one considers the quite fantastic butchery that they have been subject to at human hands, over the past few centuries. They retain their culture(s), despite this, albeit surely a damaged culture: imagine humanity, from a far lower initial base of numbers, being then taken down to about a thousandth of its size, with the burden of the slaughter often falling strongly upon the wise, the elders, the leaders. This is what we have done to cetaceans. It is incredible in its barbarity, cruelty – and stupidity. It is soul-rending. Indeed, clothes-rending: when one really tries to contemplate it, in both the horror of particular examples and the vast scale of it, one wants to do something like rend one's garments, in despair and shame.

And yet: they manage to go on. . .

Take a famous example: the singing of humpback whales. It has now been shown that their songs evoke mimetic and creative responses; that different groups alter their songs in patterns that look much the same as human fashions. We are still somewhat far from understanding what these songs are for or mean, but we already know enough about them to see that they are far more clearly cultural than are most bird songs.

Or take the increasingly strong evidence of detailed communication among orcas (Chadwick 2006, 122–3 & 134).

Or take tool use and its spread among certain groups of cetaceans.

Or take the playful habits of self-decoration that pass around some of them like fads.

Or take their care for the dying, and their enduring interest in and connectedness, often, to the dead (Chadwick 2006, 116–17).

Or take one which was a bit of a clincher for me: the way that some groups of orcas, roughly, go on holiday. They travel hundreds of miles to interesting, warm parts of the ocean, and hang out and play there. They don't eat or engage in sexual activity there. When they have had a good rest, they return, as it were, to work.

It's not all 'nicey nicey': orcas sometimes exhibit xenophobia.[16] (Though even this they tend to handle rather better than chimps or humans often do. They will sometimes form up in long 'warrior' lines facing each other like armies; but these aggressive formations rarely lead to damaging mutual combat).

All these phenomena we can probably understand to some degree by rough analogy to ourselves.

But here Whitehead and Rendell make another audacious move. They suggest that another mark of culture, which we should look for in cetaceans to confirm that the adjective 'cultural' is appropriately applied to them, is: social stupidity. It is possible for cultural beings to be stupid, sub-optimal, in ways that are not open to uncultural beings.

This we can understand at a suitably high level of abstraction by reference to ourselves (we are all too familiar with human stupidity at scale); but the point about such stupid, irrational or incoherent behaviour is that in its specificity it resists such understanding.[17] We say, in such cases, 'But that's just *stupid . . . Why* are they doing that??'

Stupid social behaviour in this manner is very unusual in the animal world. More often, we'll simply assume that they lack the cognitive capacity to be capable either of relevant intelligence or stupidity. It's not an accident that it's very rare that we say, seriously, meaning it, as we do of fellow humans, 'But that's just stupid, why are they doing that?', of nonhuman animals.

Some of what I have already mentioned *could* be called stupid: xenophobia perhaps; or self-decoration (what's the point of prettifying oneself?); or interest in or 'care' for the dead (why bother with mere pieces of dead matter?) . . .

But Whitehead and Rendell offer a more powerful, less tendentious, more novel case; one which we can't easily come to understand and find non-stupid, as we do not find self-decoration (let alone respect/grief for the dead) stupid. The case they offer, which is harder for us to understand, is: mass strandings.

Now, some mass strandings can be explained, tragically, by reference to pollution having made the cetaceans in question ill; or by reference to the sonar which we and in particular our navies are, indiscriminately and highly destructively, filling our seas with. But there are plenty of cases which don't fit this kind of model. Cases where one or some of the pod are beached, stuck, ill or wounded, while others, fit and healthy, are not decisively so. And then it appears stupid, that the latter are unwilling to save themselves even when their conspecifics are doomed – unless we change the frame, and, instead of asking repeatedly why the dolphin won't save itself or allow itself to be saved, we step back to think in this case about whether the notion of self in play here may be prejudicial.

Perhaps the cetacean sense of self transcends what for us are divisions between 'individuals'.

From a distance, of the right kind

This is the way in which we might come to understand cetacean society, broadly after Winch: by placing it initially at a greater distance from ourselves (though *not* othering or objectifying it), and thus allowing ourselves to actually see then what it is like for them.

And thus opening ourselves to possible change.

The Whitehead-Rendell account, which points in that direction, fits with other things we know about dolphins and whales too. For instance, about their terrible distress in many cases when forcibly separated from each other; about the super-intelligent way they seek to protect each other against us when we try to capture or kill them, with extraordinary subterfuges that seek to protect in particular their young and mothers; about their intense family and extended family bonds, including the way in some species the adult males will stay with and support the matriarchs on into the menopause of the latter.

Recall Deecke's remarks, quoted earlier. To understand cetacean society, we may have to let go – which is challenging – of philosophical-ideological assumptions about the separateness of living beings from one another, assumptions which seem natural to us *re* human beings (but perhaps only because we are so deeply captive to an ideology of individualism: we don't see it, for it is the sea we swim in). We may have to contemplate the lived reality of what we would call 'larger-than-self' identity being in-dividual, not sensible of division without the rupturing of internal relations ... Internal relations are a mark of wholeness, and to claim that to invoke them is to depend on dubious notions of conceptual truth is to smuggle in a commitment to a kind of atomism: to exactly what, I am suggesting, is killing us.[18]

If we are to be/become *us*, rather than just a load of warring or mutually-indifferent 'I's, if we are to undertake such a great transformation, if we are to find some harmony and not just greater dissonance under the pressure of (incipient) climate breakdown, who then might inspire us in this becoming? I suggest we take inspiration from cetaceans. Drawing on what we know now of their intense cultures, and with specific reference to strandings, I would argue that, if they were able to speak to us, what cetaceans in a pod undergoing a mass stranding,[19] and who we were seeking to lead back out to sea, might say is: 'You ask me to save *myself*. But you haven't understood. You haven't understood that it would be (part of) myself that I would be leaving on the beach, if I did as you asked'. If we could find a way to understand that,[20] then we might have a much better chance of survival on this planet. *That* would be: being *us*.

It would be better for us if we all were profoundly internally related, as communities of cetaceans typically are. Then we might be better placed to think as a civilization. And to survive. For we would feel directly the reality of all the others who we are committing to suffering or death. And we wouldn't be able to go on doing it.

Cetaceans expand our sense of what is humanly possible *vis-à-vis* relationship and community. Or perhaps they exceed it. They indicate perhaps a spectrum upon which we are far from reptiles (who have no interest in their own young, and will eat them if they come across them), but not quite as ... advanced as them, as cetaceans. They offer us a new 'model' of what it would be to be 'internally related' to one another.

What kinds of beings do we need to be(-come) in order to survive the coming ecological devastation, and in order not to accelerate it beyond the beyond of civilizational survival? I would posit the answer as: humbler, rooted communitarian animals, not liberals or neoliberals. I think that cetaceans present us with an enormous clue as to how being thus would be: if we are willing to hear them. They are increasingly appreciated as being the smartest of beings besides ourselves. I am suggesting that they are also the wisest. And that we need to seek after their wisdom; for I have laid out in this book reasons for thinking that we may not be as wise as we have cracked ourselves up to be . . .

An anthropomorphic rhetoric?

Of course, the rhetoric of seeking to speak as cetaceans would if they were able to, could itself be questioned. If a cetacean could speak, would we understand it? That is indeed the question I'm asking. But significantly less sceptically than Wittgenstein, when he famously asked a similar question of lions.[21] For framing the question as that kind of counterfactual is potentially prejudicial. Perhaps the question is actually: when cetaceans speak, do we understand them?

Either way, the enterprise (of seeking to understand a kin and yet deeply different species or society) is certainly chancy, like with speaking for future people. But attempting it may be one of the best chances we have. For, by fomenting climate breakdown, we are on the high road to destroying ourselves (and taking down many, possibly even most, other species with us). Maybe we wouldn't, if we could manage to 'model' ourselves more on cetaceans. So let us continue to see if we can understand them.[22] My suggestion, following Winch, is that such understanding forces us simultaneously to open a possibility of change in ourselves.

Does my rhetoric involve 'anthropomorphism'? We should be wary of the rhetorical move that bars us from ever being 'anthropomorphic' with regard to other creatures. As Frans de Waal, the great contemporary primatologist, notes, such a move is tacitly in the service of a scientistic refusal to allow primatology/cetology to take seriously that the being we are seeking to understand may not be able to be understood if we restrict ourselves to traditionally narrow 'animal behaviour' vocabularies (de Waal 1999). De Waal calls such restriction 'anthropodenial': a blindness to the humanlike characteristics of other animals (or the animal-like characteristics of ourselves). My rhetoric may at times be playfully anthropomorphic, but to seek too religiously to eliminate any possible anthropomorphism from one's vocabulary risks anthropodenial, and begs the question against the intelligence, empathy, politics and *morality* of the actions of some 'higher animals'. This risk is actually a worse risk to engage in than some anthropomorphism: because, if scientistic assumptions are stopping us from realizing the complexity and (as I put it above) advancedness of some animals, that's a worse crime than the risk of some exaggeration of the latter. Just as it is a worse crime to punish someone who has done no wrong than it is to let someone free who should have been found guilty. Rather than sticking with the conservative anthropocentric assumptions of science, an elementary ethical precautionary principle hereabouts ought to err on the side of allowing non-human animals to measure up to and beyond ourselves (Read 2018b). Too much is at stake to wait until we have 'proved' that non-human animals are highly intelligent, deeply caring, sophisticatedly communicative etc.: *they* are at stake. *They* are at risk.

Moreover, and more importantly, bear in mind that I am absolutely not seeking to reduce what cetaceans do to being measurable by what we do. On the contrary, *the whole point* of this chapter is to seek to extend our sense of what might be humanly possible by seeing if we can learn from the way that cetaceans are rather different from ourselves, on the crucial point under discussion. The human race is not the measure of all cetaceans. Perhaps, indeed, to some extent it can be *the other way around*.

I'm going beyond even de Waal's anthropodenial concept – because I'm suggesting that animals really do have things to teach us.

Of course, in any case, not too much weight should be put on the particular way I've expressed what I think these dolphins/whales that won't be saved are thinking. Because we can't ask them for confirmation that that's the best way to express it.[23] We have philosophical freedom, therefore, as to how to describe the situation, so other ways of expressing the matter might be just as good, such as: 'These are my friends. I simply won't leave my friends!' But I think that this suggestion is probably less felicitous than the particular way of putting the matter that I've chosen. For, can we understand *simply not being able* to leave one's friends, even if death is the outcome? Perhaps. But humans do leave even their dearest friends, sometimes, in extreme situations, in ways that cetaceans in the strandings I am talking about do not.[24] We may stand more of a chance of being able to understand the impossibility of abandoning the self, on an extended conception of the self. This is still a great challenge, in a way *more* alien to us; but, if we make the effort to reach into it, then it can 'flip' into being clear, I think . . .

Being 'internally related' to 'others'[25]

Let's now seek to express what I am trying to draw from the cetaceans' case in order to enrich our own, in terms which Wittgenstein and Winch both employed. Winch wrote that 'to be clear about the nature of philosophy and to be clear about the nature of the social studies amount to the same thing. For *any worthwhile study of society must be philosophical in character and any worthwhile philosophy must be concerned with the nature of human society*' (Winch 1990, 3).[26] When we do philosophy properly, we must be learning something about ourselves, not just about what we are studying and thinking about if that does not appear to be about ourselves. The twist, of course, is that, in the present chapter, I am suggesting that what we learn about the nature of 'ourselves' may include selves who are not human. That 'us' may be broader than just our species. Or again: that our concern with human society, and its change, may proceed by way of a non-human society.

Perhaps we should see there as being internal relations between cetaceans, as there are not, or at least not much, between (say) reptiles, which have no caring interest in their own young or in each other. Perhaps this (cetaceans') holistic understanding can change us humans; by offering us a way of being that is less quasi-reptilian?[27]

Social relations are logical relations,[28] and logical relations are internal relations. And 'internal relations' are not really relations at all: they do not connect two pre-existing separate things. They form a transitional mode of getting us to re-understand wholes that we inhabit. They express our quintessentially second-person deeper-than-deep *inter*-relation. A relation which is somehow always available, always 'there', even when we fall away from it.

But this is of course in the final analysis an ethical point; it is not available as some reliable truth of metaphysics that can simply be counted on; it is something to be real-ized, as my next quotation helps to make clear. This is from my teacher, Stanley Cavell: '[The slave-holder is] missing something about himself, or rather something about his connection with these people, his internal relation with them' (Cavell 1979, 376). To understand what he means here, consider for instance cases of sexual relations between slaves and slave-holders, which have been widespread. Such relations give the lie to propaganda that slaves are 'sub-human'.

What the slave-holder is missing is not exactly something factive. The missing isn't like what happens when one mislays one's spectacles, forgets where they are; it's more like missing that you are actually wearing spectacles that are changing the way you see. One is in a kind of denial, or a state of unaware seeing-as or seeing-by-way-of. One needs to be freed to see others clearly as not Other; such clear vision *is* relationality; it *is* owning-up to our second-person (or first-person plural) internal-relatedness.

One way of putting what I want to say we can learn from seeking to understand cetacean 'stupidity', and from being amazed and moved by it, would be this:

Many cetaceans seem to have a more solid grip on (their) internal relatedness than we do.[29] They don't tend, when the chips are down, to regard each other as ... *others* at all.

And now consider this remark:

> What sort of issue is: Is it the *body* that feels pain? – How is it to be decided? What makes it plausible to say that it is *not* the body? – Well, something like this: if someone has a pain in his hand, then the hand does not say so (unless it writes it) and *one does not comfort the hand, but the sufferer: one looks into his face.*
>
> Wittgenstein, *Philosophical Investigations* §286, my emphasis

This is Wittgenstein expressing our internal relatedness, or mutual acknowledgement. But again, this acknowledgement is also something we can fail to do.[30]

If we are to not thus fail, we probably need both literally and metaphorically to look into cetaceans' faces. Doing so will not only lead to us no longer treating them as appallingly as we have done, mostly, to date; it will also lead to us looking again at ourselves, and at what perhaps we could better seek to emulate.

Human society as non-understandable

I don't[31] understand most of my fellow humans. I don't understand how our 'advanced' society is advancing so blithely toward self-apocalypse. I think that there's something crucial about our self-destructive path that virtually all of my fellow humans are somehow seeking not to understand. As Upton Sinclair famously pointed out, it is difficult for someone to understand something when their salary depends on them not understanding it. While Wittgenstein sought to remind us that philosophical problems are at root problems of the will rather than of the intellect.

In a way, of course, I understand all this perfectly well. I'm familiar with it in the first person, not least from my frequent experience as a philosopher of not wanting to understand things that I would just rather not. But I find it very hard indeed to understand how one can allow oneself to be ruled by it, given the stakes, and once it is brought to consciousness.[32] This is about facing up to things one doesn't want to see and hear. We don't want to hear about what we are doing to ourselves and our animal kin and our descendants. We don't want to face the destruction we are wreaking on our present and future. And virtually nobody wants to hear what I am saying right now.

I don't understand my fellow humans; virtually any of them. I don't understand how we are virtually all slowly walking more or less willingly into mass-suicide. Or, more accurately still perhaps: we are helping (at least by omission) in the involuntary 'assisted suicide' . . . of our future dependents – not altogether unlike a doctor practising mass involuntary euthanasia.

And here's what I think and dare to hope: maybe reflecting deeply on how cetaceans do sometimes walk willingly into mass-suicide – because, in a way so wonderfully, they are unable or unwilling to imagine leaving each other, as we see played out in the incredibly moving way that they actively resist being saved, in mass strandings – maybe such reflection might help us figure out how not to walk into global suicide. Because perhaps we're doing so only because, unlike them, we find it too easy individualistically to imagine leaving each other: and, in particular, leaving our children to their fate.[33] Maybe we can learn to be more like cetaceans, who will not do this.

Of course, even saying out loud that I don't understand most of my conspecifics is itself *inter alia* an attempt at waking us, collectively, up. When I say, 'I don't understand most human beings (including maybe therefore you, dear reader)', it's not a dry spectatorial claim about what I do or don't know, or am not capable of, it's rather an attempt (a risky one, of course, because it might ironically seem arrogant, because seemingly self-righteous), through bringing out a rupture between us, to see how we might become closer-bound together. Putting at a distance, in pursuit of a deeply desired deeper unity. The move is rather like that made by J.M. Coetzee's *Elizabeth Costello* (2004), in the eponymous work (and in his brilliant Tanner Lectures, 'The Lives of Animals' (1997)). The move is aimed at *real-izing* our potential internal relatedness. It is a complex rhetorical move, though not a manipulative one, once exposed to view and explained as I've done here.

Coetzee's Elizabeth Costello presents herself as a wounded animal; wounded by a lack of human internal relatedness both with her and with the (non-human) animals she speaks out to defend. I'm presenting myself as a wounded animal for similar reasons. And I'm asking: can we learn from the wounded and unwounded animals we see in mass strandings? Can we learn, through reflecting on the wholeness of cetacean life, to heal the wound of our separateness, and thus to start to heal the world we have so badly wounded?

Like Winch, I put us at a distance in order to find a genuine way to bring us closer. We could realize our internal relatedness by embracing ecological (and indeed inter-specific) wholeness, by facing climate reality (Foster 2019), together. By being honest enough to admit that if we let global over-heat let rip, sea levels rise, the Amazon burn, etc., we will be in fantasy separating ourselves from a common fate: and ensuring that that fate, certainly for those who come after us, is grim.

So my stance here is *inter alia* an attempt to change us. To (re-)forge an '*us*'. And this line of thought too, I think, can be traced back to the vital feature of Winch highlighted in the little quotation I offered earlier from 'Understanding a primitive society': 'Seriously to study another way of life is *necessarily to seek to extend our own*'.

In the darkness of this time, I yearn for us to be lit up by a sense of how we are not estranged from each other: and for this sense of inter-relatedness to encompass the future ones, and to cross species-boundaries. I think that nothing less will be needed, to avert the mass-suicide/homicide/ecocide that is getting under way.

The right to believe in ourselves

Why does this chapter matter? Isn't its topic too ... rarefied? Why think that anything that I have said here could have any moment, up against rampant human self-concern / vested interest? How will it be possible for us to think more about let alone learn from animals, in the great pressure we'll be under ourselves in the coming decade(s)?

But our less or more scientific understanding of animals is improving all the time. That will continue awhile yet, especially as many people are very interested in it.

There are some great examples to hand of how the mass media has worked to mobilize concern for animals via interest in 'natural history'; the most striking case being that terrible shot in Attenborough's *Blue Planet 2* of a plastic bag attached to a sea turtle. This catalyzed a massive change in attitudes to the political acceptability of single-use plastics (Calderwood 2018; Dunn et al. 2020).

Meanwhile, the dramatic rise of plant-based/vegan activism and living in much of the 'developed' world is testament to the potential power of concern about our non-human kin.[34] If that trend continues, it too is likely to foment considerably greater interest in what we can learn from cetaceans (and elephants, and bonobos, and wolves, and octopi, and more). Philosophical reflection of the kind I've essayed in this chapter may help to make their pertinence clearer. It is not merely fanciful, I think, to think that what this chapter has been about could move and change people, were it wider discussed and reflected upon.

Especially if one bears in mind the following: as awareness of ecocide mounts, many more people will be actively casting around for ways to understand and overcome what modern civilization has done. It would be surprising if many didn't look as far as the wonders to be learnt and felt from the social whales and dolphins.

Earlier in this book, I've commented that the philosophical temptation in the face of the awesome failure to date of humanity to rein in its destructive ways, is one of nausea at ourselves (Chapter 7). But I hope that we don't give up on ourselves, because that is only a sure route to death – and to the continuation in the meantime of the unbelievably barbaric way we have treated our animal kin, including very notably our extraordinary cetacean kin.

I hope that we can (come to) understand cetaceans; including in their seeming *greatest* 'stupidity', their tragic and moving mass-strandings. And with them functioning as an ethical 'object of comparison', and with our coming to see as possible thuswise a solidarity deeper than that which we have yet real-ized, I hope we can re-assess ourselves, and change deeply. We have to do something we have never done before: to pull together radically and change ourselves almost completely in the process and in the aftermath. If we were to manage to overcome our pseudo-individualism, and rather, wisely to reconceive freedom[35] as something we exercise above all *together*, we would have a much better chance of surviving – and in a worthwhile way — the next fifty to 100 years or so than we appear at present to have. I believe that this is possible. Which in this case means that I hope, with what Williams James called the 'will' or (better) the 'right' to believe, that this is possible. I

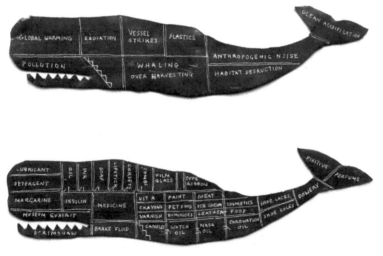

Figure 6.1 'Sing out for him'. Photograph of pewter artwork reclaimed from a church organ pipe. Reproduced here by kind permission of the artist, Angela Cockayne.

think that coming face-to-face with the beautiful reality of cetacean internal-relatedness might, in the darkness of this time, be one of our very best hopes.

If we rise to the challenge of that hope, then we will be putting our love for our fellow beings to the test. We will be showing whether in fact we actually do love each other, and in particular whether we actually do love our children.

If we do, we will not strand them on a beach with a remorselessly rising tide.

Now: can *you* mirror that hope of mine? Can you help real-ize it?

Or, better: can *we* realize it? As one? . . .[36]

7

How to Live in Truth Today

Many environmentalists say climate change is happening too fast. No, it's
happening too slowly. It's not happening nearly quickly enough to get our
attention.

Daniel Gilbert, 'Global Warming and Psychology' (2010)

No guarantees

This book began by setting out the gravity of what we face: climate and
ecological breakdown. It outlined the science (and the ethics, and risk-
analysis) of the situation without reservation.

In Chapter 1, I essayed a way out, explored already at greater length
in my previous book *Parents for a Future* (Read 2021a). This is a logical
argument based in our emotional commitments. It is based in our passion for
the future of our children, and it shows that such loving care, in the context
of incipient climate breakdown, is itself enough to 'guarantee' that we give our
all to mitigate that breakdown. For love for our own children, I showed,
equates to caring profoundly for distant future generations worldwide, and
that requires protection of nature both forever and now, and that requires
that we rise up.

But there's no way around the quotation marks around that word,
'guarantee'. I am under no illusion that the implacable logic of this passionate
argument *will* guarantee that it sweeps the world and that everything turns
fine. Agonizing though it is to admit it, the chances of anything remotely like
that happening appear extremely slim. In Chapters 2 and 3, I therefore took
you deeper into the abyss; explaining how the climate breakdown into which
we are heading is coming *despite* the fact that we know it is (and thus should
already have moved to prevent it); and setting out how, as a result, we can say
with confidence that, incredibly, this civilization is finished. That does not
mean that collapse is inevitable. It is likely, and so we ought to begin to
prepare for it (Bendell 2018), but it is not certain. We do not know the future.
To think that we do is exactly the kind of epistemic illusion and hubris that
has got us into this dire trouble. It remains possible, for all we know, that we

could transformatively adapt our way through what is coming.[1] But what we can be confident of is that, if there is such a way, it will require a transformation so thorough that in no meaningful sense will the civilization that emerges on the other side of it be the same one that we currently have. This is what too few of us are yet awake enough to hear: that we are going to have to give up much of what we have been taking for granted, if we are to get through what is coming. (And those of us who earn/own more than average are going to have to give up more than average).

But this was perhaps where things started to get really interesting. Where we started to find some hope of a radical nature, in Jonathan Lear's sense (Lear 2006). That is to say: a new hope, where all that we used to hope for (which was basically some kind of perpetuation of what we currently have) has to be let go of. For of course it can actually be on balance a thoroughly *good* thing that this unprecedentedly destructive civilization is on the way out (Servigne et al. 2020). A good thing for the living planet. A good thing for the remaining cultures and civilizations – those of some subsistence farmers, and many indigenous people – that are hanging on outside of this empire of global insanity. *And* perhaps that's even a good thing, on balance, for those of us that are inside it too. For the future can then be one in which we have (on balance) better lives, even as climate decline bites, one in which we find more meaning, have more community and less insecurity.

For real security lies in having purpose, in having not more stuff but each other, and in having more control close to our hands, as we do potentially in a relocalized future; unlike the situation of actually existing globalized techno-neoliberalism in which we find ourselves.

This – that despite (and in a certain important sense *because* of) everything, what is coming may be a better life – has been the conviction that quietly marked Chapters 4–6 of this book. In these chapters, the heart of the book, I led you 'up' from the difficult place of facing up unflinchingly to climate reality, of realizing the mad truth that the *white* swan of climate breakdown is coming for us, in plain sight, and of swallowing the 'red pill' that this civilization is finished: and being on balance happy about it, even while seeing that the process is likely to involve much further pain. That that pain is, on balance, our friend. For the surprise of Chapters 4–6 has perhaps been how this coming 'up' that I speak of has been *by way of going further 'down'*. These chapters, the guts of the 'positive' philosophy that I've had to offer in this book, have been an exploration in the upside of down. I hope that they help you to take heart, from the seemingly most-unlikely of places.

In Chapter 4, I explored how climate disasters may be the making of us. In Chapter 5, I discussed how eco-grief and eco-anxiety (and eco-anger) may be just what we need in order to really see and feel reality and act on it.

And in Chapter 6, I compared our plight with that of stranded cetaceans, and suggested that their heart-rending selflessness may be just what we need.

Like Jean-Jacques Rousseau, then, I find the remedy *in* the evil. There is saving power for us, even yet, precisely by turning to face where the danger lies. Our greatest hopes now rest *in* our greatest travails.[2] If we are to transformatively adapt and deeply adapt, then there is no alternative but to go deeper into the trouble, first, in the manner in which I sought to lead you on a journey in the second half of the book, a little like (for you Dante fans out there) a latter-day combination of Virgil and Beatrice ...

In this final chapter, I am not going to try giving a manifesto of all the things that, once we've realized the options before us, ought to be done. Excellent versions of that can be found elsewhere.[3] And, barring a deep wake-up of the kind sought in these pages, and its being acted on at scale, they are not going to be implemented, at least not enough.

Nor am I going to resort to the banality of a crude list of 'What *you* can do!' That is the way that books about 'the environmental crisis' far too often end – with a pat and utterly unconvincing sense of sudden alleged optimism, directed at the reader in the form typically of a concise list of exhortations via which you (by yourself, of course) can 'save the planet'.

The first approach operates in the third person, what ought in the abstract to be done. The second approach operates in the first person/the second-person singular, what I/you considered-alone ought to do. What we actually need is the first-person plural that I've dwelt in throughout this book: the invitational 'we'. What matters is what *we* can do (whoever exactly this 'we' turns out to be). (Constructing it – realizing in practice the way the way that we need is necessarily in togetherness – is in fact the most fundamental task of all; and I address that in much of what follows).

I want then in this concluding chapter to think, in quite plain terms, about what the knowledge of climate breakdown ought to lead *us* to do. And I assemble some final more or less novel intellectual resources for putting us in a position to do it.

Seven ways to do what we need to

The disturbing, fascinating question we need to contemplate a little more, drawing on what I've just said together with the argument of Chapter 3 of this book, is this: what comes after civilization as we know it? Is it going to be a transformed civilization? Is it going to be some kind of successor civilization? Or is it going to be nothing at all?

And critically of course the way that question matters to us takes form in *this* question: how can we influence that choice?

I've got a series of seven suggestions on that that I want to share with you, by way of this question of agency and life-purpose.

First off, wake up. We need, individually and collectively, to wake up to the reality set out in these pages. All of us need to face up to these very harsh realities that I've been sketching for you here, and no longer pretend that we can get away with just focusing on, say, changing our energy infrastructure to renewable energy, or even get away with assuming that we can and will succeed in transforming our civilization in the way that I very much hope we still might.

This waking-up process is not necessarily particularly pleasant or easy (to put it mildly). It may well involve you, for example, if you're willing to go through it, experiencing some not inconsiderable despair. Normally, we try to avoid despair. Such avoidance is no longer tenable. *There is nothing wrong with despair,* provided, as I've noted, that you don't become stuck in it and disempowered by it.

The process certainly should involve you experiencing some profound fear and sadness. If you're not at least sometimes heart-sad about what's happening, and if you're not at least sometimes distressed or afraid in the context of the things I'm saying and reminding us of, then you're not paying attention.

In fact, we can go further than that, as I did in Chapter 5. As we saw there, there's a wonderful new branch of psychology called 'eco-psychology' (Roszak 2002). What the ecopsychologists argue is that the despair, fear and anxiety, deep sadness, grief and rage that we feel in the context of ecological collapse is rational and could even be described as a kind of consciousness arising from the Earth itself. That is: we are nature coming to an awareness of what we are doing to ourselves, in the sense that we are feeling what we are doing to our beautiful planetary home; and those kinds of feelings are appropriate. If you're not feeling some 'bad' feelings, then one suspects there might be something wrong with you …! The task will be, to work with and through those difficult feelings: perhaps in therapeutic settings, and certainly via taking action with others who have been feeling them too.

Once again, a vital clue here: is to face climate reality together. What the ecopsychologists say is: don't (as conventional psychology does) focus on the individual(s). Don't say: this individual is feeling sad, therefore they need to be fixed; rather, notice that this individual, like an increasing number of others, is feeling sad for a reason, and so maybe that shared sadness tells us all something reliable about what is happening, about what is wrong beyond them (us). That sadness or fear connotes a noticing of and is an expression of what's been happening at this point in history and what's happening to the Earth. So if you're experiencing 'bad' feelings at this moment in the human adventure, then *you're not alone* and *you may well be* more *rational than the people who as yet are not experiencing those feelings.*

The only way we get to follow our bliss, now, is to follow our heartbreak.

I'm going to single out one person who's very worth reading in this connection: my teacher, the deep ecologist Joanna Macy. Her approach, 'The work that reconnects', is a guide for those involved in the difficult collective journey that she used to call 'despair work' (or 'despair and empowerment work'), which I think is quite a useful phrase for it.[4] To say it again: there's nothing wrong with despair, in the right place and time. In fact, there is a need for despair. It has a deep sense of reality and a great potential energy.[5] And it isn't somewhere one necessarily gets stuck, *once one stops trying to evade it!*

So firstly, let's wake up.[6]

And, of course: let's gently (but none too slowly) seek to wake everyone else up too.

Wake up. Time to live. And to be the alarm-clock for everyone you know. Don't expect there to be one co-arising awakening for everyone. Different people are waking up to climate breakdown at different speeds, for reasons that have been discussed in earlier chapters. It is setting oneself up for disappointment to expect that especially-grave climate mega-disasters will do the job for you. Yes, events like the North American heat dome and the German floods of 2021 are game-changers; but this is going to be an attritional job of creating attention and space for facing climate reality. Everyone is at a slightly different stage in this 'game' that isn't.

That leads directly into my second 'Do': we need to talk about this.

Isn't talk cheap? But where there *isn't* talk, the price can be dearer. Without honestly addressing what these pages have concerned, the ruling trope will remain (soft) denial. It is hard to get to the five-past-midnight space, the space of truth; it is so tempting to remain instead stuck in the domain of imagined-salvation, of Polyanna-ish 'Yes we can!', of saving *this* civilization.

But spaces can be designed that make the collective honest awakening easier. Green House, a think tank (that I co-founded) directed toward eco-realistic appraisal of the contemporary world, has had for some years now an important 'Facing up to climate reality' project (Foster 2019). This started after we decided several years ago that we needed to have an honest conversation in our core team about what was happening in relation to climate. Was what was being done enough? If not, then how long did we have before catastrophe strikes? So we started off with a 'go-round'.

We addressed the question of what we thought was going to happen and what our feelings about it were. I was the first person to go and said something like 'Well, what I think is going to happen is that probably there is going to be a collapse, and I'm terrified for myself, let alone for people who are younger than me, and I feel very lonely in this terror. I feel very alone in it, because I can't help feeling that virtually no one else is really seriously thinking this'. And then the next person went – and they said pretty much the same; and then the next person, and they said much the same.

What was interesting about that process was that by the time we'd gone around us all, a couple of things had emerged: (i) The feeling some of us had had that perhaps we could hold on to the hope that we might simply be wrong because maybe it was only oneself thinking this . . . well, that was gone. Tears of sadness and anticipatory terror welled up in my eyes as I realized that I now had to accept that my fears weren't just some psychological complex; they were probably realistic. They were certainly shared. It turned out that everyone else in my team had been secretly thinking about the (high) likelihood of collapse as well. (ii) But also, and at the very same time, was something more encouraging and more liberating. We realized that we could talk about it. We had started to break the taboo. 'It's not just me', we all understood. We can talk about it in a group, and perhaps now that we are starting to grasp that we've all really got this fear, then others are doing so – or could soon be – too.

So: find venues in which you can talk honestly about your expectations and fears.[7] After that, seek if you can to take that talk into places where its impact can leverage: the media, education, the writing and the arts (Read 2018c). Consider the striking popularity of the recent climate-allegorical film *Don't Look Up* (2021). Seize – and co-create – such opportunities to help others to look up, to wake up. Spread the word about spreading the word.

Third, there is something specific that needs to feature in those conversations, and in academic research: we need to think and talk seriously, as we haven't done yet, about my option number two out of three, from Chapter 3, the successor civilization idea. We need to think about this concept and then to start to act accordingly (Read 2018a).

This is very, very challenging. For example, we need to consider how we preserve the values of civilization through a period of partial collapse. And we need to consider carefully which values of our current civilization we want to preserve. It seems to me that writers (except perhaps for a (growing) handful of sci-fi writers, including many of those in 'solar punk'), academics of all kinds, certainly philosophers like myself, have as yet done little of this work. But the building of a new kind of 'imaginary' which can cope with the scenarios I'm talking about is vital (Earle 2017). It's hard to think of *any* intellectual work that could be more important at this time.

And when you stop a moment and think this last point through, it makes our task even harder. For, if there is to be a civilization to succeed this one, it will have to be tough enough to survive – without being turned wholly vicious – a time that is likely quite literally to test humanity more severely by far than we have ever been tested before. The signs, in terms of things like our willingness to be caring to refugees (including climate refugees) are, to say the least, thus far rather mixed.

We run two risks of losing humanity, in the coming generation(s). The more obvious risk is the outside chance that we might commit ourselves to extinction. The less obvious, but probably graver, risk is that we might lose our very humanity in the rush to try to save ourselves.

Among those who are (rightly) conscious of this risk, 'lifeboats' have lately got a bad rap. There is concern that we will make ourselves a lifeboat that stops others from getting into it. But lifeboats are a wonderful thing: provided that one saves others, wherever possible, by way of them. There have to be, there ought to be, lifeboats.

And in any case there will be, whether one likes it or not. So the question is how does one build lifeboats that are not so viciously exclusive that they undermine their own worth? For that is what we have to do, for it to be worth doing at all.

Perhaps the task then is not even as 'easy' (!) as building just one new civilization. Perhaps we need to plan on two, in sequence. The real task may be to build a lifeboat-civilization, a decent and yet realistic/pragmatic ethic, unafraid to be determined to survive at many costs, and that can create a 'container' within it, containing the seeds of a future more beautiful civilization, a true culture. A container that will carry some of us through the storms of our children, and that can somehow carry within it the seeds of a future *successor civili*zation, one that is less harsh and which might exist and truly *flourish* in a less awfully pressed time that we might one day be able to recover to.

Just as some knowledge and wisdom survived the Dark Ages in monasteries, so perhaps a key task now is for us to create 'ecosteries'[8] seed banks both literal and metaphorical for a possible civilization to come once this one has died. A superb (fictive) 'model' for these ecosteries might be Margaret Atwood's Gardeners in her novel *The Year of the Flood* (2010).[9]

If our task is creating two future civilizations, then it is even harder than at first I made it appear earlier … We may have to make some pretty challenging compromises, and yet to be very careful not to compromise ourselves and our values completely, even to be able to seed a future *civili*zation at all.

Václav Havel penned some deeply wise words that speak directly to our condition, as we contemplate this difficult balance, this voyage of *ecovery* and *then* perhaps of recovery. His idea of 'living in truth' seems particularly pertinent for times where 'post-truth-ism' (Read & Uçan 2019) – a product of consumerism applied to ideas and therethrough to reality itself – has, absurdly, become widespread, at the very time when reality is about to bite us harder than it ever has before.

I quote:

> The profound crisis of human identity brought on by living within a lie ... possesses a moral dimension ....: it appears ... as a *deep moral crisis in society*. A person who has been seduced by the consumer value system, whose identity is dissolved in an amalgam of the accoutrements of mass civilization, and who has no roots in the order of being ... is a *demoralised* person. The system depends on this demoralisation, deepens it, is in fact a projection of it into society. // Living within the truth, as humanity's revolt ..., is, on the contrary, an attempt to regain control over one's own sense of responsibility.
>
> Havel 1978, 62

To me, these words still resonate a couple of generations on (though if I were reworking the passage, I'd make it sound less purely personal, more of a social process). Havel's words can diagnose us and offer us a challenge to rise to, now. Of course, I have been seeking to go with you, reader, on a journey of such arising, in these pages. And I have suggested ways in which, through loving our children (Chapter 1), through being-with-others in disasters (Chapter 4), and so forth, we *already* have strong resources with which to avoid being 'demoralized' in Havel's sense. Perhaps via the likes of these, we can overcome the attraction of living in denial, and prove T.S. Eliot wrong in his famous claim that human beings cannot bear very much reality. Perhaps we can (as per Chapter 5) even find the route to living in truth *through* our very attraction to denial.

In the same essay, Havel wrote something that seems to me to carry over if anything even more directly to our own predicament today. He spoke of the state's 'desperate attempt to plug up the dreadful wellspring of truth, *a truth which might cause incalculable transformations in social consciousness*' (Havel 1978, 59, my emphasis). Do we dare to seek to cause such an incalculable transformation in social consciousness? One that might be enough to radically transform this civilization (Chapter 3's Possibility 1), or (more likely) to seed the new imaginary, the civilization(s) worth birthing from this one's death-throes (Possibility 2)? Havel spoke of the (totalitarian) effort to defend 'the integrity of the world of appearances in order to defend itself'. Are we willing, and able, to stop engaging in such defence? To stop 'defending' ourselves against reality itself?

Havel wrote that 'the moment someone breaks through in one place, when one person cries "The emperor is naked!" – when a single person breaks the rules of the game, thus exposing it as a game – everything suddenly appears in another light and the whole crust seems then to be made of a tissue on the point of tearing and disintegrating uncontrollably'. The East bloc regimes proved astoundingly fragile. Perhaps our civilization's hegemony, its death-embrace with the insanity of perpetual industrial-growthism (which, as part of the hegemony, feels to us like business-as-usual, but is actually a continual reckless movement into terra incognita), is less assured, less solid than it seems? Perhaps it might yet melt into air?

This seems, however, decidedly unlikely. One can take some small hope from all sorts of movements of liberation in history, including the Velvet Revolution and its fellows. But we have absolutely no precedent for a revolutionarily radical transformation that centrally involves long-termism, and care for the voiceless (including non-human animals), for a transformation that is not about deprived human beings taking seeking to join the ranks of the privileged, but is about us saying, together, 'Enough'. There is enough already, if only we share it out better (Blewitt & Cunningham 2014). We could end the endless ignorant scramble for *more*.

The closest there is to such a precedent appears to be the way that the surviving prehistoric 'future-eaters' described by Tim Flannery (in the eponymous book) (2002) seem to have managed truly to learn from their decimation of the megafauna and of their own ecosystems, and to have left to many of their indigenous descendants ways of living harmoniously and lightly on the Earth. But note: they had to go through terrible crashes and extinctions in order to learn this painful knowledge (so this was a version of Possibility 2, Phoenix, *avant la lettre*). We were hoping that there would be a precedent for the revolutionary transformation that we are in need of, without such pain and destruction; but one is not in evidence. Moreover, if we do thoroughly crash our civilization, then the danger is that it will take down everything necessary for any successor civilization with it; the collapse may be global, and complete (as suggested by James Lovelock in *The Revenge of Gaia* (2007), for instance), and even perhaps therefore irrecoverable (Possibility 3, Dodo). We have to learn from our white swan crash before it takes place, if we possibly can. (That has been a primary purpose of this book).

So we need to reach higher and longer (into the future) than we ever have before. But meanwhile, too often I hear decent people using ideas such as Maslow's alleged hierarchy of human needs as an excuse for pandering to short-term 'needs'. We are told that we have to give all the least well off human beings who are alive today much more, and that until we do so we will not be able to safeguard ecology and the long-term. But in reality, this is little more than an excuse for never addressing the long term. *We will never get to the long term, until we embrace a concept of enough.* This concept[10] is alien to developmentality (Deb 2009; Read 2019a), the mentality of trying to put the whole world on the path of growthism (Read 2019a). That mentality dominates the otherwise laudable UN 'Sustainable Development Goals': Goal 8, for endless (so-called 'sustainable') economic growth, ensures that all the rest of the goals will be trashed eventually.

Clearly, it goes without saying that the rich should have less and the very poor more; *of course*. True leadership now, in rich countries such as my own, involves us therefore being collectively willing to live lives of comparative voluntary simplicity (Read, Alexander & Garrett 2018) – being willing to prove that we mean it: *we are not all we are cracked up to be.* Our civilization is not to be aspired to. But so long as we insist (instead) on trying to 'develop' the entire world as the global North has developed, we are tacitly continuing to act as if every country should try to be like the US and the UK are now, and are simply putting off the moment of reckoning – though not, in practice, probably putting it off for much longer. Far, far too often, parties of the 'Left' and even would-be Greens can be heard saying that we'll seriously address the environmental crisis *after* we've 'grown' some more. *This simply means that we will never address the crisis, full stop.* And in turn *that* means that we will collapse. Unless we manage to question the develop-mentality.

Maslow's famous thinking on this point, as he came in part to recognize in his later years, is in a crucial respect bogus anyway: what the experiences and the thinking of concentration camp survivors Victor Frankl (and Primo Levi) teach (and they have much to teach us, as we head into a time when many of us are quite likely to experience death-like conditions *en masse*) is that there is a need more basic even than the allegedly 'basic' needs, of food and water etc.: namely, for *meaning* (Markert 2018; Tay & Diener 2011). As we gamble with our very future and risk gambling away our posterity and descendants, we risk stripping ourselves of that meaning. Life not going on, as per Alfonso Cuarón's superlative film *Children of Men*: this is a potent meaning-destroyer. We need to be less obsessed with raising everyone's 'standard of living' and more concerned about ensuring that life has a chance of going on; without that, quality of – i.e., the meaning of – life is going to evaporate, however 'high' our short-term standard of living.[11]

What Chapter 5 brought out was the way in which faith in humanity and in life makes for a deep difficulty in accepting the emerging reality of this climate-desecrated Earth. It is somewhat similar to how it made (and still sometimes makes) for a deep difficulty in accepting the reality of the world of the concentration and extermination camps. It contradicts the ground of our shared lifeworld like the loss of a loved one contradicts our lifeworlds (resulting in grief and more). The question is whether we can face reality and harvest what the emotions of eco-grief, eco-anxiety etc. are offering us, or whether we will be charmed deeper by the more immediate consolations of petro-fuelled techno-life.

The real charm of modernity has proven to be its 'democraticness': it promises all of us all the conquest we want (just look at the way that this promise is now literally consuming the great ancient civilizations of India and China). We are all living downstream from conquest, from 'empire'. That stream is now poised to sweep us all away: for, by 'conquering' nature, we end up only vanquishing ourselves.

If that is where we head, will it really have been worth it?

One thing is for certain. We cannot change this trajectory except by a radical attack on the normal. Our civilization's death-embrace will not melt into air, *unless we are willing to break the rules.* (See 'Sixth', below, for development of this point). We have to be willing, for starters, to tell the truth. We have to be willing – and this isn't easy – to admit that this civilization is finished. That we really are like one of those cartoon characters that hovers in space, frantically running a while yet, after crossing the limit of the cliff-edge.

Continuing to mouth feel-good pseudo-platitudes risks, in this context, simply repeating the absurd self-deceptions of 'positive thinking'. Staying within the confines of 'positive thinking' at the present time, and refusing in particular to face the utterly desperate prognosis that is afforded by climate reality, simply *is* denial. (And will without doubt conduce to a true nightmare).

Once more, this was the vital contribution of Chapter 5: taking us deep into 'negative' emotions, and seeing/feeling their power actually to aid us in a profound manner. It is actually the relentless call for 'positive' thinking that leads into genuinely negative thoughts. If one thinks to oneself 'I oughtn't to be feeling these "negative" emotions; I ought to think positive', then one is doing violence to one's feelings/thoughts that are based on attunement to a difficult reality. Beating oneself up like this for having 'negative' emotions/ thoughts is tantamount to deepening one's depression (and denial). Far better to accept one's 'negative' emotions and see where they lead. My suggestion has been that ultimately they lead through our difficulties to the possibility of something truer and better.

But the way through is hard. What we are talking about, what we are trying to face, what is at risk of unfolding, is the potential death and morbidity of billions. We need somehow to seek to build down the human footprint (especially, thus, that of the rich), fairly rapidly, and without a brutal authoritarianism; there is as yet no prospect of this happening, and without it happening collectively/voluntarily, then we face collapse, which means, sooner or later, horrific life or non-life for billions. Talk of (ending) 'civilization' then risks being euphemistic; what is being talked about boils down quite simply, in part, into people. Thus one can of course hardly wish for the perishing of what might, from a distanciated perspective of thinking civilizations, be said not to deserve to survive: for one would be wishing for a far greater set of genocides than has ever occurred in history.

If we do not start living in reality, then reality will eject us (starting with our present civilization) from the gene pool.

And, just as important perhaps (for we may well get ejected anyway): if we do not face climate reality, if we do not speak truth not only to power but first at least to each other, if we do not work to make our/a civilization civil, then we won't even die with fellowship and integrity. Which brings me to my next point:

Fourth, we need, as I started to describe above, to actually build good lifeboats to carry as many as possible of us through the storms that are coming. What kind of things do I mean by that?

Well, I mean many things, but can sketch only a few examples of them here. I will start out by suggesting that you engage in a bit of individual 'prepping' for potential collapse.

For example, I recommend that you do not keep all your money in the bank and instead keep some 'under your mattress'. Why? Because it may well be that that the banking system, the financial system, as we know it, will not with us for very much longer; but money will probably be with us for quite a while before any fuller collapse-event. (By the way, just in case any criminals are reading this: the money in my house is not literally under my mattress ,so don't go looking there; you'd have to tear up the whole house to find it and you still might well not). And I recommend that you store some food, as I'm doing. Dried food, canned food, etc . . . It's an elementary precaution.

And undertaking it teaches one something helpful: *how very little one can accomplish by way of such individualistic prepping.*

What else, then?

We are going to survive as communities, or not at all.

We must (re-)build community, as per Chapters 4 and 6. The relations that we have with each other have become very fragmented by the kind of society that we live in: a pseudo-individualistic neoliberalized economistic society.

Those relations are going to be vital if there is some kind of partial collapse at least, as I'm suggesting there is very likely to be. The Transition Towns movement is a good model here and has already achieved a certain amount.[12] This movement seeks to bring communities together to engage in some of the work of transformative adaptation by creating less polluting and more resilient localities. That work needs to be built upon and expanded. We need to work on how to preserve things which will be useful to future people through a potential collapse.

The creation and preservation of seed banks is a great example of work that needs to be done here. Although, admittedly, this is quite challenging in the context of escalating climatic change. The great seed bank at Svalbard was seriously disturbed recently by the massive increase of temperatures in the Arctic (Griffin 2018). It was previously thought to be pretty much invulnerable, given that it is based deep in the 'perma'-ice; but that ice started melting.

Despite these challenges, we have to think actively about how to preserve seeds through unpredictable dangerous climatic change; and we also have to think about the kind of seeds which are going to be useful for us. We should be planting native species and varieties, of course; but we should also be planting some non-native species which will cope with higher temperatures (and potentially drier/drought conditions). This is a key part of the work of transformative adaptation.[13]

We need to take seriously the attempt at (such) adaptation 'deadly',[14] and that means that we need to rethink it: as I've indicated in earlier chapter, it means we need to deepen as well as transform our concept of it. We need to shift far more resources of all kinds to it (while we still can).

Deep adaptation, remember, considers the uncomfortable thought: what if (as, to a clear-eyed view, must now appear almost overwhelmingly likely[15]) we fail and things start to collapse? We need to be, for example, preparing for sea-level rise. This means not doing completely absurd things such as building nuclear power stations by the coast, which is where virtually all such installations are constructed. To build these things – which we know are super-toxic for hundreds of years, and dangerous for hundreds of thousands of years – in such places that are quite obviously vulnerable to sea-level rise, is almost the very definition of insanity, hubris and chronic short-termism. And if civilization does collapse even partially, how confident can we be that all the resources that are needed to keep nuclear power plants and waste safe are going to remain intact? For example, what will keep spent fuel rods from catching fire and burning if their cooling pools dry out? We already saw at Fukushima a little bit of what can happen even in the middle of an intact civilization when something hits a nuclear power station hard. Remember that there are going to be more and more 'natural' disasters; because there will be worsening climate disasters coming in the next generation, even if, as seems unlikely at present, the world really gets its act in order to start being in earnest about steep greenhouse gas emissions reductions.

There is a slight chance that we might transform to stop climate catastrophe, but in the meantime there will definitely be more climate disasters as we are seeing right now. Building nuclear power stations in the context of that scenario is plain foolish.

I explored the dangers of geoengineering in Chapters 2 and 3. The deep adaptation agenda is a further reason for thinking that there is something very wrong about the ambition of geoengineering. Because the would-be geoengineer, to have this incredibly hubristic idea along the lines of 'humanity is going to control the climate of the whole earth' work – the very kind of madly controlling thinking, note well, that got us into this mess – would have to have a technological infrastructure which we are confident that we can support for the long run. Imagine, for example, that we put hundreds of mirrors in space' to deflect sunlight away so that we can avoid some of the effects of global overheating. We would need to be confident that those mirrors will be able to stay up there for a very, very long time for this to be viable, and not to risk the danger of a sudden, overwhelming heating if they were removed fairly suddenly (Paul & Read 2019; Read 2015b).

In fact, most of the proposals for 'mirrors in space' do not refer to literal mirrors. They are rather lots of very small sulphur particles that could be pumped into the atmosphere. Inevitably, these particles then start to fall, and so more are needed to replace them. This begs the question of what would happen if we had a project like this and then suddenly were unable to continue it – if, for example, because the country that is supposed to do this has collapsed. The consequence would be a sudden catastrophic spiking in temperature, something far worse than a gradual increase.

Mirrors in space, so-called 'Solar Radiation Management' [SRM], is shallow, defensive adaptation on steroids. It is a last-ditch effort to keep our failed civilization kicking its can down the road. Don't be fooled by the emerging calls for it, which this decade will grow and grow, as climate-despair deepens and the system flails around for a way of keeping itself staggering on for a few more years.

The thing that worries me the most of all about SRM is that if it works, it will enable us to go on polluting, to continue the fossil economy. That could very well have utterly catastrophic effects, especially via continued ocean-acidification. There appears to be a vicious feedback loop developing in the oceans, between ocean acidification, accumulated chemicals and plastics hurting ocean wildlife, consequent loss of carbon sequestration (and of oxygenation), and thus further acidification (Dryden & Duncan 2021). If

SRM enables this vicious feedback to continue or even accelerate, extinction-cascades in the ocean could bring about a Dodo scenario for humans and many, many more, *even as* we get global temperatures temporarily 'under control'.

There are more potential 'side effects' (although really there are no such things as side effects; only *effects*) from (other) geoengineering schemes. Some have suggested seeding the oceans with iron to create plankton blooms that will then sink to the bottom and subsequently be sequestered. We cannot know what the ecosystemic effects of that approach would be. Maybe we can monitor those effects and then stage further interventions to counter the horrible negative side effects quite likely to result from an intervention like that, launching us into a possible spiral of further complexification; but we cannot do any of that if the civilization in question has collapsed. You might then get some kind of vast oceanic dead zone opening up, with nothing human beings can do about it.

One of the morals here is that *there are worse things that could happen even than civilizational collapse.* I think humans are quite bad at thinking about collapse, but even worse about thinking unselfishly beyond it. What could be worse than our civilization collapsing? Well, here is something that could be worse: our civilization could collapse in a really horrific uncontrolled way and poison or more than decimate the remaining ecosystems long term at the same time.[16] So be very careful what you wish for. The deep adaptation agenda says we need to be thinking and acting *now* in ways that take seriously into account the possibility that we will not be able to do the kinds of interventions in future that we can do currently.

It adds momentum to an idea that has gradually been gathering steam in these pages:[17] what if we were to deliberately simplify our society, relocalizing, avoiding hyper-technologization, rather than endlessly creating further complexity that we cannot control or even understand and that ever adds to our exposure to harm at scale?

Seeking to facilitate such a relocalizational de-complexification would be great work for our time.

At my best moments, I am *grateful* to be alive now. Grateful to be the recipient of this awesome gift: that we are the ones who have the chance to save the future, one way or another. At minimum, to help design the 'lifeboat(s)' in and from which, like in the very final scene of the highly salient film, *Children of Men*, the future can set sail and survive.

This film gives us lifeboat-thinking at its most inspiring.

As I noted above, some people think it is wrong to even think about 'lifeboats'. I think that ship has plainly sailed; in my view, more and more people are thinking about them, if mostly on the quiet. I try to bring this

Figure 7.1 The ending of *Children of Men*: a rowing-boat lifeboat containing the first of a future generation encounters, through the mist, the larger lifeboat, the 'Tomorrow'. *Children of Men,* dir. Alfonso Cuarón © Universal Pictures 2006. All rights reserved.

matter into the light. The challenge that we need to seek to rise to, as I have said, is to produce lifeboats that are not unethical. Let's aim to build lifeboats that are good – not just at keeping afloat, but actually good, decent, enough.

Fifth, 'holding actions'. This is a term from my teacher Joanna Macy. By this phrase she means actions to hold the damage at bay and slow it down. A wide variety of things come under this heading, from consumer boycotts and divestment campaigns to political action, lobbying and becoming involved in electoral politics. Do not make the mistake of thinking that because I am saying that civilizational collapse in some form or another is likely to happen, we should give up on these conventional methods. Not at all! They are absolutely vital right now. It is just that they are not enough by themselves anymore. We should think of them primarily as holding actions, as holding back the potential catastrophe rather than actually either being able to stop it completely or being able to genuinely ameliorate its consequences.

So holding actions are of course a vital part of what we need to do.

And at this point in the journey, it's appropriate to focus on how you can start contributing to such holding actions directly, particularly if you happen to be one of the many in the global North who (like me) have more than you need.

Consider: some of us have been really suffering economically in the time of COVID-19. There has been rank injustice in the rich getting richer and the poor getting poorer. But *some of us*, even if we aren't rich, *have not* been suffering economically. On the contrary, some of us are sitting rather pretty on bank balances that have grown unabated. For many months on end, during the time since March 2020, we have been hardly spending anything while stuck at home.

This money is something that radical movements – such as Extinction Rebellion, School Strikes for Climate, Local Futures, Parents For Future, and whoever comes next – that are poised to struggle right now for the world we so badly need. So, if you find yourself in a position of comfort today, then consider investing that into the holding-actions and activism that just might preserve a tomorrow for us all. I've even got some advice for you on how to do so, which I'm going to update regularly, at **https://rupertread.net/ ecologically-effective-altruism**. I've included hyperlinks there to some of the causes I recommend most.

Sixth point: as I've said, holding actions are not enough. We should, we must, do something more. If you're with me so far, then you need to go with me one more step: you need to be prepared to rebel. Act so as to do what is necessary now, regardless of its legality or otherwise.

That is actually why I got heavily involved with Extinction Rebellion. Governments have almost completely failed us. We should no longer feel bound to accept their authority. They have abrogated the 'social contract'. In response, it is not enough to do consumer boycotts and vote and so on. We should also use non-violent direct action as well. We should disobey, civilly. We should be ready to break the rules in earnest!

In April 2019, Extinction Rebellion held protests across the globe demanding immediate action on the climate and ecological crises. In the United Kingdom, where I am based, we shut down parts of central London for 10 days, with over 1,000 protestors arrested for peaceful disruption. Incredibly, this led to the British Parliament partially capitulating to our three demands: the declaration of a climate and environmental emergency (Walker 2019); the bringing into by law for the first time ever of a net zero target; and the setting up of a citizens' assembly for climate (Carrington 2019). This was a *start*, but that's all: progress has stalled since summer 2019. Indeed, partly in response to these successes, the UK government has introduced new laws to crack down on the right to protest. This is at once a partial vindication of our tactics and an assault on our ability to continue with them.

People sometimes say to me, 'Oh Rupert, you talk too much in terms that are kind of fearful. You make people sad and scared and you don't give them enough hope'.[18] My reply is: I do not think that this is really a time where hope, *at least in the sense of a kind of passive attitude of wanting things to turn out 'alright'*, is necessarily the most appropriate emotion to feel. What we most need right now is *courage*. Which is, as one might put it, hope transmogrified into action. What we need is courage to level with what is; courage to face the reality that is trying to stare us in the face; and to try to do the right thing in the face of it. That courage is what the Extinction Rebellion movement have shown: a real and manifest courage, a willingness to put their (our) bodies on the line etc., and if enough of us manage to find the courage to do that too, then we could yet change the course of history and we could, even now, bring about conceivably this transformed civilization, this transformed normal, which of course must be a much more 'hopeful' idea than the succession of civilization after collapse.

Do I think Extinction Rebellion is likely to succeed in getting its demands actually answered, fulfilled? No. (Its task was far harder than precedents sometimes cited (Read 2018e), such as the suffrage or civil rights movements). Extinction Rebellion is no longer growing. It has almost certainly reached its ceiling, at least for the foreseeable future (It might well at some point have a new lease of life as future mega climate disasters engender more waking up). Extinction Rebellion was born in 2018. Over half the time has passed before its target date (2025) for net zero emissions and net zero biodiversity loss! It is a fantasy to think that Extinction Rebellion is going to get its demands fulfilled.

Is that 'game over', then? No. It never is. The chances for some things pass, and they have to be relinquished. But there is always the chance to do the right thing, to reduce harm, to build a less bad tomorrow, to become more conscious and to spread that consciousness. With climate, unlike a giant Earth-bound asteroid, there is always time to look up. And to look down, at the abyss we are opening.

My argument now is that what we most need now is a broader, much larger movement. Something *between* conventional holding actions and full-on rebellion. Extinction Rebellion has functioned as 'a radical flank' (Samuel 2020) to the previous environmental movement. It has successfully changed the conversation (most dramatically, in the UK (Read, 2020d)); it opened up a space. We now need a moderate flank *to it*, something that can have much wider appeal (in part, through being just a little less demanding of participants), and be more genuinely inclusive of those who are not 'woke', not into identity politics, including citizens on whose politics are on the Right or are centrists. Those many, whose numbers will without doubt increase in the next few years as we enter further into climate breakdown, who will feel called to try to mitigate it, whether or not they think of themselves as g/Green (Read & Eastoe 2021).

The suggestion I made in *Parents for a Future* (Read 2021a) was that this new mass 'moderate' movement should be focussed on us parenting the future together. In particular, it should bring together parents (and aunts, and uncles, and godparents (and 'Gaiaparents'?, etc.) to struggle for their children to have a future. It could be unifying, in the way I imagined in Chapters 1 and 6 alike. The next, larger, 'post-Extinction Rebellion' wave, I am suggesting, could be: us at large.[19] Not 'them' – the activists – alone.

Such a mass movement could take diverse forms, but likely to be key among those forms will surely be workplace-based action. Marx remains correct in thinking that our work is the place we spend most of our time and have most of our power. Imagine if across our workplaces we were to turn our determination to the question of how to make our work compatible with climate sanity – in everything from greening supply chains to radically rethinking commutes, from greener use of employer-owned land to getting employers to permit political climate action on their time, from trades unions including green demands in their negotiations to firms lobbying government to level up the playing field in terms of eco-regulation. And much, much more. Imagine if, when this agenda gets stymied, we were to be willing to undertake climate strikes. After all, our children have shown the leadership to do so, in the last few years. Shouldn't we adults be willing to be as brave? It would be shameful to leave all the leadership to our most vulnerable, our young ones. We must take up the mantle! Let's make it so that there are some adults finally in the room.

The key point implied by *this* suggestion in turn is that it is essential for those of us already involved to be welcoming, as more and more increasingly wisely troubled souls recognize the need to stay with the trouble, and to seek together to adapt to climate decline in a manner that is transformative, ethical and effective. By definition, not all of these souls will be what is today called 'woke'. *Awakening*, the process of getting to grips with the full reality of our plight (and the full depth of our needful response to it) that this book seeks to help midwife, should not be confused with the political agenda that is called 'woke'. Many of those who join the ranks of climate action in the 2020s will not be left-wing or Green, nor most likely in many cases will they be into identity politics, nor will they be familiar with environmental activism (nor will they necessarily come to consider themselves as 'activists' at all), nor will they necessarily be scientifically literate, etc. It will be crucial that those of us who are already on the bus are ready to welcome them in. If you reject these new recruits, on the grounds of them not being ideologically 'pure' enough, they will find less salubrious ways of pursuing their enthusiasm or their collapse-anticipation. The wonderful opportunity contained in the bitter fruit of climate decline is for the building of an increasingly broad, genuinely inclusive (including of those with different politics from our own) climate movement that can generate some critical mass and some power to make change: at every level of society.

All this is why I have suggested it is time for a 'Parents for a future' movement. Extinction Rebellion has shown the way. Can a wider/parents' movement take up the mantle, and win? That cannot be said to be likely; but, as offered up broadly in Chapter 1 above, it is at least *possible*. That is the wonderful thing about human action. In regard to the future, one can never *know* what is going to work and what is not. I certainly would not *bet* on something like 'Parents for a future' succeeding; but I am throwing myself into trying to help make such a movement succeed, and the more of us who are brave enough to do that, the greater the chance that it might just succeed; and even if it does not succeed, it will at least have shown some courage and some willingness to look what's coming in the face. (Which means that we will be able, even if we fail, to face ourselves in the mirror, and not have to die of shame before our betrayed children).

My hope is that *this* book might help cement our courage for the tremendous challenge ahead. And in order for that to happen, we are going to have to create 'space' for all this to land.

That brings me to the seventh and final thing on my list. Perhaps an unexpected, almost paradoxical one. Stop. We need to pause – by which I mean we need to slow down and actually give ourselves a chance to take all of this in, to really think about it and to really feel it.[20]

If we do not do that, then we will not wake up properly and we will not be in a good position to wake anyone else up. We need to stop and give ourselves time to talk about this and work through our issues in relation to it. And only if we stop will we actually be in a good position to do the dramatic, courageous things that we'll need to do under these headings if there is to be something worth calling (a new) hope emerging from all of this.

Paul Kingsnorth, who saw a lot of the way things were going some years ago and was one of the founders accordingly of the 'Dark Mountain' group, has said the following (Kingsnorth 2017): that there is an abyss opening up before us. We need to be brave enough to look into it; and only if we do that will we then know what to do next ... and that's what I mean by stopping.

This my seventh and final recommendation in this seventh and final chapter of my book. Some readers will note an affinity in it to a central Daoist/ Buddhist recommendation – 'empty *yourself*, so you can truly engage responsiveness, what in Daoism is known as wuwei, 'non-action'. We might note a kinship with the important non-violence principle, of not taking any action that will cause harm (as in the famous 'preface' to the Hippocratic oath: 'First, do no harm'). I would recast it thus for our time: not taking any action that is not in accord with life (Read 2007). Not rushing in. The principle of wuwei is obviously in accordance with the precautionary principle. It is a prime example of the kind of paradigm-shifting that will be characteristic of the true civilization that could/will succeed this one. And it begins in the willingness to pause, to be in 'negative capability' awhile.

Lenin's famous question was, 'What is to be done?' I have substituted a subtly different question: 'What shall we do?'[21] For it is particularly crucial, given the vast, grinding nature of the threat, that we rise to our full collective *agentiality* in response to it.

I urge you to join with others in doing some of these various seven things that I have just explored; use your abilities, use your intelligence and your potential in the way that the best fits you to them. I would say do not restrict yourself to just one of them, though; we need to be giving ourselves multiple options, and we need to be more rounded and joined up than our atomized society encourages.

We have gambled too much to date on being able to stop the juggernaut of 'growth' and business-as-usual from destroying our civilization. We need to think very seriously about what will happen if we fail and that is why the things I have spent most time here discussing are important, and more novel than they should be. But the final thing I have wanted to suggest to you is that what we need to do is to stop so as to give ourselves a chance to *reflect* on all of this; and only if we do *that* will we be actually well placed to make the next moves forward.

And that is *philosophy*. This is the great task of philosophy today: to facilitate and undertake the right kind of pause. This is what philosophers are called to do. The kind of deep reflection about what really matters now that I have sought to intimate and initiate.

Philosophers have too often only *interpreted* the world. The point, however, is to *face it as it is*. When one truly does so, one has no choice but to seek to change it. Paradoxically, the route toward complete change is complete acceptance: of the bitter reality of climate breakdown.

Vulnerability – and vision

In October 2019, I appeared on BBC *Question Time* – Britain's most watched political panel TV programme – on behalf of Extinction Rebellion. It was a nerve-wracking experience and I faced a tough crowd. The way I won them around was by arguing that the *terra incognita* that Earth is becoming, with incipient climate breakdown, is making *all* of us *vulnerable*. I have found that this message of shared vulnerability – of our communities, our ecology, and even our energy and food supplies – is one that can cut through effectively. Like with the matters that I explored in Chapters 4 and 5, that vulnerability, when we admit to it, can bring with it real chances for change.[22]

'Even' in countries like the UK, we are highly vulnerable (in part because we have patently failed to undertake serious adaptation, so far (Committee on Climate Change (2021)). And as a species we are moving into a new world where tragically we are ever *more* vulnerable. We have therefore, as I've outlined, to prepare, to adapt. If we allow ourselves to be just *hit* by the kind of crisis of vulnerability that could result, for example, from an unprecedented heatwave of the kind that we had in the UK in the summer of 2018, but worse, then we are in terrible trouble. Imagine if that heatwave had continued on into August and September, roasting and shrivelling our crops in the fields. Maybe you think: that's OK, we're a rich country here, we're a 'developed' country. We can always buy food from abroad. But what if there aren't any foodstuffs for sale for us, abroad? Or at least, not enough at a price that most inhabitants of the UK can afford? (Here again we see how economic inequality is *de facto* threaded through the whole issue (Kenner & Read 2019); once again, this is why I think it high time we consider emergency responses or preparednesses such as food rationing (Lang 2020)). Or what if we *could* buy food from 'abroad', but only at the terrible, unacceptable cost of fomenting famine there?

What if we have a situation like we had on Earth in 2008, but even worse? Most people don't know what happened in 2008 because everyone's attention was on the financial crisis. At about the same time, a number of key countries in the world stopped some or all staple food exports. There was a weather-driven (probably climate-driven) food crisis and many countries banned exports of rice, wheat and so on. We are vulnerable in this country. This eco-crisis that we're in the middle of is not just about Bangladesh and the Maldives and Nigeria (and Australia! And Greece! And California!). Those places are really suffering right now, and they need our solidarity. But don't let that fool you into thinking that it's not going to hit us too. We, here, where I'm writing from, in the midst of (and in part of course *because* of) all our complacency, are vulnerable.

There's a cliff, called climate breakdown. Some are still warning us not to even talk about the cliff, because it will allegedly 'put people off'. They are often secretly the most scared of all; they can't bear fully to face reality. Because here is the reality I've been driving at since the beginning of the book: we're not being driven towards the edge of a cliff. We're not being shunted off the precipice. We're already *off* the cliff. We're already tumbling down towards the jagged rocks below. What we have to do is to painfully, with great difficulty, try to arrest our descent; and then start to climb back up the steep cliff. That's how difficult the task is going to be.

But that's what we have to seek to do. There is no alternative. The only other thing that I mean, when I talk about adaptation is that it will be better to try to sort of remain at the point we've reached in our descent, and learn how to hang on by our fingertips halfway down the cliff, than to fall onto the jagged rocks at the bottom. That's worth doing, too. That's worth fighting for. Hanging on by your fingertips is better than lying impaled and dead down below.

But we've really got to not fool ourselves about how hard it will be even to do that. As I laid out in my seven suggestions, above, we've got to wake up thoroughly, and remain awake, and wake up the rest of our society and (as much as possible) of our species. We've got to stop looking for excuses to spectate. We've got to *act*. We mustn't fool ourselves by thinking that, as things stand, those rocks are not our destination. They are very much our destination. We are already off the cliff. We have a massive job to turn everything around. We will probably fail, and fall. But the thing you really don't want to do is have to face your children or grandchildren in twenty to thirty years' time, if/when it's clear that we're all broke down among the rocks dying, and have to say 'I wish I'd tried harder'.

Don't be that person. Make this your mission: let's do *enough*.

Are there any precedents for what we need to do? The case of the Byzantine Empire

Earlier in the chapter, I asked whether there are any precedents for the transformation we need to co-create. I have canvassed possible such precedents periodically during this book, but never found one that really fitted the bill. Let me very briefly now mention one that occurred within recorded history, and that seems to me more promising. It is the most challenging period in the history of the Byzantine empire, which, according to the great theorist of collapse Joseph Tainter,[23] survived – in that it avoided collapse – in an extraordinary way when under severe pressure from invaders in the seventh century: it did so not by staying within the narrative of 'progress', not by creating a larger army and higher taxes, but by turning half its army into a sort of glorified peasant militia and telling them to simply defend the land where they lived. The economy shrank, urbanization went into reverse and money itself went largely out of fashion; but the empire survived, rather than falling as (famously) the western Roman Empire had already done – perhaps because it had never attempted anything as radical.

This successful relocalization offers us a kind of model, I would suggest. The best way to survive what is coming is not by trying to create a high-tech brave new world, but by actively welcoming the process of putting 'progress' (growth, development, complexification) into a significant degree of reverse (Tainter 2000, 24–9; Tainter 1988). The Byzantine empire chose to be less … byzantine! They chose to risk simplifying, localizing – the very opposite of conventional 'progress' or imperial majesty. It was a very unusual choice, in historical terms but is certainly one to ponder.

Imagine being there at the court of this the so-called Eastern Roman Empire, at the start of this process. Imagine being one of the senior courtiers who dares to imagine, 'What if, instead of trying yet again to increase the size of the army to fight off the disasters that these "barbarians" are bringing us, and bankrupting ourselves in the process, or debasing the currency further and forfeiting trust, or fomenting mutiny … what if, instead, we *reduced* the size of the standing army, put the process of centralization and civil-ization *as we know it* into reverse, and relied on a new, relocalized peasantry to defend us and thus defend ourselves? What if we became, willingly, a little more like some of the "barbarians"?' Imagine being not just wise enough to think this, but brave enough to *say it*. Imagine, most encouraging of all, implementing this bold, virtually unheard-of simplifying, localizing response … and seeing it work!

You are imagining the kind of thing that *we* need to do.

That said, while the content of the simplificatory course-change we need to execute is in some respects very similar to the Byzantine example (for example, with regard to relocalization), in other respects it's completely different. An example: our position is even more paradoxical than that of the Byzantine empire under pressure. In order to survive an external threat, they paradoxically chose to 'downsize' their centre, but *not* their population. Whereas in our case, the threat is, in a way, of course … ourselves. I have emphasized, especially in the early portion and in this closing portion of this book, our literally vital role in parenting the future. For the sake of our children, one of the things we plainly need now to do is: have fewer of them. No one is more determined than I that we do miles better than we have in caring for unborn future generations. But I am also one of the increasing number of people who have recognized that a prime way of symbolizing in our life the reality of this care can be to *not* have kids of our own.[24] This is especially important for those of us living in richer countries, where kids have a footprint that is typically much greater than those in poorer countries.

Imagine a future in which rather more of us (though not of course all of us!) make a similar choice. You are imagining the kind of thing for which the children of the future will be grateful.

Why does climate breakdown matter?

In the light of the point that we have now reached, here's a final re-seeing of what this book has been about.

After the pretty epic darkness most of the first half of this book, the second half has taken us into some possible light – by way of greater darkness. The light that flickered on in Chapter 1 (via the hope for the world that our love for our kids could bring) has been enriched since then in our journey together by considering the communities formed under pressure of disasters (i.e., by the spontaneous care and love we show each other, under such pressure) as an unexpected upside of the greater weight of disasters we'll now encounter; by our less pleasant emotions (all of which come back in the end to being forms or consequences of love), which again will increase under the pressure of what is coming; and by what we can learn from our kin, our fellow social animals (a kind of love, of unity, that we can perhaps aspire to), when under the gravest pressure of all. In this concluding chapter, I have drawn these threads together and sketched what on the back of them we can and should intelligently and intelligibly think and do.

In the light of this hope of the hopeless, we are now in a position finally to answer properly the question posed in the title of this book, now slightly reframed:[25] Why must climate breakdown matter to us, come what may?

It matters because, whatever happens, what we do makes a difference: it shows (or otherwise) the love and care we are willing to *be*.

Because some of what we do at the least makes any destruction of our civilization less painful, literally. Even just slowing down the coming of a potential apocalypse is potentially well worth striving for, if it preserves some more relatively good years, or reduces the suffering that occurs in the process, or even if it merely manifests some sane loving joyful consciousness amidst the madness that surrounds us.

We *are* the light in the tunnel

There's virtually no light at the end of the tunnel.

But that doesn't absolve us from at bare minimum trying to extend the tunnel rather than have its roof collapse on us.

And, crucially, *we can create light* within *the tunnel*. Rather than always peering toward the end in a hopeless attitude of passive hope, we can make things brighter right here, right now. By acting nobly, regardless of outcome.

By building community, in the face of disaster. By feeling and expressing our grief and the love that lies within it. By being whole, by being one. By becoming more ourselves than we've ever been before.

One way this will happen is quite literally by sitting around campfires together. To the extent that, emerging from the time of corona, we reconnect with our deep history, lovingly with each other, and with the land, thereby putting ourselves in the best possible position to weather whatever climate-crazed weather comes our way.

Even if there's no escape from the tunnel, we can *be* the light that shines *within* it.

We – you and me, and the *us* we co-create – can manifest the awakening of a species. We can show the will to manifest a new civilization, drawing on the ancient and the tested, and abandoning the failed experiments of recent centuries (and millennia).

The whales might inherit the Earth

How much we degrade the Earth's ecosystems matters profoundly even if we fail to awaken enough, and so fail to build a new civilization out of the materiel of this one. Because, even if we (humans) almost or completely vanish, we are pretty unlikely to eliminate complex life completely or anything like it. Our first priority must be to seek to reduce the chances of a near-exterminatory event such as the end-Permian mass extinction (Steffen et al. 2018). That should be doable, even for us.[26]

Moreover, if we manage to preserve more of nature rather than less, then – even if we do vanish, or become hemmed climatically or geographically or toxico-chemically into some restricted zones of the Earth – what we will have done, in preserving more rather than less of life-not-ours, is hugely important: because life can then go on.

And so can evolution, too.

Imagine a future in which we mismanage things so utterly that humanity goes extinct, or becomes drastically reduced and highly geographically restricted for a geologically significant period but in which we don't nihilate so completely that complex life goes extinct. That is, a scenario in which, as I warned earlier, we at least don't create a result even worse than terminal civilizational collapse: namely, civilizational collapse that takes out most other species with us. In that case, what next? What might happen over the tens of millions of years to follow?

Imagine for instance that some kind of a runaway heating effect ends human civilization with extreme prejudice. *But* that some non-human life continues to flourish, in some corners of the oceans. Over some millions of years, biodiversity gets 'restored' (Gabbatiss 2019) to levels not dissimilar to prior to human 'mismanagement' of Earth.

Return to the topic of Chapter 6. Imagine, say, that some orcas survive. And over time, no longer massively depleted by humanity, their cultures flourish and spread (Read 2017d).

Imagine them becoming even more sophisticated over the next several million years. And then, partly by pressure and ability of evolution, and partly by *choice*, they notice substantial chunks of the Earth under-inhabited by anything like them.

It is entirely possible that, given 10 or 20 million years or so and some open ecological niches, social species of whales or dolphins could evolve biologically and culturally so as to take to the land (from which, of course, they originally came, about 40 million years ago). They could re-evolve those vestigial hands or feet.

And perhaps if they ever get to make civilizations of their own, on the basis of the splendid cultures they already have (as outlined in Chapter 6), they will do so in a way that is less short sighted than the world's dominant culture of empire has done.

What I've been asking you to do here is something very difficult for us, almost conceptually impossible. Namely: to imagine the world without us; and to imagine that we fail to imagine enough to actually prevent this.

Imagine, in other words, that therefore *we fail,* but that we *don't* acidify and pollute and overheat and de-oxygenate the oceans to such an extent that we completely take out the cetaceans, in the course of our down-going. Imagine that we manage to do enough to head off such worst-case scenarios, scenarios in which our mass-suicide turns into complete ecocide. Imagine even that, in our travail, we use some of our remaining agency to try to stop whales and dolphins (and elephants, and bonobos, and all the other animals whose cultures show promise that ours sometimes lacks) from being wiped away. Imagine that they survive, and then prosper, in the millions of years to follow.

It could happen.

It *might* even happen in a world where humans had not been eliminated, but only geographically restricted in the long term (perhaps, to the poles). So imagine too a perhaps more thrilling prospect: a future world in which humans and cetacean-descendants co-exist, and learn from each other. The implication of my argument of course is that, even if we are/were doomed (which of course we most certainly do not yet know ourselves to be), then every 'holding action' we take on nature's behalf could still turn out to be of incalculable value. If we stop the seas from filling with plastic, not to mention from boiling off in a runaway greenhouse effect, then we increase the chance that some marvellous scenario such as those sketched above could be made room for.

When we think of civilizational succession (Chapter 3; Read 2018a) – when we take seriously the idea that our civilization will be replaced by something – we tend not to factor non-human animals into what may succeed us. But if we start to think long term enough (which is *exactly* what we now need to learn once more to do), then such a possibility starts to become real. Perhaps one day there will be an eco-sane, communitarian civilization descended from our present-day cetaceans, living on and off the ruins we left behind. If that happens, they will be very glad indeed that we didn't destroy and kill even more than we already have. And, if there are humans around then too, so will they.

It is arrestingly sad to face the possibility of humanity vanishing from virtually all of the Earth (if not entirely from it), because we have the capacity to be great-hearted, and to do and create beautiful things and relationships. (Consider Emil Cioran's deep, dolorous quip: 'Bach's music is the only argument proving the creation of the Universe cannot be regarded as a complete failure. Without Bach, God would be a complete[ly] second-rate figure').

Cetaceans have some such capacities, too. In fact, some of their capacities in these spheres appear already to be potentially even greater than ours (as per my argument in Chapter 6).

Once we are fully woken up to the extremity of our vulnerability, and no longer complacent about the staying power of our civilization, we are better placed to be able to learn from the past, from peoples that we have falsely labelled as 'primitive', and even from non-human animals, than we have been for a long, long time. For we no longer feel veiled in superiority.

We can then potentially overcome presentism, ethnocentrism, speciesism – and (then) anthropocentrism. 'Ecocentrism' is ultimately non-negotiable in that what has to be at the centre of our concern is nature. Without viable ecosystems, we are nothing. The fundamental unit in nature is of course not the biological individual or the species, but the community, i.e., the ecosystem.

We can credibly hope for such natural communities to be less vulnerable to destruction in future – if we humans are willing to learn for example from the social whales and dolphins. Or, failing that, if we end up making way for them. (Or for corvids, wolves, elephants, orangutans, bonobo chimpanzees, perhaps even cephalopods). Any of those species could easily evolve, over the vast course of the time left to Earth before the Sun starts to chronically over-heat it and Gaian balancing feedbacks can no longer operate, into a species capable of doing on balance a better job than we have so far done of enjoying a rich cultural life at scale.

While our extinguishing ourselves would be unutterably stupid and tragic, extinguishing species such as these too would be far worse still. There is a very high premium on keeping these species in particular intact, unextinct – both for the glories of their life now, and for the richer-still glories that might await them in an evolutionary future.

Biodiversity hotspots are the new monasteries, in the likely coming Dark Ages. It is going to be almost impossibly difficult to preserve the social cetaceans through what is coming. We have nevertheless to try to do what we can to stop the oceans becoming gigantic dead zones; one implication of this is to underscore one final time that (and how) geoengineering schemes are wrong (Paul & Read 2019), for they recklessly imperil ecosystems, in pursuit of an (understandable, but monomaniacal) desperate focus on arresting global over-heat. Remember: acidification and loss of life and of oxygen through this and pollution could turn out to be a graver threat even than over-heat.

Then there is the unsmall matter of stopping our contemporaries and descendants from directly killing those that should be given a chance at inheriting the Earth. Civilizational collapses will be unlikely to be to hospitable environments for zoos (or aquaria). These glorious fellow beings need to be given enough 'rewilded' space in which to live and thrive. And that is a lot: because there is likely to be much human predation upon them in failed states and collapsing civilizations.

We should struggle with determination, on the macro and micro scales, to give whales and dolphins and bonobos and more as strong a shot as can now be managed at surviving the near future, the 'Anthropocene'. This process – and the vital, deeply-challenging aspect of it that has to do with rendering these our kin sacred so that fewer and fewer of us are minded to be willing to kill them, even if doing so would feed us for a while – begins with reflection, imagination and with feeling.

And then actions which speak more urgently than any words.

Senseful acts of beauty.

Hopefully it won't come to that. Hopefully the arising of global consciousness of which this book is, I hope, a small 'for instance', will head off humanity's downgoing.

But my point has been: *however bad the future gets,* what we do continues to matter, across the piece.

That's pretty much all I've got it. I hope it may be enough.

The politics of paradox

The politics our time needs is a politics of paradox (Read & Baldwin 2021). The 'post-Covid' Glasgow climate COP has failed us, failed humanity. So have the vast majority of governments. This civilization is finished. There is just one way we get to have the slightest chance of society not collapsing, in this context. And that is if we junk traditional 'optimism', face up to these harsh truths, accept that the status quo is a cartoon character pumping its legs in the air off the edge of a cliff, and react with the rage and love and determination the situation merits. That's what this book has been about.

Only if we have the courage to give up the hope we've had do we get to find a new hope. A *radical* hope; the hope that is born from the ashes of our fantasies.

Remember: typically, philosophers have only interpreted the world. What we need now is a (maybe philosophically inspired!) willingness to help change it out of all recognition. (Preferably *before* it breaks down).

And if you are still wavering, consider, finally, this:

Only if we give up active, radical hope – hoping for something new when all we previously hoped for is implausible – is hope gone.

Only if we don't rely on hope as a quasi-passive attitude but *act* like never before *is* there (any) real hope.

Only if we envisage our descendants, our children's children, *as* real will they have a strong chance to *become* real. Only if we see them staring us in the face will we *get* to stare them in the face.

Only if we envisage the breakdown, the catastrophe, as real, staring us in the face, will we just maybe act enough.

In sum, our only hope is that the beyond-dire reality that I have outlined in this book is faced, comprehended and acted upon. Starting with you, reader.

You cannot proceed from here without re-examining your life. And the joy of it is: doing so makes life matter much more. Makes it, in fact, worth living.[27]

Notes

Preface

1   My first further acknowledgement is to the good people at Bloomsbury, especially Liza Thompson, and to my colleague and friend Constantine Sandis, who originally came up with the proposition of me doing this book (or something along its lines). They have been endlessly understanding of the long delays that have plagued its writing, some of which were a result of my life turning upside-down when my talk at Cambridge University went viral (Read 2018h), and I threw myself into the launch of Extinction Rebellion (Read 2020d). More recently, I suffered a severe and disabling bout of eco-anxiety in summer 2020 that further delayed this project (The Poetry of Predicament 2021).
    My only complaint is that Bloomsbury wouldn't let me title this book 'Why *ecological* breakdown matters'. As I'll explain in the Introduction, our predicament is far broader than even the broad word 'climate' suggests.
    I want to acknowledge also the truly tremendous help that Tim O'Riordan, Tom Greaves, Victor Anderson and Peter Kramer have given me throughout this book manuscript. (Acknowledgements of help I've received from many on particular chapters can be found in those chapters).

Prologue: The Attention-shift from Climate to Corona – and Back Again?

1   Throughout this book I am using the Harvard referencing style. Whenever you see an author name and date of publication appear in brackets like this, it is an invitation to look up that reference in the Bibliography and follow up by reading the source it is from. These sources will either contain more information or be examples of authors who have made similar points to those I am discussing in the sentence preceding their appearance.
2   Since then, of course, President Biden has part-restored the US's reputation on the world stage. But it is a complete illusion to think that his election somehow puts us on a path to climate sanity. The illusion is encapsulated by the horrific fact that, as I finalize this book (in early 2022, not long after COP26 at Glasgow), the USA is in the process of undertaking a sale of licences for fossil-fuel extraction larger than any that occurred even under the Trump administration. ('Undertaking' being, tragically, the precisely-operative word for what it is doing).

3 African countries have suffered from patent monopolies (I am thinking especially of the coronavirus vaccines), and from depleted health services. This makes all the more remarkable the comparative success of countries like Sierra Leone in relation to the virus.

Introduction: On Climate, Ecological and Societal Breakdown

1 This is the fundamental point made in Bruno Latour's important recent book, *Down to Earth* (2018), the original French title of which, *Où atterrir?*, might be better translated 'Where to land?' or even 'A place to land'). (A note to the reader: here, as often in this book, I will use the footnotes to provide a juicy expansion on something in the main text; and, sometimes, moreover, an expansion which is of a more academically or technically philosophical nature. Just skip these, if you don't want the juice. But if you are keen on philosophical juice, be sure to read these footnotes: they might even be the best bits of the book, if you like that type of thing).

2 Political philosophers will spot that here, at the opening of this book, I am indicating a foundational disagreement with the ideas of John Rawls, as laid out at the opening of *A Theory of Justice* (Rawls 1971; Read 2010c).

3 For how easy it may be to set off a decades-long fatal 'nuclear winter' (Caldicott 2017; Schlegelmilch 2020, ch. 5). Translated into the terms of my work, Schlegelmilch draws on the specialist literature to suggest that even a 'nuclear autumn', which could be caused by very few nuclear weapons being detonated, could be enough to terminate our fragile civilization with extreme prejudice.

4 I'll discuss in subsequent chapters (especially Chapter 2) the philosophically principled basis for such slowness: known in the trade as precaution.

5 Later in the book, I'll discuss one such emerging threat which really terrifies me: ocean acidification (Dryden & Duncan 2021). The tragic destruction of our coral reefs may turn out to be the least of it, where this threat is concerned.

6 I am happy to import my colleague Jem Bendell's definition of 'collapse' here (Bendell 2019).

7 This premise is defended in detail in *Deep Adaptation* (Bendell & Read 2021).

8 See Morgan Phillips (2021) for an excellent treatment of how to do adaptation right and how to overcome the semi-taboo on talking about it that exists even now in most climate-activist/NGO circles.

9 This is not, obviously, to denigrate technology across the board, still less science! It is to begin to set out how an uncritical positive attitude toward technology across the board is part of what is killing us (Read & Rughani 2020).

10 Not to pretend to 'define', but to give the reader a vivid sense of 'climate/ ecological breakdown'. 'Breakdown' is not a term used much in science, but it can help evoke appositely what we are facing. There is no need to seek a strict definition of the term up front, and little point in trying to do so. It will become clear throughout this book just what it means.

11 If there are echoes here of Buddhist (and Heideggerian) teachings that only by facing the reality of death can we truly appreciate living, that is no accident. One thing I am doing in this book is taking such philosophy, which has often been heard as timeless and individualistic, and turning it into something for our time and for us as a collective body.

12 Who is this 'us', this 'we' that I keep invoking? I hope it is contextually obvious usually how to interpret this term in my text, but it is worth remarking upfront: (i) that it is often directed at (including, co-forming) those who are the likeliest readers of this book: i.e., thinking citizens, not living hand to mouth (as many in our world, utterly unjustly, are), of our globalized civilization; and (ii) that it is often invitational. I invite you to join me in an emerging sense of who we have been and who we can become, in a more unified way, as a society/civilization/species, as we wake up to our greatest-ever challenge. This is a challenge that will be flubbed if we do not lean into it together (Read & Alexander 2019, ch. 17). At bare minimum, the invitation is extended at least to the person reading the sentence, i.e., 'we' is at the very least you and me! But in aspiration at least, it is usually far, far wider than that.

I try to hold (i) and (ii) 'in balance'. By this I mean that the rich and most of those living in the global North are much more responsible than the poor, and most of those living in the global South, for committing us to climate breakdown (and this has many implications, including who should pay the lion's share of climate finance); *and yet* we are all in this together, in the sense that an emergency is above all a time for common action for the common good, not for bickering or *resentment* about who started it.

Note further that on occasion there is a sense in which the 'we' part- excludes myself and hopefully yourself, as in occurrences like 'We are driving our children over a cliff'. If you and I are trying actively to stop our children being driven over the cliff, this may seem a peculiar usage of this pronoun. The reason for nevertheless invoking 'us'/'we' here is to avoid any complacent 'othering', any too easy breaking of the unity of the first-person *plural* that is needed – and needs – to face this crisis. If I am willing to be counted as part of the society that is driving its children over a cliff, then that increases at least somewhat the chance that *we* can pull back together from doing so any longer (Read 2020d). (I return to this matter in Chapters 6 and 7 of this book).

Note finally that in a different book with a slightly different purpose, I'd emphasize more the injustice aspect of the equation and the need to push in the direction of economic equality (these have been central to my academic work in this area (Read 2011a & 2011b)). Others have of course done this job brilliantly, such as Jason Hickel, whose books I strongly recommend (Hickel 2020). For why I strongly suspect that the implications of the argument of the present work are radically redistributive, see Read 2019b. I explain there how the changes we need will resemble those in Left/Green manifestos, even though they need not be 'leftist' in ideological terms. There is precedent for this. In the UK, radically redistributive measures, such as food rationing, were brought in during the Second World War by a Conservative Prime Minister leading a National Unity government.

13 Although the very thrust of my book is that sometimes, breakdown can be breakthrough: thus I have employed the word 'seems' in this sentence!

14 There is no longer any 'safe' level of heating; we are seeing climate chaos aplenty already at 1.2°C. And 'even just' 2°C means for example the death of over 99 percent of the world's coral reefs – permanently, horribly and dangerously defacing the ecology of our planet. The International Panel on Climate Change is unambiguous in its latest report that 2° means a much greater frequency and a higher magnitude of the extreme weather events that are increasingly and scarily blighting our world. It means a further increase in violence and war globally because of resource scarcity and hotter temperatures. It means increased frequency of pandemic and pestilence, with greater threats to our health and the food supply we rely upon to nourish us. And it likely means the complete erasure of ice from both the North and South Poles. For more on all this, see David Wallace-Wells' *New York Magazine* article, 'The Uninhabitable Earth' (2017), and his 2019 book of the same name, although there are reasons to think that even Wallace-Wells might be understating the severity of our predicament (Read, Foster & Bendell 2019).

15 I examine these downsides of Paris in greater detail in Chapter 3. See in the meantime Anderson (2015), and below on the geoengineering sting in Paris' tail.

16 For the situation is now one of 'post-normal' science, in which, as I'll explain in the body of the book, the employment of precautionary reasoning is essential (Read 2018b).

17 See n.12 above for why in this book I am emphasizing the collective aspect of this, rather than (as I have sometimes done previously (Kenner & Read 2019)) emphasizing the undoubted much greater responsibility for this outcome of some companies, such as fossil-fuel corporations.

18 Eileen Crist's paper 'Beyond the Climate Crisis' (2007) argues against climate-centric discourse and for a move towards focussing more on 'biodiversity' – but even that latter has to some extent all too easily been made part of the technocratic accounting system in the meantime (Anderson 2016). For more on this, see Charles Eisenstein's problematic but useful book *Climate: A New Story* (2018), which critiques 'climate fundamentalism', and Ginny Battson's article on this (2021).

19 In my book *Parents for a Future,* I argue that thinking of nature as valuable for its own sake and thinking of humanity's enlightened self-interest almost

entirely coincide (Read 2021a, ch. 3). In this book I'll also touch on the tensions between the humanity-centric and eco-centric worldviews.

20 Iain McGilchrist's work offers, in my judgement, the best such full examination.

21 I continue to be amazed by the number of comments from climate deniers that, even now, periodically appear under my talks on YouTube. Their number has decreased in recent years, but has certainly not vanished entirely. This denial is of course completely and categorically refuted by the scientific consensus on the climate emergency, even if it does occasionally (though again, significantly less often now (Read 2018f)) make its way into sections of the mainstream media. A recent worrisome example of the BBC in effect greenwashing and greenlighting denial of the brutal realities of climate breakdown is discussed in Monbiot (2021). While overt climate denial is thankfully now a niche demographic, groups espousing this nonsense remain well organized and invested in their message of prevarication on ecology and climate. They are tending now to seek subtler ways of undertaking their deadly enterprise, such as arguing that strong action on climate is too expensive, or that there is a clash between our freedoms and such action. Look for example at the rhetorical moves made by Bjørn Lomborg and the output of media such as talkRADIO.

22 In Chapter 2, I outline the precautionary case for radical action on climate *even* if the science was as cloudy as deniers claim it is. While the uncertainty in climate modelling may mean that it is *less* bad than all the evidence suggests, the uncertainty also means that it could be far *worse* than we are anticipating. Because the harms (and import) of *far worse* are of such a greater magnitude than the benefits of *less bad*, we ought to take aggressive regulatory steps in response to the very uncertainty involved in climate modelling. In Chapter 2, I argue that to create a civilization that would be as robust as possible to any potential catastrophic uncertainties present in climate modelling, we must seek to go further in our climate goals than most models suggest or entail is necessary.

23 This is especially peculiar since 2019, when the boldly named Extinction Rebellion proved that it is possible to succeed in dramatically shifting public opinion with a framing that is alarming and 'negative'.

24 As I argue in Chapter 4, coming to terms with that reality is crucial to help guide effective public policy and community action going forwards.

25 John Foster's work is critical for understanding why climate breakdown isn't really a 'problem' at all. It is something much 'larger': something like a tragic condition that we are inevitably inhabiting for a very long time to come.

26 I do not dwell explicitly in this book on the long and often tedious debate between those who focus on individual responsibility and those who focus on systemic responsibility. Instead, I emphasize repeatedly the ways in which systemic responsibility is clearly paramount, when it comes to climate, and yet each and every one of us has a profound and inalienable responsibility to

do whatever we can to change that system (together). (See also n.12, above).
Talk of systemic responsibility must not be an evasion of responsibility.

27 It is unfortunate that the technical term in climate discourse for GHG
emissions-reduction is 'mitigation'. It would have been better had there been
more emphasis on preventing dangerous climate change, by reducing such
emissions to zero. Then we could more easily have spoken of mitigation in
the same breath as adaptation: as the enterprise of handling as well as
possible, in the round, the effects of whatever climate damage has been done
(Read 2020a).

28 I mean by this that it is absurd to seek to pursue one's favoured issue without
at minimum compatibility between it and a great turning toward eco-sanity;
because without that turning, one's efforts will before too long be swept away.
I suggest in these pages that serious pursuit of that turning will lead us
toward a more just society/world, for various reasons, including crucially
that the long emergency requires the giving up of 'luxury emissions' (and in
due course, to reduce our growing exposure to food insecurity, of luxury
food-consumption) much like it required the giving up of much luxury
food-consumption in the shared emergency of the Second World War (Shue
1993; Read 2019b). One could go further, and credibly argue that portents of
social breakdown that we see – a loss of hope for the social contract, a rise in
near-despair – have in fact been co-responsible for making plausible climate
breakdown, and that these portents are due in significant part to the
abandonment of 'social democracy'. (Think of the rise of Trump, or of the
gilets jaunes (yellow jackets), fuelled by a festering sense of injustice and
abandonment, and by the green banner being seemingly hitched to that
economic injustice). This point would of course add further to the profound
importance of a just building-back from Covid, a just transition.

29 Sharon Beder's 2002 analysis of this phenomenon still stands the test of time.

30 It is all very well, a critic might say, speaking of the need to overturn the soft
denialism present in the way we speak about climate and ecological collapse,
but to truly do that we must replace the soft denialism with something else,
something *better*. We must reframe emotions like grief over climate
breakdown (as a good thing, as necessary) and start to speak with
psychological honesty about the emotive aspect of our global predicament.
In Chapter 5, I explore some of the ideas of the growing 'eco-psychology'
movement that seeks to do just this. I argue against the idea that honesty
about ecology demotivates and leads into unproductive hopelessness. Indeed,
I argue that hope is not in the end the appropriate emotion that our
predicament most demands. Hope, if it is naive, can blind us to reality.
Rather than hope, the facts about impending ecological collapse demand
courage. The courage to look honestly at our situation, to interrogate its
causes, to face its likely consequences, and to act to minimize harm and
prepare for an environment more hostile to human life.

31 The definitive analysis here is still Clive Hamilton's (2013). See also the
critique of geoengineering that I develop in Chapters 2 and 3, below.

32 As Ludwig Wittgenstein's work shows most clearly (Read 2012b).

33 Here I am thinking of John Foster's recent work; this is one of a number of important moments in the present work where I owe him a debt.

34 To echo the words of Greta Thunberg's rebuke of British parliamentarians in April 2019, 'You are only interested in solutions that enable you to carry on like before'. The truth is that there are no solutions that will enable us to carry on consuming like before. No green capitalism or consumerism that can 'solve' this crisis. No fully automated luxury communism that keeps material consumption at extreme levels but simply widens the franchise of who can participate in the festivities of eco-destruction (Mariqueo-Russell & Read 2019; and see the section on 'On those who deny planetary boundaries' in Chapter 3). And no techno-fix that will dispel climate and ecological breakdown with the flick of a switch. Letting go of these enticing and convenient delusions, and recognizing the ephemeral nature of our unsustainable civilization, is a liberating practice that can enable us to think creatively and wisely again about how to live on a finite planet (Read 2016a).

   I will set out in more detail in Chapter 2 that and how our faith in techno-science is unfounded.

35 Though there was a hopeful moment during the Covid pause when we were reminded that it doesn't have to be this way (Read 2020e).

36 The 'white swan' of climate catastrophe is bearing down on us (Chapter 2); we are not pulling together to stop it, we are not even staying stationary: we are racing toward it at roughly the speed of economic growth. And yet a change in this ludicrous state of affairs cannot be ruled out.

37 More generally, the trend of nearly every technological development, in its net effects (i.e., in a context of growthism and of reliance upon open-market mechanisms), to propel us closer to (i.e., over) planetary limits. To increase entropy (Read 2016b). (Even renewable energy is no exception, because of the 'rebound effect'. It is no good making energy systems greener and more efficient if the net result is only to free up more money and resources for people to fly more, etc.)

38 There are also those who see robots as a likely future existential threat to humans. Conversely, I think that the most likely effect of accelerated robotization is accelerated climate breakdown, which will take us out first (Read 2016b).

39 I elaborate a little on this painful thought experiment (painful, because our present and future would be very different, had this happened) early in Chapter 3.

40 This means relocalizing not only as a way of retreating from the wider world, but as a way, globally, of reimagining the world! This requires protection of the local (so that viable relocalization is possible, and mutual), globally (Norberg-Hodge & Read 2016).

41 Cf. chapter 1 of Williston's *Philosophy and the Climate Crisis* (2020). The most likely end for the globally hegemonic culture, tragically, appears to be far from that hoped for by Williston (and us all): it is that most people will

mostly seek to carry on living roughly as they are, and that governments will mostly facilitate this until they are decimated by climate decline. This is why, as I will detail in Chapter 3, it is no longer reasonable to imagine our society, this civilization, surviving, unless one imagines entirely – absurdly – unlikely technological outcomes. Sure, there will gradually be more and more concern; and anger; and bitterness. There'll be pious declarations (as in Paris and Glasgow). Some of us will really try to do something, and there will be some great achievements and moments of hope along the way. But it appears likeliest that the net result will be – faced as we are with the mother of all collective-action problems, and unable or unwilling to rise to a higher state of consciousness at a lower level of impact – humanity signing its own death warrant. We will act as the brilliant allies of our own gravediggers. Or, more simply, as our own gravediggers.

Seeing this clearly is realism, and is a *sine qua non* for any realistic (even if long-shot) prospect of changing it.

42 And this thought of mine is, moreover, evidence based; there is strong evidence from opinion polling that collapse-anticipation is actually pretty rife in the contemporary 'West' (Cassely & Fourquet 2020).

43 Doing both these things – seeking to prevent collapse, and to mitigate its impact should it come – is a complex ask (Bendell & Read 2021, ch. 11). Our civilization doesn't like complex asks, one of many reasons it is failing. But, as I have already intimated, the ask is in practice largely answered by approaches which embody a transformative mode of adaptation. By and large the complexity is resolved by the beautiful coincidence that the very things we need to do in order to make our lives actually better (not materially richer, but better) are the very things we need to do in order to make collapse less likely are the very things we need to do in order to make any actual collapse more endurable.

44 This phrase is intended to evoke Wittgenstein's key methodological device of 'objects of comparison' (1958, §130–2).

1 Just How Much do you Care About the Future of Humanity?

1 If you have already read my book *Parents for a Future*, you may wish to skip this chapter, which is in part a recap of that book. (However, the presentation here is novel, and so you may profit from reading it even if you have read that book already). If on the other hand you have not, and you find in the reading of some of this chapter a lack of sufficient depth or support, then I invite you to consult that book.

2 I recently discussed the extent to which Rawlsian liberalism is ill equipped to respond to climate breakdown on BBC Radio (Freethinking 2021).

3   This critique is developed throughout Green House think tank's book, *The Post-Growth Project* (Blewitt & Cunningham 2014). Needless to say, such growthism – the fantasy of unending growth on a finite planet – is the ideology preferred by profit-seekers. A capitalist economy militates systematically in favour of such a nonsensical 'philosophy'.

4   I explore this further in 'Some thoughts on "civilizational succession"' (Read 2018a) and 'Fully automated luxury barbarism' (Mariqueo-Russell & Read 2019).

5   I consider this and other such examples (historic and contemporary) of future care built into politics in my 'Guardians of the future' report (Read 2011).

6   We should, however, note that there are some hopeful partial past precedents for such deferral. For instance, the collective sacrifice undertaken during the Second World War. There are of course some signs of a degree of change now in the present, too. Extinction Rebellion, the School Strikes for Climate movement and increasingly visible indigenous activism, have all helped partially shift the dial on the expectations placed on politicians. Countries like Bolivia and Ecuador have historically faced far more pressure from their populations to act on climate ecology than their counterparts in the global North. Consequently, these countries have taken more radical approaches to enshrining protection for ecology in their legal systems (Tabios Hillebrecht & Berros 2017), at least in theory.

7   Cowen and Parfit outline the arbitrariness this type of discounting (1992). Notably, even minor discount rates aggregate to make the far future count for very little.

      Economists would say there is a reason for employing such a practice of discounting: they are reflecting everyone's (i.e., 'current consumers') way of looking at things – following the 'revealed preferences of consumers' rather than 'imposing their own values'. Insofar as this is true, it makes clear once again the importance of the topic of this chapter: seeking to show everyone that their own values actually have the consequence that it makes no sense to value the future less than the present.

8   I discuss the awful *and yet* deeply hopeful rise in ecological anxiety and climate grief in Chapter 5 of this book.

9   Perhaps partly because it is sometimes still very unclear to people how to act on it. I will endeavour to rectify that in the final chapter (Chapter 7) of this book.

10   With regard specifically to the 'Left', see 'Fully Automated Luxury Barbarism' (Mariqueo-Russell & Read 2019), and the section entitled 'On those who deny planetary boundaries' in Chapter 3 below.

11   See for instance, the far-sighted *Dark Mountain Manifesto* (2009) and associated movement, which has risked the appearance of dalliance with doomerism since its own inception. With regards to deep adaptation, the picture is more complex. Jem Bendell, its brilliant founder, shares the sense of inevitability motivating Dark Mountain. As I have set out already in this

book, I am sceptical of the knowingness present in this attitude. I think we cannot yet rule out the chance of our making a great turning. However, as made clear already, I think the chances of our doing so are slim. That is why I have co-edited with Bendell the first book on Deep Adaptation (2021), in which we discuss at length our disagreement as well as expounding our large measure of agreement.

12 This was most brilliantly expounded by Hans Jonas. For discussion, see the interview Nigel Warburton conducted with me in late Spring 2021: https:// fivebooks.com/best-books/eco-philosophy-rupert-read/.

13 And by nuclear war, and perhaps also by 'unaligned' AI, by natural or genetically-engineered pandemics, and more. These too deserve serious precautionary attention, more than they have been being given by governments and in politics. As already intimated in the Introduction, my reason for focussing, in this book, on climate and ecology, is that climate and ecological breakdown is, as the next chapter will show, a *white* swan. Unlike these other existential threats, which are potential dangers only, it is actually and actively poised to sweep human civilization aside, unless we accomplish something absolutely extraordinary.

We should remember too that climate breakdown is increasingly accepted to be the ultimate 'threat-multiplier'. Thus, if you are worried about nuclear exchange (accidental or deliberate; global, regional or even terrorist-fomented), as you should be, then you ought to be very worried about what this book is saying. I would suggest humbly that the most likely scenario now for the use of nukes is in increasingly climate-stressed nations such as India and Pakistan.

14 Toby Ord makes this argument in *The Precipice* (2020), where he carefully surveys a range of existential threats and reflects on our collective responses to them. Ord is however far more willing than I am to numericize and probabilitize the likelihood of the existential threats we face. I regard this as an overly 'knowing' and under-agential form of approach. It pretends to know what the future will be like, and takes insufficiently seriously the radical ways in which we may change it.

15 Harry Frankfurt takes broadly this approach in his definition of love (2004).

16 For a classic taxonomy about different theories, see Derek Parfit's *Reasons and Persons* (1984), appendix I. For a more comprehensive list, see Chris Woodard's paper 'Classifying Theories of Welfare' (2013).

17 And indeed, as I'll argue later in the book, 'paradoxically' it may be that the best way (or at least, a genuinely good way) proactively to help co-parent the children of the future is not to have children of your own, but to seek to devote your life to the children of the future that others bear – as I myself have chosen to do.

18 One cannot use the uncertainty surrounding the identity or even existence of future people decently as a basis to argue that they don't matter as much (as we living now); for the uncertainty as to whether they will exist and under what conditions is precisely the problem! The issue is that, unless we

pull out all the stops, their *existence,* let alone their flourishing, will become ever more uncertain. We ought by contrast to have as a default our continuation under the best possible circumstances.

I take my line of thought to draw upon the broad thrust of the thinking of Samuel Scheffler (2013) and of Mark Johnston (2011), both of whom have influenced me. John Passmore (1974) and Richard Howarth (1992) have also influenced me positively. A position that is somewhat like-minded can be found additionally in Robert J. Barro (1989). Barro argues in effect (though without any reference at all to matters ecological) that infinite horizons result from taking seriously the indefinite temporal (and spatial) extension of the family. For a more popular presentation of similar ideas, see Cuarón's magnificent film, *Children of Men.* (I take my line of thought also to overcome alleged problems of potentiality associated with the thinking of my teacher, Derek Parfit, and of my colleague, John Foster).

19 My thinking in this section was, I found out after writing it, partly anticipated by Ophuls (1997, 163f).
20 If this invitation resonates strongly with you, and you feel its importance and potential power, then you may wish to read my book *Parents for a Future* (Read 2021a).
21 The idea explored in this section is an extension of the example considered briefly in the Introduction to this book, the theme of Ishiguro's *Never Let Me Go.*
22 Of course, we are in practice already doing this: most notably, via de facto healthcare rationing. But it is striking that we don't wish to admit that we are doing it. Healthcare rationing is a taboo topic.
23 I return to this theme in Chapters 5–7.
24 In the way, roughly, proposed by Giorgios Kallis (2018) and others, in the 'degrowth' movement, and familiar to many of us already from wisdom traditions, that have flourished across the world and especially in the East.
25 The real figure, wait for it, is likely to be closer to (gulp), six, eight, or even ten planets (Alexander 2015).
26 Consider, for instance, E.O. Wilson's visionary 'Half Earth' (2017) proposal, which suggests devoting half the planet to non-human life and nature. It is very important, of course, that any implementation of Wilson's goal should not compromise the rights and needs of indigenous peoples and of peasant peoples who are frequently Mother Earth's best defenders.

2 Is Climate Breakdown a *White* Swan?

1 Of course, it is possible that they fantasize that they can escape altogether the consequences. But, as I already argued in Chapter 1, this is highly improbable, and in a certain sense entirely impossible. Rushkoff (2018) already shows some of the conceptual and practical difficulties involved.

These multiply, once one starts to think long-term enough in the way this book is recommending.

2 See Christopher (2019), for this key aspect of Nassim Taleb's argument as to why we should think of the history we have had as one of a myriad of possibilities, and how in many (probably most?) of these possible histories we did *not* escape mutual nuclear annihilation in the twentieth century.

3 See Helen Caldicott's (2017) edited collection, *Sleepwalking to Armageddon*, and Chapter 5 of Schlegelmilch (2020), about the possibility of a global nuclear winter (which could extinguish humanity and end most life on Earth) following upon the heels even 'just' of a regional nuclear exchange, such as in the (climate-stressed, thus perhaps increasingly hair-triggered) India–Pakistan 'theatre'.

4 In an interesting illustration of the broadly predictable but yet in detail wildly unpredictable chaotic and exponential nature of pandemic events, I drafted most of this segment of this chapter in 2017. I came to rewrite it in early–mid 2020, and had of course a new and terrible example to contemplate and refer to.

5 See the early part of Sinclair & Read (2021) for some account of the 'more or less' here. The COVID-19 case was not by any means as entirely unforeseeable and un-prepareable-for as some in the UK Government have pretended.

6 This fact was central to the argument made by my colleagues in January 2020, that we faced in COVID-19 an unprecedented foe requiring unprecedented precautionary action (Norman et al. 2020). I also wrote about applying the precautionary principle to the pandemic in early March 2020 (Read 2020b).

7 This is why the fantasy of geoengineering – engineering the entire planet's climate, as if we were gods – is an utterly reckless response to the climate emergency (Read 2015b; Paul & Read 2019). See the next section for discussion.

8 This is of course a brief overview of our case. We have published more thorough articulations elsewhere (Taleb et al. 2014; Taleb et al. 2015). In the philosophical literature, the precautionary principle faced renewed attention in response to an important paper by Stephen Gardiner (2006). A more recent in-depth treatment is available in Daniel Steel's book, *Philosophy and the Precautionary Principle* (2015). These approaches differ in some respects from our/my own, but they are nevertheless instructive of the debates around the precautionary principle; and the differences are I think not determinative *vis-à-vis* what I am seeking to accomplish in this chapter and this book.

9 I develop the consequences of this point about geoengineering as a reckless unprecautious endeavour in Chapters 3 and 7.

10 Recall the discussion on this point in the section 'Why does this book matter' in the Introduction to the present work, including the critique I offered there

of the IPCC's overly conservative approach (see also Harrabin 2021, for scientists themselves finally speaking out on this publicly).

11 True, there are some grey-flecked feathers in the white plumage. We don't know the exact climate-sensitivity of the Earth system, and we don't know all the feedbacks that are likely to kick in, nor just how bad (or, if we're very lucky, innocuous) most of them will be. And we don't know how long we've got. Crucially, such uncertainties, properly understood, *underscore* the case for radical precautious action on climate: for uncertainty cuts both ways. It may end up meaning that the fearful problem one was worried about turns out to be relatively tractable . . . Or it may end up meaning that it turns out even worse. There is an asymmetry here: for the worse the worst-case scenario for something potentially ruinous gets, the more strongly we need to guard against it. Uncertainty around the detail of climate science means that we might well still be *under*estimating the scale of our exposure to ruin (and perhaps drastically so).

So, even the grey matter among the swan's plumage only underlines how we not only (very probably) have a (broadly) predictable catastrophe facing us but furthermore one that may exceed most of our models and even our imaginations.

For further discussion of this consequential point, see Read (2018b).

12 How can we look our children in the eye, while we contemplate this potential cataclysm? But maybe this is why we typically *don't* look our children in the eye, on this determinative issue, why we tacitly engage in soft denial.

13 How can we, as I've put it previously in the prologue to this book, learn to be 'wise frogs' (Read 2017)? How do we learn to jump out of the saucepan before we boil ourselves alive?

The situation we are in is an unprecedented one. It indicts us all, and it indicts our 'leaders' perhaps most of all. We are staring now down the barrel of ecocide, which means a mass-suicide into which the voiceless and powerless and unborn future generations and most of our non-human animal kin will be dragged down with us. It's like Jonestown, only on a scale thousands upon thousands of times bigger. We're all slowly drinking the Kool-Aid, but this time it isn't only those drinking it who are going to suffer or die. (And of course, to make the metaphor more accurate, it will tend to be those in the global South who are (as it were) force-fed the Kool-Aid on our behalf – they will, typically, suffer most, and first).

14 The coronavirus crisis has put a dent in that. But no more than a dent, and one that looks worryingly temporary (Tollefson 2021).

15 I develop this thought at some length in Chapter 5.

16 The Green House think tank's book, *Facing Up to Climate Reality* (Foster 2019) to which I have co-contributed three chapters, seeks to do just this. In particular, Nadine Andrews and Paul Hoggett's chapter in that collection looks at the emerging 'eco-psychology' movement and considers how we can psychologically process ecological devastation in a way that motivates us to act to minimize it. I discuss eco-psychology in Chapter 5 of the present work.

17 But let's recall early 2020 once more. It was not easy to imagine that everything was about to change. Governments had only to look a few weeks ahead, at most months, to see what was coming. They only had to see just around the corner (e.g. at Wuhan, and then at Italy), to see the impending potential decimation of their citizens. And yet still, for months, countries like the US and UK essentially did nothing, until it was too late to stop this part-white, part-grey, part-black swan of COVID-19 scything through the old and vulnerable.

During the coronavirus crisis, those states which took forthright precautionary action (such as, after a very rocky start, China; and, more consistently, South Korea, Taiwan and New Zealand), moving ahead of the evidence and thus keeping ahead of the virus, suffered far less grievously than those that did not. The same will be true of the world/of different countries, *vis-à-vis* climate. The difference is that first and foremost, there is no escaping the climate crisis, barring dangerous fantasies of escape to Mars etc. (dangerous because they are a lie, as John Henry Greer's 'The Terror of Deep Time' (2017) shows succinctly and powerfully; and because they may persuade us for a while longer to do nothing of a genuinely precautionary nature), we really are all, in that sense, in this one together. And second, that the consequences of getting it wrong will be way worse than they were in 2020–2 with corona.

3 Is This Civilization Finished?

1 If you have already read my little book *This Civilization Is Finished* (Read & Alexander 2019), you may wish to skip this chapter, which is in part a recap of that book. (However, part of the presentation here is updated, and so you might profit from reading it even if you have read that book already). If, on the other hand you have not, and you find some of this chapter lacking in sufficient depth or support, then I invite you to consult that book.

2 We have failed to get governments to treat climate breakdown as an emergency. This inertia should trouble us deeply. Just how much worse must things get for transformational green policies to be implemented? Every further delay only increases the magnitude of the changes needed to turn things around. Yet still short-term thinking prevails unabated.

We have seen this hardwired short-termism more recently in the government response to COVID-19 (Prologue). Despite the World Health Organization and epidemiologists making it clear that tough action was needed to curb the spread of the virus through February and March 2020, some governments continued to operate on a near 'business as usual basis', prioritizing porous borders and economic activity above human health and well-being. The UK was an extreme, particularly egregious, example of this (Sinclair & Read 2021). The precautionary principle was not applied

(Norman et al. 2020; Read 2020b). It was only when things got so undeniably horrific in late March 2020 that governments were spurred to action. This was far too late to prevent hundreds of thousands of unnecessary deaths. This is a stark illustration of how our politics are uniquely ill equipped to act pre-emptively on catastrophic risks.

Our response to climate breakdown is in the same mould as COVID-19. The differences between the two are in the potential scale of harm and the timeframe that we have had to act. As noted earlier, climate breakdown is a far greater threat to human health than a global pandemic, and it is a threat that has given us a wider timeframe to ameliorate. Yet, as with COVID-19, too many of our leaders have preferred to shuffle their feet and buy more time to preserve business as usual. The currency that this time was purchased with is one that will cost not just millions of lives, but quite possibly the future of (our) civilization itself.

3 Though it's important that we remember that there have been some successes. Think of the Montreal Protocol that has massively reduced ozone-depleting (and climate-damaging) CFCs from being emitted. Think of the various effective measures that have helped nurture the renewable energy industry, and so forth. Certain measures have been taken but emissions continue to grow. However, had these measures not been taken, they would have grown faster still; so there is something to build on for the future. It is most probably not viable to expect zero emissions any time soon and thereby to avoid ever-increasing net levels of destructiveness for the foreseeable future, but it is possible to make it less bad than it would be without these efforts.

4 As of course should the gross historic and contemporary exploitation by the global North of the global South, which links with this picture. See Hickel (2017) and (2020), and the Foreword to the latter by myself and Kofi Klu, which explicitly links the two.

5 I discuss how we can develop a better cultural narrative and psychological processing of climate breakdown in Chapter 5 of this book.

6 To anticipate: the fact that this has not happened, that Glasgow in 2021 still got nowhere near implementing it, is a hammer blow to the hopes of sufficient international climate-action. Global South nations are losing patience with the global North countries who should have provided most of this climate-finance already.

7 Christiana Figueres, a key architect of Paris, tends to emphasize that Paris has/is a ratcheting mechanism (Cleaning Up 2020). This is true, but it does not succeed in countering the multiple interlocking levels of concern with Paris that I develop below. Moreover, we saw at (and, worse still, after) Glasgow that the ratchet is ineffective; it is not mostly occurring, on the ground (as opposed to in promises of jam tomorrow).

8 For instance, in the celebrated Heathrow Third Runway court case (Carrington 2020).

9 That such transformation cannot quite be ruled out is what makes our position so tantalising and, as I will lay out in this chapter, deprives us of the

certainty that 'doomerism' is one instantiation of. Politics sometimes moves surprisingly fast – see the recent decision by the German constitutional court forcing the government to change its plans, or rather to make them more specific with regards to the next few years (Oltermann & Harvey 2021). The court case was initiated among other people by representatives of Fridays for Future in Germany, and the court's decision may well under the radar have been influenced by the consciousness-shift coming from the high profile that Fridays for Future demonstrations had achieved in Germany. This contributes to one key 'moral' of this book: it is worth getting engaged now and working towards a better world, because sometimes one succeeds more than one can dream of, and *out of* despair.

10 It is sometimes objected to me that the precautionary principle opposes innovation. This is false: often it will lead to more innovation (though not necessarily taking the form of new technological inventions; there is more to innovation than tech-wizardry), rather than the continuance of a dangerous but profitable practice (Gee 2013, ch. 27; Corporate European Observatory 2018).

I sometimes hear the objection (often with an air of its being a knock-down argument against me) that the precautionary principle would have meant the Industrial Revolution never happened. This is false; what the principle would have suggested is that we undertook this Revolution far more slowly and cautiously, experimentally rather than uncontrolledly at scale, and with a view to ethics and asymmetries (such as between those risked and those benefitted). And if we had done so, perhaps (more accurately, almost certainly) we would not by now have pushed our world into incipient ecological breakdown. So perhaps this objection is not so decisive after all ...

11 The 'planetary boundaries' framework (Rockström & Gaffney 2021) is the contemporary successor to the better-known 'limits to growth' framework discussed in this section.

12 The crucial implication of the Tim Jackson's work is that even if and where absolute decoupling and so net green growth is possible (and in some cases actual) it is not happening fast enough to bring us back within the planetary safe zone, especially so far as the climate planetary boundary is concerned.

In the emergency we're in, in any case, it just isn't good enough to undertake actions that make our situation harder to fix. Growth does this, because every bit of economic growth requires a higher rate of decoupling, just to stay still.

13 Think of the unacceptability today in significant chunks of the world of homophobia and anti-Semitism, for instance. This is an achievement, relatively recently wrought, that has been won ... *as* we overcrowd ourselves and 'develop' ourselves to death.

14 The 'Left' just seems to love to attack certain factions on/in the 'Left', and intersectionalist Identity Politics has become an 'ideal' vehicle for such divisive factionalism. On a hopeful note, one should note that the vicious infighting is mostly taking place mainly within a tiny minority of highly

educated middle-class people in Western countries; is it possible to build global majorities without fixating on, and around, them? I think it is. I sketch lightly how in Chapter 7.

15 Unless you are unlucky enough to be a well-off straight white male, etc., in which case, so long as that remains your 'chosen' identity (there is of course a temptation therefore to take on for yourself somehow a self-identity that is more oppressed), there is virtually 'nothing you can do'.

16 There is an alternative to identity politics (or as I call it, Ipolitics: the politics of 'I'): 'co-liberation' (the politics of *we*) – freeing ourselves *together* (Rathor & Read 2021).

17 To vary Orwell: you want to know what the likely future looks like? Picture a massively oversized human footprint stamping on all of nature and on our very children, forever. Except: that 'forever' may not last long, because the stamper will before too long end up stamping himself out, too.

18 This could be in the form of the 'opportunity cost' of not pursuing particular types of career.

19 Have I not omitted another more 'optimistic' eventuality? Namely, the deeply-unpleasant scenario of 'Resource Earth', the Earth bent wholly towards humanity's will, without wildness, and without space or buffering (Crist 2012).

   I omit this possibility because I do not consider it to be one. For such a turbo-charged continuation-version of our civilization is a radically-unprecautious scenario, a virtual complete impossibility organizationally and practically given the utter chaos that climate chaos is going to introduce into the system, and most fatally of all, an entropic absurdity. It imagines a future in which our current civilization takes over and manages the entire planet; but this will not be possible, even with a 'circular economy' (De Decker 2018). 'Resource Earth' might be pursued for a while, but is on a hiding to nothing. [Thanks to Tom Greaves for discussion that has prompted this note.]

20 I won't address in this book extreme 'anti-natalist' positions/philosophies that hold that the best future for humanity is one (and for Earth) in which it does not exist. These philosophies seem to ask, to borrow a phrase from the late Bernard Williams, 'one question too many'.

   I once witnessed Joanna Macy being asked by a fellow student, 'Wouldn't the best thing be for humanity to just die?' Joanna paused before replying with a question of her own: 'Isn't that just the most bloodless thing to say?' I like that. It seems to me bloodless, a kind of denial of ourselves, to give up on ourselves, by *wishing* ourselves gone.

   In effect, I'll develop that counter-denial, in the rest of this book.

21 I discuss the prospects for fast civilization changes in Chapter 4 of this book.

22 Including those likely to be chosen by any proper citizens' assemblies (Chapter 4; Read 2021a).

23 Thus actually it is highly likely that a successful successor-civilization, beyond monocultures of the mind, will be civilization*s* (plural). One of the

main problems with our globalized world is that it is becoming one
civilizational monoculture. That fragilizes it.

24 So wanting the kind of connection expressed so very powerfully at the very
   end of the most magnificent movie yet made about overcoming climate
   denial, *Take Shelter*. I am referring to the moment in which the two
   protagonists at last silently share an acceptance of what is happening, and a
   determination to act on that acceptance.

4 The Great Gift of Community that (Climate) Disasters Can Give Us

1 This chapter draws on a paper that I published in *Global Discourse* (Read
   2017b). (That material is thoroughly revised, updated and much expanded).
   Thanks to the editors of *Global Discourse* for permission to reprint some of
   the material from that paper in this chapter.

2 The future will contain far more climate disasters. The last few years, tough
   though they have been, were merely an overture (Steffen et al. 2018).

3 Far more likely (than a civilizational transformation without megadeaths), I
   argued in Chapter 3, is that some level of civilizational collapse occurs in
   response to compromised supply lines and almost unimaginable ecological
   disasters (including perhaps as yet unseen collapses in pollination).
   Ecological collapse at scale entails some degree of civilizational collapse
   (Bendell & Read 2021).

   Either way, we can say with confidence that the world that we are set to
   bequeath to our children is one that will be beset with disasters: climatic,
   ecological and social. And that truth can seem almost too terrifying to
   contemplate.

4 For discussion, and a positive take, see *A Film-Philosophy of Ecology and
   Enlightenment* (Read 2018c, ch. 3). I emphasize the way in which *The Road*
   centres upon the miraculous, angelic old and new possibility for humanity
   represented by the boy, of 'carrying the fire' of morality through an extreme
   process of breakdown.

5 Possibly one should say 'Hobbesian', with quote marks, i.e., according to the
   public image that has been grafted onto Hobbes by posterity. Such a
   description may not necessarily be correct according to the subtlest reading
   available of his texts. For one could alternatively read Hobbes as follows:
   disaster breaks down the maladaptive social bonds that we have in place (as
   in the English Civil War, when Hobbes wrote; as in our civilization today?),
   but that gives us the impetus to create new and stronger social bonds – and
   all will then agree to those bonds so that the new community is less of an
   imposition of force and more of a bond of consent. One doesn't have to agree
   with the 'individualist' basic social ontology that I mention above or with the
   idea that the new social bond has to come in the form of a state machine

(though for sure some of what we need, in a true post-growth Green New Deal for instance, will come through a strong state) to get this very convincing and helpful (in my view) set of thoughts from Hobbes.

I am not enough of a Hobbes scholar to be able to judge between these readings of his work (and so in what follows I shall continue to speak mostly of the 'Hobbes' of popular understanding). Thanks to Tom Greaves for pointing out to me the possibility of this subtler, less individualistic and potentially less Levianthanic part-reading of him.

6 Dorothy Day, the founder of the Catholic Worker movement, was inspired to change her life and to found that movement by her tremendous youthful experiences in and after the 1906 San Francisco earthquake. She used to speak of the 'sense of solidarity which made me gradually understand the doctrine of the Mystical Body of Christ, whereby we are the members of one another' (Solnit 2009, 68*)*. My view is that, bold as it may sound to contemporary ears, something like that vision of (what Buddhists call) *inter-being* is ultimately what is needed, for us to emerge from our contemporary predicament.

7 The possibility of a positive programme of 'disaster-localization' in response to the historical moment in which we find ourselves is sketched by my colleague Kristen Steele (2019).

8 It is already weakened (Caeser et al. 2021).

9 I will return to this point in the next section by examining a couple of such movies (already mentioned).

10 Sometimes, sadly, the authorities and/or the media will describe a favoured group as 'gathering supplies', when the same activity engaged in by a non-favoured group is referred to as 'looting'. Solnit documents this as having happened in New Orleans, *vis-à-vis* white and black people, respectively (Solnit 2009).

11 This phenomenon of 'convergence' was particularly striking in the case of September 2001 (Solnit 2009, 195).

12 Thus something like the Grenfell Tower fire in London in 2017 was not able to *bouleverser* our social system, our political economy. That would have been a much more likely outcome, had the fire affected much of London, rather than 'only' one tower.

13 This switching of figure and ground is a feature we shall encounter again in Chapter 5.

14 More recent research supports this claim by highlighting the extent to which people underestimate the pro-social nature of other people (Common Cause Foundation 2016).

15 See the closing chapters of my 2020e for detail on how this was how many of us experienced the onset of the coronavirus. Even many of those enduring the hellish conditions of hard healthcare in full PPE etc. found the time one of intense meaning; otherwise, drop-out rates from healthcare workers would have been far higher.

16 Consider as a case-in-point once again the coronavirus pandemic. In the UK, some wobbles in March 2020, with a pandemonious rush at one point for supermarket food (and, famously, toilet paper), were outweighed by citizens largely moving ahead of a complacent government to take care of each other. 'Social distancing' was a misnomer in that the physical distancing we began was *a way of being* pro-social. Or then again, maybe it wasn't a misnomer: for the distancing was in that very way in its essence social, caring. We physically distanced, pro-socially. And we found an amazing solidarity in the coming out of our houses to applaud the heroes of the NHS weekly; I don't think anyone who experienced that will ever forget it. I remember vividly the first evening, worrying that there would be hardly anyone on my street joining me out on the doorstep; and the tears that came to my eyes as we assembled and began to clap and cheer. Elsewhere I give a full account of these beauties and revelations that lay concealed in the avoidable and terrible tragedy of COVID-19 (Read 2020d, ch. 26). I am thinking here for instance of the mutual aid activities that sprung up almost ubiquitously and spontaneously; and of citizens pressing for and initiating actions to achieve 'social distancing' (Read 2020c).

17 I argue in Chapter 3 of *A Film-philosophy of Ecology and Enlightenment* (Read 2018c) that actually this catastrophe is so extreme that it exceeds the very bounds of conceptual possibility.

18 This is the kind of thing that I seek to do in *A Film-philosophy of Ecology and Enlightenment* (2018c). (See also Octavia Butler's great apocalyptic novels, *Parable of the Sower* and *Parable of the Talents*).

19 Not entirely incidentally, a side benefit of Fritz's work becoming widely read by those whose job it is to prepare for disasters, such as the military, would be that they would be less likely to engage in thoughtless aerial bombardment. For Fritz's work explains more clearly than I have ever seen it explained before why aerial bombardment alone, *even when enormously devastating*, usually fails to cow a population. For it is experienced as a disaster imposed deliberately upon the community – and the community pulls together remarkably against it. As Fritz documents, this phenomenon probably also goes a long way to helping explain the (phenomenal) success story, which has left many scratching their heads, of the Japanese and German economies after 1945.

20 My idea here is developed by loose analogy with what Mahmood Mamdani recommends as the kind of ethos ultimately needed in post-genocide situations, as opposed to an ethos of retributive justice (Mamdani 2002).

21 Part of the genius of Extinction Rebellion was its insistence – rare, among 'Green' organizations/movements (but then, in the terms of spiral dynamics, Extinction Rebellion was explicitly an endeavour to create a 'teal', and not just a 'Green', movement) – upon a no-blame, no-shame ethos. This often wrong-footed Extinction Rebellion's opponents (Read 2019c).

22 Those based on the philosophy of John Rawls (Freethinking 2021; Read 2011b). I hinted early in this chapter that the kind of philosophy made

popular among intellectuals in our time is in fact in its paternity worrisomely Hobbesian.

23 Let me here salute some of those who have been part of that small band of brothers and sisters: Dufresne (2019) (whose argument is often very close to mine, especially in this chapter); Williston (2020); Jamieson (2014); Gardiner (2011); and Mulgan (2011).

24 Especially to unborn future generations of all classes.

25 I develop this point further in the latter part of Chapter 7.

26 This raising of gaze, I've agreed, is a near-impossibility right now for many whose lives are grindingly difficult in the present, especially in the global South (*although* some of these have been in effect thrust already into the terrain of paradises made in hells, and are already living in the way this chapter foregrounds (Shareable 2019). Thus, once more, it falls to all those of us contextually capable of raising our gaze to redouble our efforts to do so, for others' sake as well as for our own. (This speaks to the implied audience of this book, to who is addressed in many of my invocations of 'we').

    The critical message of the present chapter is of community renewal and new solidarity. But 'left-behind' communities may well, as things stand, mostly be shattered by climate/civilizational breakdown, and may have not sufficient capacity for resilience except through self-help. That's exactly why the message of this chapter is vital (for their sake). Many very poor peoples do band together successfully for survival as in slums and in indigenous cultures. But there are swathes at present with little such capacity and any hope for them to gain that capacity (flourishing) risks being snuffed out even before the (societal) breakdown begins, or, as some say, has already begun. Again, that's exactly why this chapter matters. It isn't enough to leave disasters to save us, obviously! We need to learn from them, proactively, to help our fellows (and ourselves) be ready for them; and the ultimate such learning and proaction (to anticipate!) is to be wise enough to grow a determination to build their incidence down, to head them off, just as much as is now humanly possible.

27 What do the rest of us do in this case? We need to be clear-eyed about the likelihood that many elites will oppose the restructuring suggested here. Such elites will then need to be labelled enemies and treated accordingly. Let us hope it doesn't come to this, and that enlightened mutual self-interest prevails. But if it does not, then let us be ready.

28 Earlier in this chapter, I spoke of the likelihood that our rupturing of the limits to growth (of which dangerous climate change is only the most developed example) may lead to an irrecoverable civilization collapse, within the next generation or two. The remainder of this chapter since then can naturally be read as an attempt to think through how yet to avert such an outcome.

    But there is another way of reading it, too, both more pessimistic and more optimistic than that. For, if Fritz, Solnit and Schlegelmilch are right – and I am confident that they are – then perhaps our worry about 'irrecoverable civilizational collapse' can be downgraded further. Perhaps what we should assume instead is that, *even if* our rupturing of the limits to growth continues and humankind proceeds on the trajectory of collapse through rapidly rising mortality, so on, that we find in most of the Club of Rome 'Limits to growth' scenarios (Meadows et al. 1972), still human beings will rally, and will keep on and on turning the hells that we've created by so recklessly tampering with the conditions of our collective life-support system (the living planet) into mini-heavens.... And in contemplating 'dark' times, that really is an encouraging thought.

29 Has our society already become too atomized even to be capable of a 'paradisical' response to disaster? I have already given my answer to this question: no. Let me put the point slightly humorously: if twenty-first century New Yorkers can manage it, then anyone can ... (they probably actually have one of the greatest *hungers* for it, being more deprived even than most of everyday community).

30 See especially Homer-Dixon's *The Upside of Down* (2006, 226–33) for his take on Painter and (especially) on Holling's 'panarchy' concept, giving us a clear upside of down: the chance to refresh and simplify our systems – much as ecosystems do, when they break down. I'll return to this point in the Conclusion of this book, with reference to Painter's inspiring example: of the Eastern Roman Empire in the seventh to ninth centuries.

31 A worry here explored by Healy & Malhotra (2009) is that voters appear to reward politicians who respond well to disasters far better than they do politicians who act effectively to prevent disasters. The trouble with prevented disasters being of course: they are hard indeed to see, to witness, to learn from! (Schlegelmilch 2020, ch. 6).

    The issue here is whether the next run of climate disasters prompts proactive 'catagenesis', or whether we have to wait for full-scale collapse to literally force it upon us.

32 The form of this argument recurs in Chapter 5, where I argue that the only ultimately affective antidote to eco-grief is to tackle its causes.

33 And thus, when I contemplate now our likely collective response in the face of disaster(s), I see the very real possibility of us coming through, stronger. If in a country like the UK, deeply vulnerable because of our inability to feed ourselves (and because of other factors, plainly visible in the corona crisis, such as a political class without vision and with increasing cronyism, and chronic over-centralization leading to lack of local knowledge and to decision-paralysis (Sinclair & Read 2021), we heed the warning that disastrous shocks are delivering to us already, then it seems to me more than possible that we could move to implementing intelligently something like food rationing (Lang 2020), and to bringing into cultivation areas such as some horse-pasture and horse racing/training areas, some brown-field sites, and yes, some golf courses, which at present contribute absolutely nothing to

our food needs. These are the kinds of things we need to be at least ready to do, if we are to *adapt transformatively* to what is coming.

34 See the film *The Response* (Shareable 2019) for a beautiful case in point of this kind of response to disaster.

35 Thanks to Peter Kramer and Ian Christie for invaluable comments on earlier drafts. Thanks also to John Foster.

5 How Climate Grief May Yet be the Making of Us

1 Later in this chapter, we will as promised come to eco-grief. And I've had terrible experiences of that, too, and of its close cousin, eco-anxiety (The Poetry of Predicament 2021).

2 I make the personal philosophical here by making it broadly phenomenological. That is to say: I trace the logic of the phenomenon of grief, through giving a description of experience. If you want to avoid the stress of encountering any vaguely 'technical' philosophy, then just skip the next section. (This chapter draws loosely on some of the material I wrote in a *more* technical presentation of a philosophy of grief; Read 2018d).

3 That is: finding, if one can, a possible place and time for the form of words in question. For, roughly: no form of words is intrinsically nonsense. Nonsense, understood after a resolutely Wittgensteinian fashion, is just forms of words for which no use has been found. It is always a provisional category. In this connection, the 'New Wittgensteinian' understanding of nonsense and sense is closely akin to that of the Ordinary Language philosophers at their best (Crary & Read 2000). For what is Ordinary Language philosophy, the practice of Austin and Ebersole et al., after all, except for a marvellous pursuit of how the kinds of weird things that philosophers say might actually be found a linguistic home in real life?

4 And this is the founding insight of the philosophy of pragmatism, based on the conception of belief promulgated by Alexander Bain.

5 Think here about Wittgenstein's salient remarks in *On Certainty* (1975). There are commonalities between the difficulty of fitting 'Matt is dead' into this 'system' – a system that usually functions relatively harmoniously (albeit *always* with some Merleau-Ponty-style *indeterminacy*) – and the kinds of difficulties Wittgenstein considers in relation to ideas such as 'Some people have been to the moon' (recalling that Wittgenstein wrote in the days before space travel).

6 In my terms, Solomon doesn't take seriously enough the ghostly semi-presence of the lost beloved (Solomon 2004, 87–9). This is a prejudice against the phenomenology of deep grief. (Lacanians, employing the slogan '*Je sais bien, mais quand même*' ('I know very well that it can happen, but nonetheless . . . I cannot really accept that it can happen'), are likely to come closer to the truth of this phenomenology).

7 Or alternatively: cases where the *only* way to express oneself adequately is to yield to the temptation to utter nonsense. Wittgenstein held that such cases include ethical language (see the 'Lecture on ethics' (Wittgenstein 2014)) and properly religious language (ditto) – and properly philosophical language (see the *Tractatus Logico-Philosophicus* (1922)).

8 I am thinking here of Wittgenstein's delicate use of expressions such as 'I'm inclined to say . . .' in the course of his philosophizing. The modality here is part of the philosophical point (Morris 1994).

9 Note that the good sense of saying in the circumstances I have been in things along the lines of 'I know that Matt is dead, and yet I can't believe that he is' shows the crudity of philosophically-standard 'Justified True Belief' analyses of the nature of knowledge; and the far greater subtlety present in our actual language than in the doctrines of philosophers (except for philosophers such as Ebersole, Austin and Wittgenstein who are properly attuned to our actual language) about it.

10 For some discussion, see section 2.3 of *Wittgenstein Among the Sciences* (Read 2012b) and the work of Louis Sass.

11 For detail on the idea that there are paradoxes that are not merely philosophers' artefacts but that must be or at least sometimes are lived, see Part II of *Wittgensteinian Way with Paradoxes* (Read 2012a), and especially the Conclusion to that work. Compare also Merleau-Ponty's argument that all being in the world has a paradoxical moment/aspect characteristic of it (Merleau-Ponty 2002, 95).

12 Thus I will suggest below that, while ordinary common-or-garden sadness is a figure on a world with a secure taken-for-granted ground, grief involves rather the reconfiguring of the ground itself.

13 This challenge will reach its apogee in Chapter 6, which details an alternative to liberal individualism that we might live.

14 I am thinking here of the early Charles Taylor and the early Sandel, and their criticisms of liberalism (in particular, of Rawlsianism) as individualism.

15 I am thinking here of the early Rawls' famous criticisms of utilitarianism.

16 Consider in this context the following dream I had about Matt, some months after his death: I dreamt Matt was alive again. I was shocked and delighted to find this, but the shock outweighed the delight, because I had the uncanny feeling that his alive-face somehow could not be real. (This part of the dream especially, and the dream as a whole, itself manifests the process of denial-as-acceptance that I am claiming in this paper to be an essential part of the logic of significant grief). What then happened was that it came to me that his face wasn't alive in itself; it wasn't him as such that had survived. I started seeing his face morphing into that of other people who were alive, *myself* eventually included.

   The meaning of the dream seems clear to me: it is a mistake to look for Matt's survival in his bodily resurrection. The place to look for it is in the rest of us. He survives, the more his values, his dream, his wonderful self, are manifested in – actively re-membered by – the collective (Johnston 2011), what ethnomethodology calls 'members'. (What I am saying at this point could be put as Wendell Berry's character Burley Coulter famously puts it, drawing on St Paul: 'We are members of each other').

17 Liberal individualism cannot understand revolutionary sacrifice, the kind of sacrifice that is increasingly likely to be necessary in 'the climate war', and of which portents can be seen in the brave 'sacrifice actions' of those willing to go to jail for non-violent direct action for the sake of the future. A key part of my task in the present chapter is to comprehend grief without making it seem intolerable to the point of madness or breakdown that people die, and sometimes that they die young and avoidably, and even sometimes voluntarily.

18 Including, as Edmund Burke saw, and as indigenous peoples have long known, the dead, and the yet-to-be-born.

19 It is not encompassable within the logic of what the philosopher Maurice Merleau-Ponty calls 'objective thought'.

20 For the distinction between 'internal' and external relations, see Wittgenstein's *Tractatus Logico-Philosophicus* (1922), and the exegesis thereof given by Denis McManus in *The Enchantment of Words* (2010). (See also Winch's classic work *The Idea of a Social Science* (1990). Relations between persons treating each other *purely* administratively, purely externally, are not really relations between persons at all any more. This point is implicit, I believe, in Arendt's famous critique of Nazism.

21 In this way, the euphemistic expression 'biodiversity loss' makes a sense: this loss (aka destruction) can put us *at a loss*. Our sense of loss at the loss is real-ized, is essential.

22 Does this put into doubt the stance, for which I am well known, that we are best advised not to debate with climate deniers, but to insist that they should not be debated with at all, merely passed over, so that we can engage in the real debates (e.g. for and against geoengineering; the kinds of debates I engage with in this book)? I think not. The point stands. Climate deniers need to be bypassed strategically, if we are to get serious about climate breakdown. But what I've said *supra* does have three implications worth marrying to this bypass: (i) We should not engage in ad hominem unpleasantness against climate deniers. We shouldn't name, shame or blame them, at least if they show any willingness at all to reconsider their perpetration. They deserve the respect due to human beings struggling as the rest of us, even though their views taken at face-value are catastrophic. (ii) We should not take their views at face value. They are either liars, or (and this is the more common case, I believe) they are in denial in a manner that has some similarities with the denial of someone grieving, as I have characterized it. In the latter case, we should look to find ways of engaging with their real concerns and leading them towards the painful acceptance of reality. (iii) Every time we call out denial, we should turn remove any remaining blinkers on our own eyes, too. This is the sense in which the

greatest purpose of climate denial is to enable us, if we are courageous enough, to see the soft denial that we ourselves may yet be subject to.

This latter point is far the most important of these three, in the sense that it is a key purpose of my book, which aims to manifest our key purpose as truth-tellers who can come to greater clarity, with ourselves and with our fellow citizens, as to our potential shared human purpose, in the face of climate breakdown.

23 This is my hypothesis as to the explanation of most experiences of ghosts (which are typically of fellow humans that it is sad that we have lost, or whose deaths were sad): ghosts are the ghostly presence of the lost one; grief keeps them almost alive, even as we know that they are dead.

24 But see n.21, above.

25 The parallel with my conclusion in the previous chapter is close: the ultimate moral of disasters is to prevent them; the ultimate moral of grief is to prevent the kids of events when such prevention is possible. (And here we see another difference between climate-grief and ordinary grief. Often, ordinary grief concerns losses that are unpreventable. But part of the pain of climate-grief, and how it is more closely related to anger, is that the losses are by and large preventable).

26 Though I confess that even I am nervous of our letting our anger have too much sway; for that reason, I've quite often tended to change the Extinction Rebellion's 'slogan' of 'Love and rage' into 'Love and trust' or 'Love and truth'.

27 'The myriad voices of ecological warning – those of scientists, novelists and filmmakers, teen school strikers, religiously inspired protectors of Creation, indigenous peoples who have lived with Gaia's rhythms for thousands of years, brightly festooned extinction rebels dancing in the streets of London and Bratislava, and more – are enunciating Gaia's own thoughts, performing her pain. But our political and economic elites are either ignoring them outright or merely paying them lip service, and that is a key aspect of our tragedy" (Williston 2020, 146). That will change only when there is a much bigger uprising – a massive movement mainly of adults, making even the school strikers' upsurge appear small in comparison.

6 Can We Understand Cetacean Society? Can We Change Ourselves?

1 To find *that* we would be better off looking at the work of Wittgenstein than that of Hobbes and Locke and their recent descendants (Read 2021c).

2 As in 'social contract' theory from Hobbes on, and as diagnosed for instance by Charles Taylor (1985).

3 Thus in this chapter (and the next) we come explicitly to address the question of the nature of the 'we' that I invoke, that may have hung over you as you read this book.

4   The latter may always be riven by agons (here I have in mind for instance the
    work of Arendt, and of Mouffe), but that doesn't prevent them from being
    the fundamental units of existence, not sensically susceptible (except under
    special circumstances) to being further sub-divided. (I'll come back to this
    point, in discussing 'internal relations', below).

5   And in this particular respect our starting point should be broadly Humean,
    as per David Hume's great critique of the fantasy of the social contract (a
    critique with which Wittgenstein's leading follower in the field of social
    philosophy, Peter Winch, had huge sympathy).

6   The long temporality whose true form begins, as I set out in Chapter 1, with
    understanding how our children are what we become, and so on forever;
    such that together we parent the future, into deep future time, by way of what
    we choose to do or not do, right now.

7   See Chapter 3 for argument and references.

8   We have in fact, as Simone Weil epochally showed (1952), a dire need for
    roots. For locality, for place. 'Earth-citizenship' needs complementing by and
    basing in localization, and in identifications that occur usually on a far less
    than global level.

9   On the inclusion of past and future, I am following Edmund Burke. For
    development, see my 'Guardians of future generations' proposal (2021a,
    ch. 4). On the inclusion of non-human animals, see Kymlicka and Donaldson
    (2013).

10 See also the brilliant satire 'Resolute Anti-anthropocentrism' by Jonas Ahlskog
    and Olli Lagerspetz (2015), which indicts virtually the entire Wittgensteinian
    tradition on this score, up to and including Wittgenstein himself.

11 Some may be concerned that this claim must involve 'anthropomorphism'.
    For my rejoinder to that claim, see the section specifically on this, below.

12 Philosophy of 'social science', the understanding of understandings of
    understandings, *always involves - requires - ethical* thinking. This I would
    suggest should make sense to any Wittgensteinian. For his entire career,
    Wittgenstein suggested a sense in which ethics saturates life. It is not a
    separate topic, not an area of expertise. It is a discipline not in the sense of
    academic discipline but of needful cognitive and existential (self-)discipline.
    Winch was never a philosopher of social science in some narrow sense. He
    was always alive to questions such as 'Who is my neighbour?' (See the
    chapter of that name in his 1987 work).

13 Here's an important moment in his late paper:

> [T]here is *a kind of understanding* of [Azande] practice that we ... do
> not have. I will try to express this by saying that we cannot imagine
> what it would be like for us to behave as the Azande do and make the
> kind of sense of what we were doing as the Azande, we assume, do
> make of what they do; or perhaps: we cannot imagine taking the
> consultation of the oracle *seriously*, as the Azande do.
>
> Winch 1997, 199

It would be laughable, stupid – just impossible – to *do* so seriously. The
challenge is that this is so while we *are* seeking seriously, non-prejudicially to
understand, to enter imaginatively into what it would be like to live
according to the poison oracle; and *not* to assume that so to live is to live in a
way that fails to embody living as one ought allegedly to live, according to
the prejudice characterizing our time, 'scientifically'.

14 I.e. the standard academic mode is, as we might put it: *overstanding*, rather
than understanding. (Thanks to Nigel Pleasants for this point).

15 Which it seems as if they may not always have been. I am thinking here of
the important fact that across much of the world humanity appears to have
eliminated most mega-fauna. For argument, see Flannery's *The Future Eaters*
(2002). However, it is *very important* to note the powerful moral that
Flannery draws from his own story: that those indigenous peoples who
survived learnt from the destruction of their megafauna and thus of much of
their ecosystems, and that this explains the way that many indigenous
peoples today live in a remarkable (to us) harmony with nature. And thus
how and why we have typically so much to learn from them.
  Of course, it is also worth bearing in mind, to avoid romanticisation, that
indigenous peoples are not homogenous and have not all risen in recent
times to the challenge of inter-being and of ethical long-termism. This is the
downside, for instance, to the story of the Crow people that Jonathan Lear
put together both inspiringly and problematically in his *Radical Hope* (2006).
Arguably, they sold out (under, admittedly, extreme, existential pressure).

16 What cetaceans have to offer us is not global consciousness (it is nothing like
cosmopolitanism), though there are remarkable and inspiring incidents of
altruism (including cross-species) in the whale world. What they have to
offer us, above all, is something that might prove even more important than
global consciousness: a more profound caring than we know, an inter-
relation of a kind that we might aspire to.

17 Except when we ourselves acknowledge that it is stupid. But this must in fact
be an acknowledgement that it *was* stupid: there is something absurd,
nonsensical, about doing something in the present tense that one calls stupid.
(The point here resonates with that made in *A Wittgensteinian Way with
Paradoxes* (Read 2012a, ch. 9). There is an ineradicable paradoxicality, akin to
Moore's paradox (Chapter 5), in knowingly doing something stupid).

18 Another good example – stimulating the sense of inter-being, taking us
closer to age-old indigenous wisdom – is new work on forest ecology, which
suggests that trees exist in inter-species communities connected by lines of
communication in the form of mycorrhizal fungal networks. See Wohlleben
(2017); and Simard (2021). See also Richard Powers' magnificent (2018)
fictionalization of this in *The Overstory*.

19 An intriguing question, one deserving of further research, is whether the
kind of 'larger-than-self' strandings that I'm here discussing are cultural
phenomena in the sense not merely of being limited to some species of
cetaceans only (which is undoubtedly true) but in the sense of being limited

to some cultures – some groups – *within* those species. If that were true, it would be very strong evidence indeed that these phenomena are genuinely cultural! (Of course, tragically, this question will be much harder to answer with confidence now than it would have been a few centuries ago – i.e., before most entire cetacean cultures were eliminated or decimated).

But if it isn't true, that isn't reason to doubt the culturality of the phenomenon: just as the ubiquity among human beings of some things, stupid or otherwise (e.g. language, concern for corpses) is hardly evidence that these things are not cultural in their nature. As Peter Hacker, John McDowell and others have argued, it is in our nature to be cultural beings.

20 In the sense that we can't do with the Azande poison oracle (as per the quote from 'Can we understand ourselves?', above).

21 This is, incidentally, not the only point, either, at which I would query and move beyond Wittgenstein's attitude toward non-human animals. In *Philosophical Investigations* Wittgenstein remarks:

> It is sometimes said: animals do not talk because they lack the mental abilities. And this means: 'They do not think, and that is why they do not talk'. But: they simply do not talk. Or better: they do not use language — if we disregard the most primitive forms of language.
>
> 1958, §25

This is a ringing, brilliant passage. But it is no longer obvious that cetaceans are correctly characterized as using only the most primitive forms of language. In respect of their songs, and in respect of their still barely understood intense discourse of 'clicks' and echo-location, it may be that this is an inadequate characteriszation.

Worse still is what Wittgenstein says at *Philosophical Investigations* §281, where, in plain anthropodenial, he denies that animals have even sensations, see, hear, are conscious, etc.

22 In the sense in which Winch says we can't understand the Azande (see n.13 above and supra).

23 The Wittgensteinian (post-Freudian) move of seeking their acknowledgement is not available to us.

24 If the concept of friendship is understood in the very demanding way outlined by Joel Backström (2007), such that leaving one's friends is basically proof of non-friendship, then this suggestion would basically equate to mine.

25 In thus titling this section, I'm thinking of Wittgenstein's intriguing phrase, 'internal relations', which plays a pivotal role in his first masterpiece, *Tractatus Logico-Philosophicus* (Read 2012b, part 2; McManus 2006; Read 2007). Consider this quote from the Preface to the revised edition of Winch's *The idea of a social science and its relation to philosophy*:

> Had I paid proper heed to [Wittgenstein's *Philosophical Investigations* §81–2], I might have avoided the impression sometimes given in this book of social practices, traditions, institutions etc. as more or less

self-contained and each going its own, fairly autonomous way ... Again, and connectedly, the suggestion that modes of social life are autonomous with respect to each other was insufficiently counteracted by [the] qualifying remark ... about 'the overlapping character of different modes of social life'. Different modes of social life do not merely 'overlap'; they are frequently internally related in such a way that one cannot even be intelligibly conceived as existing in isolation from others.

Winch 1990, xiv

Just as Winch does *not* mean to offer an 'autonomous communities' thesis, so we can see the transitional concept of 'internal relations' as taking us not only to the acknowledgement of the profound holistic nature of human practices, but also the profound holistic nature of communities and even at times of humanity itself (Hutchinson, Read & Sharrock 2008). And perhaps not even merely of humanity; perhaps also the field of animate being. Or at least those parts of it in which there are internal relations. On which, see below.

26 The first portion of the sentence that I have italicized here has received a great deal of emphasis in the reception of Winch's seminal book. The second, interlinked portion of it has not. But it is crucial, not least for our purposes here.

27 I've often thought of writing a satirical book called 'Political philosophy for reptiles'. It would be a pastiche of liberal individualism ...

28 The other side of the coin here, the oft-neglected import of the oft-neglected second part of the title of Winch's revolutionary little book, is that the internal relationship of philosophy and the social studies goes both ways. It's not only that social relations are logical relations, *logical relations are also social relations*. (This is also what Wittgenstein is intimating in *Philosophical Investigations* §240–2). As Winch puts it: 'criteria of logic are not a direct gift of God, but arise out of, and are only intelligible in the context of, ways of living or modes of social life' (Winch 1990, 100).

29 They understand deeply what Knud Løgstrup would call the ethical demand that their very presence exerts upon one another (1995).

30 We can fail to be 'Levinasian'; we can fail to look into each other's faces. One way of putting the philosophical issue here would be this: can we find it easier to adopt the cetacean practice of feeling closer than closer to each other than the Azande poison oracle practice?

31 In the sense at issue in the quote I gave earlier from 'Can we understand ourselves?'.

32 Perhaps this is half-way between the two kinds of cases mentioned in my quotation earlier from 'Can we understand ourselves?'. I take my fellow humans' practice of sleepwalking into eco-catastrophe seriously because I can understand how one could come to be caught up in that kind of thing; but I certainly can't make it my own.

33 Or do we? In Chapter 2 I argued that we may also be able to take huge succour and fortitude from our love for our children. If we were to real-ize

that, then surely we would find it much harder to destroy the future than we are currently doing? Perhaps our key failing to date has been to engage in a serious enough imaginative effort to vision the future? I think that this should be a remediable failing.

34 On this front, I particularly recommend watching the remarkable BBC film, *Carnage* (Amstell 2017).

35 In roughly Arendtian fashion.

36 Thanks to colleagues at an online audience in Bergen in September 2019; at the Symposium celebrating sixty years since the publication of the Idea of a Social Science, at Pécs University, Hungary, 30–1 March 2018; at the 'Truth and metaphysics' event on Peter Winch at King's London, June 30–July 2 2017; at the UEA Philosophy Society; and to colleagues at the 'European society of rhetoric' conference at UEA on 3–5 July 2017, for helpful comments on presentations of this material. Particular thanks to Dimitris Akrivoulis, for vital orientation especially to the concept of 'standing under'. Thanks also to Olli Lagerspetz, Niklas Toivakeinen, Nigel Pleasants and Gavin Kitching for very helpful comments.

7 How to Live in Truth Today

1 See www.transformative-adaptation.com

2 In my next book, I'll explore these matters from an explicitly spiritual point of view. I'll explore there in full how accepting just how things in their totality are can, paradoxically, be the truest route to being able profoundly to change them.

3 It very probably is still entirely possible decisively to head off full-scale climate breakdown and societal collapse – there is still time for an 'Apollo-Earth'-style unprecedented transformation that could save the humans (Read & Rughani 2017, especially the section on 'Restoration'). That is absolutely worth striving for; we need to try our utmost, so long as there is a chance, for even a small chance is far better than none. It's not over until it's over.

For greater depth on what ought to be happening (but isn't), start perhaps with Woodin & Lucas (2004). For an update on the institutional changes needed globally to relocalize effectively, see Norberg-Hodge & Read (2016). For a philosophically informed picture of how this can and should work at the vital level of agriculture, see Chris Smaje's brilliant book, *A Small Farm Future* (2020). See Green House's books and reports for work covering almost every aspect of the policy changes required. And see Anna Coote's work with the New Economics Foundation, and especially her & Percy's 2020 work, for what should be at the heart of the national programmes for redistribution and transformation: Universal Basic Services.

The bottom line is that there should be a swift ecological revolution tied in with a massive redistribution of wealth. My judgement is that this is unlikely to happen without political revolution, and that that is unlikely to happen. Leaving us with my list of 'Seven ways to do what we need to do', below, as a more realistic alternative.

4   For more information on this approach, see https://workthatreconnects.org/

5   If you allow your despair, and work through it, rather than suppressing or holding it at bay as so many of us have been doing for so long, then remarkable new possibilities open up.

6   I explore this waking-up process via art in *A Film-philosophy of Ecology and Enlightenment* (2018c). The popular arts will have a pivotal role to play in the process of waking us up collectively. *Don't Look Up* (2021) appears to have achieved exactly this kind of effect, despite, intriguingly, being panned by most critics. Its popularity is a very encouraging straw in the wind.

7   The Deep Adaptation Forum is one such place: https://deepadaptation.info

8   See, for instance, The Ecostery Foundation: http://www.ecostery.org/default. htm

9   See also Lewis Dartnell's (2015) non-fiction account of same.

10 Which played a key role, as you may recall, in the latter part of Chapter 1.

11 We have some reason to believe in fact that a sense of meaning is easier to obtain/enhance under bad conditions; recall Chapter 4 (and indeed Chapters 5 and 6).

12 For more information, see https://transitionnetwork.org/

13 Recall that transformative adaptation means adaptation that is not merely defensive, but that contributes directly to transforming our society in necessary and beneficial ways, and that simultaneously prevents/mitigates further climate damage.

14 While recognizing that it cannot possibly fully succeed; as I explored back in the Introduction to the present work, 'adaptation' to ongoing dangerous climate change is only partially possible. To simply say, as insouciant capitalists do, 'We're very adaptable; we'll adapt!' is the height of selfish stupidity. And it shows a barbarically callous attitude to those on the climate front lines who are already pressed against the limits of adaptability.

15 Though note: from a strict philosophical point of view, this talk of the 'likelihood' of our failure is suspect. Strictly speaking, we cannot strictly speaking compute the likelihood of something that depends upon our own agency. That is why I more often turn to speaking of what bets one would make. It would be incredibly rash now to bet everything, as basically we have been doing, upon our winning the climate 'war'.

On the other hand, the nonsensicality, strictly speaking, of talk of the 'likelihood' of our failure, is deeply encouraging, in that it reminds us of how vast our agency may be(-come).

16 I discuss this – and the obverse possibility – at greater length in the final section of this chapter, by returning to cetaceans with a very long-term view.

17 This idea will reach an apex of focus in the section below on 'Are there any precedents for what we need to do?'.

18 Perhaps my interlocutors have wanted something different from me than hope: namely, assurance that, appearances to the contrary notwithstanding, things will probably turn out alright. In other words, perhaps they wanted illusion (Williston 2015, ch. 6).

19 I.e. The first-person plural I have often imagined in this book. (For a brilliant convivial applied philosophical analysis of this first-person plural, see Norris (2017).

20 The Deep Adaptation movement has wisely encouraged us to do this.

21 Critically, both of us are agreed that the question is definitely not: what you as an individual can do. Though if you want to know what I judge you can best do with your money to help the collective effort, please go to https://rupertread.net/ecologically-effective-altruism.

22 And, as noted in n.5 of chapter 4, Hobbes *can* be read as the patron philosophical saint of this argument from vulnerability. That is arguably the thrust of his argument for Leviathan. As I mention there, that argument need not perhaps be nearly as black as it has been painted (including, to some degree, by myself, elsewhere in that chapter).

23 I'm relying here on Tainter's account of the Byzantine empire. I am aware that it is not uncontroversial either conceptually or in simple historical terms; but I take it to have considerable merit on both fronts, and for the purposes of the present work I will simply assume it here. The episode (as Tainter construes it) is not nearly as well known as it should be.

24 A choice I myself made in my twenties, by having a vasectomy. (And I'm sympathetic with Donna Harraway's wonderful, provocative, zoocentric injunction to 'Make kin, not babies').

25 I recognize that there has been some 'repetitiousness' in these pages. I plead 'guilty' to that: on the grounds that the struggle we are engaged in here is not one of setting out facts that merely need to be noted. It is not about learning something in that conventional way. What we are seeking to do in this book is to *unlearn* together some of the habits of our civilization that have doomed it to end. And to have the courage necessary for seeing this. That sometimes demands that things get rubbed in/dwelt on/processed by circling back to them, repeatedly.

26 I draw here on my piece published by *Dark Mountain* (2021f) by kind permission.

27 Thanks to my colleagues and friends the collapsologists/collapsosophers (as well as, obviously, to Socrates!), for the inspiration behind the final paragraphs of my text here.

Bibliography

Ahlskog, Jonas, and Olli Lagerspetz (2015). 'Resolute Anti-anthropocentrism', *Übersichtliche Darstellung*, 3(1): 12–20.

American Psychological Association (2000). 'Studies show normal children today report more anxiety than child psychiatric patients in the 1950s.' [online] *American Psychological Association*. Available at: https://www.apa. org/news/press/releases/2000/12/anxiety.

Amstell, Simon [dir.] (2017). [film] *Carnage*. BBC. Available at: https://www.bbc. co.uk/iplayer/episode/p04sh6zg/simon-amstell-carnage.

Anderson, Kevin (2015). 'The hidden agenda: how veiled techno-utopias shore up the Paris Agreement.' [online] *Kevin Anderson*. Available at: https:// kevinanderson.info/blog/wp-content/uploads/2016/01/Paris- Summary-2015.pdf.

Anderson, Kevin (2017). '2 degrees: We have a 5% chance of success.' [online] *DW*, 16 November. Available at: https://www.dw.com/en/2c-we-have-a-5- percent-chance-of-success/a-41405809.

Anderson, Kevin, and Joseph Nevins (2016). 'Planting Seeds So Something Bigger Might Emerge: The Paris Agreement and the Fight Against Climate Change', *Socialism and Democracy*, 30(2): 209–18.

Anderson, Kevin, John Broderick and Isak Stoddard (2020). 'A Factor of Two: How the Mitigation Plans of "Climate-Progressive" Nations Fall Far Short of Paris-compliant Pathways', *Climate Policy*, 20(10): 1290–1304.

Anderson, Victor (2016). 'Nature vs natural capital.' [online] *The Ecologist*, 26 July. Available at: https://theecologist.org/2016/jul/26/nature-vs-natural- capital.

Atwood, Margaret (2009). *The Year of the Flood*. London: Bloomsbury.

Attenborough, David, and Johan Rockström (2021). [film] *Breaking Boundaries: The Science of Our Planet*.

Backström, Joel (2007). *The Fear of Openness: An Essay on Friendship and the Roots of Morality*. Åbo: Åbo Akademi University Press.

Barasi, Leo (2019). 'Polls reveal surge in concern in UK about climate change.' [online] *Carbon Brief*, 10 May. Available at: https://www.carbonbrief. org/guest-post-rolls-reveal-surge-in-concern-in-uk-about-climate- change.

Barro, Robert J. (1974). 'Are Government Bonds Net Wealth?', *Journal of Political Economy*, 82(6): 1095–1117.

Barro, Robert J. (1989). 'The Ricardian Approach to Budget Deficit', *Journal of Economic Perspectives*, 3(2): 37–54.

Battson, Ginny (2021). 'On Climate as the Dominant Meme.' [online] *Seasonal Light*, 10 May. Available at: https://seasonalight.com/2021/05/10/on-climate- as-the-dominant-meme/.

Beckerman, Wilfred (1999). 'Sustainable Development and Our Obligations to Future Generations', in Andrew Dobson (ed.), *Fairness and Futurity: Essays on Environmental Sustainability and Social Justice*, Oxford: Oxford University Press.

Beder, Sharon (2002). *Global Spin*. London: Green Books.

Bendell, Jem (2018). 'Deep Adaptation: A Map for Navigating Climate Tragedy.' *IFLAS Occasional Paper 2*. 2018. Available online: *http://www.lifeworth.com/deepadaptation.pdf*.

Bendell, Jem (2019). 'Responding to Green Positivity Critiques of Deep Adaptation.' [online] *Jem Bendell*, 10 April. Available at: https://jembendell.com/2019/04/10/responding-to-green-positivity-critiques-of-deep-adaptation/.

Bendell, Jem (2020). Deep Adaptation Q&A with Rupert Read hosted by Jem Bendell. [online] YouTube. Available at: https://www.youtube.com/watch?v=y5t4slvjfQs.

Bendell, Jem (2021). 'Should we discuss our anticipation of collapse?' [online] *Jem Bendell*, 18 February. Available at: https://jembendell.com/2021/02/18/should-we-discuss-our-anticipation-of-collapse/.

Bendell, Jem, and Rupert Read (2021). *Deep Adaptation: Navigating the Realities of Climate Chaos*. Cambridge: Polity Press.

Benjamin, Walter (2002). *The Arcades Project*. Edited by Rolf Tiedemann. Translated from German by Howard Eiland and Kevin McLaughlin. Cambridge, MA, and London: Harvard University Press.

Beuret, Nicholas (2018). 'If the richest 10th of the planet reduced consumption to the average EU level, it'd cut global emissions by 30%.' [online] *City Monitor*, 19 December. Available at: https://citymonitor.ai/community/if-richest-10th-planet-reduced-consumption-average-eu-level-it-d-cut-global-emissions-30.

Blewitt, John, and Ray Cunningham, eds. (2014). *The Post-Growth Project*. London: London Publishing Partnership.

Brennan, Pat (2020). 'Stunning forecast: a century of ice-loss for nearly 100,000 glaciers.' [online] *NASA*. Available at: https://climate.nasa.gov/news/3008/stunning-forecast-a-century-of-ice-loss-for-nearly-100000-glaciers/.

Brody, Hugh (2002). *The Other Side of Eden*. London: North Point.

Brysse, Keynyn, Naomi Oreskes, Jessica O'Reilly, and Michael Oppenheimer (2013). 'Climate Change Prediction: Erring on the Side of Least Drama?', *Global Environmental Change*, 23(1): 327–37.

Caesar, L., G.D. McCarthy, D.J.R. Thornalley, N. Cahill and S. Rahmstorf (2021), 'Current Atlantic Meridional Overturning Circulation Weakest in Last Millennium', *Nature Geoscience*, 14: 118–20. Available at: https://doi.org/10.1038/s41561-021-00699-z.

Calderwood, Imogen (2018). '88% of people who saw *Blue Planet II* changed their lifestyle.' [online] *Global Citizen*, 1 November. Available at: https://www.globalcitizen.org/en/content/88-blue-planet-2-changed-david-attenborough/.

Caldicott, Helen, ed. (2017). *Sleepwalking to Armageddon*. London: The New Press.

Carbon Brief (2021). 'Mapped: How climate change affects extreme weather around the world.' [online] *Carbon Brief*, 25 February. Available at: https://www.carbonbrief.org/mapped-how-climate-change-affects-extreme-weather-around-the-world.

Carrington, Damian (2019). 'UK citizens' assembly on climate emergency announced.' [online] *The Guardian*, 20 June. Available at: https://www.theguardian.com/environment/2019/jun/20/uk-citizens-assembly-on-climate-emergency-announced.

Carrington, Damian (2020). 'Heathrow third runway ruled illegal over climate change.' [online] *The Guardian*, 27 February. Available at: https://www.theguardian.com/environment/2020/feb/27/heathrow-third-runway-ruled-illegal-over-climate-change.

Cassely, Jean-Laurent, and Jérôme Fourquet (2020). 'La France: Patrie de la Collapsologie?' *Jean-Jaures*, 10 February. Available at: https://jean-jaures.org/nos-productions/la-france-patrie-de-la-collapsologie.

Cavell, Stanley (1979). *The Claim of Reason: Wittgenstein, Skepticism, Morality, and Tragedy*. Oxford and New York: Oxford University Press.

Chadwick, Douglas (2006). *The Grandest of Lives: Eye to Eye with Whales*. San Francisco, CA: Sierra Club.

Christopher (2019). [Real name: Pete Best] 'Nassim Taleb versus Steven Pinker.' [online] *Jamesian Philosophy Refreshed*, 1 September. Available at: http://jamesian58.blogspot.com/2019/09/nassim-taleb-versus-steven-pinker.html.

Cleaning up (2020). 'Christiana Figueres.' [online] *Cleaning Up Podcast*, episode 6. Available at: https://www.youtube.com/watch?v=4YSzUJ_nMV0.

Climate Action Tracker (2021). 'Glasgow's 2030 credibility gap.' Available at https://climateactiontracker.org/publications/glasgows-2030-credibility-gap-net-zeros-lip-service-to-climate-action/.

CMCC Foundation (2020). 'Why Whales Are Important For Carbon Sequestration.' [online] *Medium*, 1 September. Available at: https://cmccclimate.medium.com/why-whales-are-important-for-carbon-sequestration-65a6fd2713ab.

Coetzee, J. M. (1997). 'The Lives of Animals: The Tanner Lectures on Human Value.' [Talks] Delivered at Princeton University, 15 & 16 October. Available at: https://tannerlectures.utah.edu/_documents/a-to-z/c/Coetzee99.pdf.

Coetzee, J.M. (2004). *Elizabeth Costello*. London: Vintage.

Committee on Climate Change [UK] (2021). 'Progress in adapting to climate change.' Available at: https://www.theccc.org.uk/publication/2021-progress-report-to-parliament/.

Common Cause Foundation (2016). *Perceptions Matter: The Common Cause UK Values Survey*. London: Common Cause Foundation.

Conroy, Gemma (2019). '"Ecological grief" grips scientists witnessing Great Barrier Reef's decline.' [online] *Nature*. Available at: https://www.nature.com/articles/d41586-019-02656-8.

Coote, Anna, and Andrew Percy (2020). *The Case for Universal Basic Services.* London: Wiley.

Corporate European Observatory (2018). 'The "innovation principle" trap.' [online] *Corporate European Observatory*, 5 December. Available at: https://corporateeurope.org/en/environment/2018/12/innovation-principle-trap.

Cowen, Tyler, and Derek Parfit (1992). 'Against the Social Discount Rate', in Peter Laslett and James Fishkin (eds), *Philosophy, Politics, and Society*, 144–61. New Haven, CT, and London: Yale University Press.

Crary, Alice, and Rupert Read, eds. (2000). *The New Wittgenstein.* London & New York: Routledge.

Crist, Eileen (2007). 'Beyond the Climate Crisis: A Critique of Climate Change Discours', *Telos*, 141: 29–55.

Crist, Eileen (2012). 'Abundant Earth and the Population Question', in Philip Cafaro and Eileen Crist (eds), *Life on the Brink: Environmentalists Confront the Population Question.* Athens, GA: University of Georgia Press.

Dark Mountain Manifesto (2009). [online] *The Dark Mountain Project.* Available at: https://dark-mountain.net/about/manifesto/.

Dartnell, Lewis (2015). *The Knowledge: How to Rebuild Our World after the Apocalypse.* London: Vintage.

De Decker, Kris (2018). 'How Circular is the Circular Economy.' [online] *Resilience*, 12 November. Available at: https://www.resilience.org/stories/2018-11-12/how-circular-is-the-circular-economy/.

De Waal, Frans (1999). 'Anthropomorphism and Anthropodenial', *Philosophical Topics*, 27(1): 255–80.

Deb, Debal (2009). *Beyond Developmentality.* London: Earthscan.

Diamond, Jared (2012). *The World Until Yesterday: What Can We Learn From Traditional Societies?* London: Allen Lane.

Dryden, Howard, and Diane Duncan (2021). 'Climate regulating ocean plants and animals are being destroyed by toxic chemicals and plastics, accelerating our path towards ocean pH 7.95 in 25 years which will devastate humanity.' Available at SSRN: https://ssrn.com/abstract=3860950.

Dufresne, Todd (2019). *The Democracy of Suffering.* Montreal: McGill–Queen's University Press.

Dunn, Matilda Eve, Morena Mills and Diogo Verissimo (2020). 'Evaluating the Impact of the Documentary Series Blue Planet II on Viewers' Plastic Consumption Behaviours.' [online] *Conservation Science and Practice,* 2(10). Available at: https://conbio.onlinelibrary.wiley.com/doi/full/10.1111/csp2.280.

Earle, Sam (2017). 'Imaginaries and Social Change.' [online] *Medium*, 1 February. Available at: https://medium.com/@samraearle/imaginaries-and-social-change-2e0c8c093c25.

Eisenstein, Charles (2018). *Climate: A New Story.* Berkeley, CA: North Atlantic Books.

Flannery, Tim (2002). *The Future Eaters: An Ecological History of the Australasian Lands and People.* New York: Grove Press.

Foster, John (2008). *The Sustainability Mirage: Illusion and Reality in the Coming War on Climate Change*. London: Routledge.

Foster, John, ed. (2019). *Facing up to Climate Reality*. London: London Publishing Partnership.

Frankfurt, Harry (2004). *The Reasons of Love*. Princeton, NJ: Princeton University Press.

Freethinking (2021). 'John Rawls's A Theory of Justice 1971.' *BBC Radio 3 Arts & Ideas*. BBC Radio, 21 January.

Fritz, Charles (1996). 'Disasters and Mental Health: Therapeutic Principles Drawn from Disaster Studie.' [online] *Disaster Research Center*. Available at: https://udspace.udel.edu/handle/19716/1325.

Gabbatiss, Josh (2019). 'Earth will take millions of years to recover from climate change mass extinction, study suggests.' [online] *The Independent*, 8 April. Available at: https://www.independent.co.uk/climate-change/news/mass-extinction-recovery-earth-climate-change-biodiversity-loss-evolution-a8860326.html.

Gardiner, Stephen (2006). 'A Core Precautionary Principle', *The Journal of Political Philosophy*, 14(1): 33–60.

Gardiner, Stephen (2011). *A Perfect Moral Storm: The Ethical Tragedy of Climate Change*. Oxford: Oxford University Press.

Gee, David, ed. (2013). *Late Lessons from Early Warnings II: Science, Precaution and Innovation*. Brussels: European Environment Agency.

Gilbert, Daniel (2010). 'Global Warming and Psychology.' [online] *Harvard Thinks Big*. Available at: https://vimeo.com/10324258.

Greer, John (2017). 'The Terror of Deep Time.' [online] *Ecosophia*, 20 September. Available at: https://www.ecosophia.net/terror-deep-time/.

Griffin, Andrew (2018). 'Norwegian seed bank built to withstand the end of the world is having trouble already.' [online] *The Independent*, 27 February. Available at: https://www.independent.co.uk/life-style/gadgets-and-tech/news/norway-seed-bank-svalbard-frost-upgrade-government-norwegian-latest-a8231361.html.

Groves, Christopher (2014). *Care, Uncertainty and Intergenerational Ethics*. Basingstoke: Palgrave.

Gustafson, Donald (1989). 'Grief'', *Nous*, 23: 457–479.

Hamilton, Clive (2013). *Earthmasters: The Dawn of the Age of Climate Engineering*. New Haven, CT: Yale University Press.

Hansen, James (2009). *Storms of My Grandchildren: The Truth About the Coming Climate Catastrophe and Our Last Chance to Save Humanity*. New York, Berlin & London: Bloomsbury.

Hansen, James (2010). 'The Runaway Greenhouse Effect – James Hansen.' [online] YouTube, 31 August. Available at: https://www.youtube.com/watch?v=ACHLayfA6_4.

Harari, Yuval Noah (2015). 'Industrial farming is one of the worst crimes in history.' [online] *The Guardian*, 25 September. Available at: https://www.

theguardian.com/books/2015/sep/25/industrial-farming-one-worst-crimes-history-ethical-question.

Harrabin, Roger (2020). 'Climate change: The rich are the blame, international study finds.' [online] *BBC*, 16 March. Available at: https://www.bbc.co.uk/news/business-51906530.

Harris, Mark, and Denise Ferreira Da Silva (2021). 'The war on indigenous rights in Brazil is intensifying: The Bolsonaro government is using legislation and the courts to try to deprive indigenous people of their rights.' [online] *Open Democracy*, 29 June. Available at: https://www.opendemocracy.net/en/democraciaabierta/the-war-on-indigenous-rights-in-brazil-is-intensifying/.

Harvey, Fiona (2018). '"Tipping points" could exacerbate climate crisis, scientists fear.' [online] *The Guardian*, 9 October. Available at: https://www.theguardian.com/environment/2018/oct/09/tipping-points-could-exacerbate-climate-crisis-scientists-fear.

Harvey, Fiona (2020). 'Tropical forests losing their ability to absorb carbon, study finds.' [online] *The Guardian*, 4 March. Available at: https://www.theguardian.com/environment/2020/mar/04/tropical-forests-losing-their-ability-to-absorb-carbon-study-finds.

Hausfather, Zeke (2017). 'Mapped: The world's largest CO2 importers and exporters.' [online] *Carbon Brief*, 5 July. Available at: https://www.carbonbrief.org/mapped-worlds-largest-co2-importers-exporters.

Havel, Václav (1978). *The Power of the Powerless*. Armonk, NY: M. E. Sharpe.

Healy, Andrew, and Neil Malhotra (2009). 'Myopic Voters and Natural Disaster Policy', *American Political Science Review*, 103(3): 387–406.

Heraclitus (1889). *The Fragments of Heraclitus of Ephesus*. Translated from Ancient Greek by G.T.W. Patrick. Baltimore, MD: N. Murray.

Hickel, Jason (2018). *The Divide: Global Inequality from Conquest to Free Markets*. London: W. W. Norton.

Hickel, Jason (2020). *Less Is More*. London: Random House.

Heidegger, Martin ([1954] 1977). *The Question Concerning Technology and Other Essays*. New York, NY: Garland.

Higgins, Polly (2015). *Eradicating Ecocide: Laws and Governance to Prevent the Destruction of Our Planet*. 2nd edn. London: Shepheard-Walwyn.

Hillman, Mayer (2008). *How We Can Save the Planet*. London: SMP.

Hobbes, Thomas (1998) [1651]. *Leviathan*. Oxford: Oxford University Press.

Hockett, Charles, and Robert Ascher (1964). 'The Human Revolution', *Current Anthropology*, 5(3): 135–68.

Holman, Bob (2010). 'How the Blitz created the welfare state.' [online] *The Guardian*, 31 August. Available at: https://www.theguardian.com/society/2010/aug/31/second-world-war-blitz-survivor.

Homer-Dixon, Thomas. (2006). *The Upside of Down: Catastrophe, Creativity, and the Renewal of Civilization*. Washington DC, Covelo, CA, and London: Island Press.

Howard, Adam (2016). '"Delivering on 2 degrees": Kevin Anderson presents 'Triumph and tragedy in Paris.' [online] *Carbon Neutral University*. Available at: https://www.carbonneutraluniversity.org/delivering-on-2-degrees---kevin-anderson.html.

Howarth, Richard (1992). 'International justice and the chain of obligation', *Environmental Values*, 1: 132–40.

Hutchinson, Phil, Rupert Read and Wes Sharrock (2008). *There is No Such Thing as a Social Science*. Aldershot & Burlington, VT: Ashgate.

International Scholars Warning on Societal Disruption and Collapse (2020). [online] *Initiative for Leadership and Sustainability*, 6 December. Available at: http://iflas.blogspot.com/2020/12/international-scholars-warning-on.html.

IPCC (2019). 'Summary for Policymaker'. In *IPCC Special Report on the Ocean and Cryosphere in a Changing Climate*. Available at: https://www.ipcc.ch/srocc/chapter/summary-for-policymakers/.

Ishiguro, Kazuo (2005). *Never Let Me Go*. London: Faber & Faber.

Jackson, Tim (2017). *Prosperity without Growth*. London: Routledge.

Jackson, Tim (2021). *Post-growth*. Cambridge: Polity.

Jamieson, Dale (2014). *Reason in a dark time*. Oxford: Oxford University Press.

Johnston, Mark (2011). *Surviving Death*. Princeton, NJ: Princeton University Press.

Kahn, Brian (2021). 'The scientists are terrified.' https://gizmodo.com/the-scientists-are-terrified-1847973587.

Kenner, Dario, and Rupert Read (2019). 'XR UK: Telling the truth through targeted disruption.' [online] *Open Democracy*, 29 November. Available at: https://www.opendemocracy.net/en/opendemocracyuk/xr-uk-telling-truth-through-targeted-disruption/.

Kikoy, Herbert (2018). 'Vasily Arkhipov: Soviet hero that prevented World War 3.' [online] *War History Online*, 4 July. Available at: https://www.warhistoryonline.com/cold-war/vasili-cuban-missile-crisis.html.

Kindy, David (2021). 'Permafrost thaw in Siberia creates a ticking "methane bomb".' *Smithsonian* Magazine [online]. Available at: *https://www.smithsonianmag.com/smart-news/ticking-timebomb-siberia-thawing-permafrost-releases-more-methane-180978381/*.

Kingsnorth, Paul (2014). *The Wake*. London: Unbound.

Kingsnorth, Paul (2017). *Confessions of a Recovering Environmentalist*. London: Faber & Faber.

Klein, Naomi (2007). *The Shock Doctrine: The Rise of Disaster Capitalism*. London: Allen Lane.

Klein, Naomi (2014). *The Changes Everything: Capitalism vs. the Climate*. London: Allen Lane.

Knorr, Wolfgang (2020). 'The climate crisis demands new ways of thinking from climate scientists.' [online] *Resilience*, 4 August. Available at: https://www.resilience.org/stories/2020-08-04/the-climate-crisis-demands-new-ways-of-thinking-from-climate-scientists/.

Kübler-Ross, Elisabeth (1969). *On Death & Dying*. New York, NY: Macmillan.

Kymlicka, Will, and Sue Donaldson (2013). *Zoopolis: A Political Theory of Animal Rights*. Oxford: Oxford University Press.

Lang, Tim (2020). 'Coronavirus: rationing based on health, equity and decency now needed – food system expert.' [online] *The Conversation*, 23 March. Available at: https://theconversation.com/coronavirus-rationing-based-on-health-equity-and-decency-now-needed-food-system-expert-133805.

Latour, Bruno (2018). *Down to Earth: Politics in the New Climatic Regime.* Translated from French by Catherine Porter. Cambridge: Polity Press.

Lean, Geoffrey (2020). 'From this awful nightmare there is one glimmer of hope – maybe we can get a cleaner, healthier planet . . .' [online] *Daily Mail*, 6 April. Available at: https://www.dailymail.co.uk/debate/article-8193807/GEOFFREY-LEAN-awful-nightmare-one-glimmer-hope-cleaner-healthier-planet.html.

Lear, Jonathan (2006). *Radical Hope: Ethics in the Face of Cultural Devastation.* Cambridge, MA, and London: Harvard University Press.

Lenton, Timothy M., Hermann Held, Elmar Kriegler, Jim W. Hall, Wolfgang Lucht, Stefan Rahmstorf and Hans Joachim Schellnhuber (2008). 'Tipping elements in the Earth's climate system.' *Proceedings of the National Academy of Sciences of the USA*, 105(6): 1786–93). Available at: *https://www.pnas.org/content/105/6/1786.*

Lenton, Timothy M., Johan Rockström, Stefan Rahmstorf, Katherine Richardson, Will Steffen, Hans Joachim Schellnhuber and Owen Gaffney (2019). 'Climate tipping points – too risky to bet against', *Nature*, 575: 592–5. Available at: https://doi.org/10.1038/d41586-019-03595-0.

libcom.org (2014). 'Disaster communism part 1: disaster communities.' [online] *Lib Com*, 8 May. Available at: https://libcom.org/blog/disaster-communism-part-1-disaster-communities-08052014.

Løgstrup, Knud Ejler (1995). *The Ethical Demand.* Notre Dame, IN, and London: University of Notre Dame Press.

Løgstrup, Knud Ejler ([1956] 1997). *Beyond The Ethical Demand.* Notre Dame, IN, and London: University of Notre Dame Press.

Lovelock, James (2007). *The Revenge of Gaia: Why the Earth is Fighting Back and How We Can Still Save Humanity.* London: Penguin Books.

Lynas, Mark (2007). *Six Degrees: Our Future on a Hotter Planet.* New York, NY: Harper.

Machiavelli, Niccolò (1950). *The Prince and the Discourses.* New York: Modern Library/Random House.

MacPherson, C. B. (1962). *The Political Theory of Possessive Individualism: From Hobbes to Locke.* Oxford: Oxford University Press.

Makoff, Ruth, and Rupert Read (2016). 'Beyond Just Justice: Creating Space for a Future-Care Ethic', *Philosophical Investigations*, 40(3): 223–56.

Mamdani, Mahmood (2002). *When Victims Become Killers: Colonialism, Nativism, and the Genocide in Rwanda.* Princeton, NJ: Princeton University Press.

Mariqueo-Russell, Atus, and Rupert Read (2019). 'Fully automated luxury barbarism', *Radical Philosophy*, 2.06: 108–10.

Markert, Kilian (2018). 'The ultimate driver of human motivation – on the quest of finding meaning.' [online] *Medium*, 26 April. Available at: https://medium.com/@kilianmarkert/the-ultimate-driver-of-human-motivation-on-the-quest-of-finding-meaning-fb6652e851f4.

Marvel, Kate (2018). 'We Need Courage, Not Hope, to Face Climate Change.' [online] *The On Being Project*, 1 March. Available at: https://onbeing.org/blog/kate-marvel-we-need-courage-not-hope-to-face-climate-change/.

McCarthy, Claire (2019). 'Anxiety in teens is rising.' [online] *Healthy Children*. Available at: https://www.healthychildren.org/English/health-issues/conditions/emotional-problems/Pages/Anxiety-Disorders.aspx.

McGrath, Matt (2021). 'Climate change: Biggest global poll supports "global emergency".' [online] *BBC*, 27 January. Available at: https://www.bbc.co.uk/news/science-environment-55802902.

McKie, Robin (2019). 'Global heating to inflict more droughts on Africa as well as flood.' [online] *The Guardian*, 16 June. Available at: https://www.theguardian.com/science/2019/jun/14/africa-global-heating-more-droughts-and-flooding-threat.

McManus, Dennis (2006). *The Enchantment of Words: Wittgenstein's Tractatus Logico-Philosophicus*. Oxford: Oxford University Press.

Meadows, Donella H., Dennis L. Meadows, Jørgen Randers and William W. Behrens III (1972). *The Limits to Growth*. New York, NY: Universe Books.

Merleau-Ponty, Maurice ([1945] 2002). *The Phenomenology of Perception*. Abingdon: Routledge.

Monbiot, George (2021). 'How the BBC let climate deniers walk all over it.' [online] *The Guardian*, 8 July. Available at: https://www.theguardian.com/commentisfree/2021/jul/08/bbc-climate-change-deniers-fossil-fuel-broadcasters.

Moore, G. E. (1993). 'Moore's Paradox', in Thomas Baldwin (ed.), *G. E. Moore: Selected Writings*. London: Routledge.

Morris, Katherine J. (1994). 'The "Context Principle" in the Later Wittgenstein', *Philosophical Quarterly*, 44(176): 294–310.

Mulgan, Tim (2011). *Ethics for a Broken World*. Cambridge: Cambridge University Press.

Mumford, Lewis (1971). *The Myth of the Machine: Volume 1*. London: Mariner Books.

Murray, Jessica (2021). 'Half of emissions cuts will come from future tech, says John Kerry.' [online] *The Guardian*, 16 May. Available at: https://www.theguardian.com/environment/2021/may/16/half-of-emissions-cuts-will-come-from-future-tech-says-john-kerry.

Norberg-Hodge, Helena (2000). *Ancient Futures: Learning from Ladakh*. London: Rider Books.

Norberg-Hodge, Helena, and Rupert Read (2016). 'Post-growth Localisation.' [online] *Local Futures*. Available at: https://www.localfutures.org/wp-content/uploads/Post-growth-Localisation.pdf.

Norman, Joseph, Rupert Read, Yaneer Bar-Yam and Nassim Nicholas Taleb (2015). 'Climate Models and Precautionary Measures.' [online] *The Black*

Swan Report. Available at: https://www.blackswanreport.com/blog/2015/05/
our-statement-on-climate-models/.

Norman, Joseph, Yaneer Bar-Yam and Nassim Nicholas Taleb (2020). 'Systemic
risk of pandemic via novel pathogens: Coronavirus: A note' (online). New
England Complex Systems Institute, 26 January. Available at: https://necsi.
edu/systemic-risk-of-pandemic-via-novel-pathogens-coronavirus-a-note

Norris, Andrew (2017). *Becoming Who We Are*. Oxford: Oxford University Press.

Nussbaum, Martha (2004). *Hiding from Humanity: Disgust, Shame, and the Law*.
Princeton, NJ: Princeton University Press.

O'Neill, Brian C., Michael Oppenheimer and Rachel Warren (2017). 'IPCC
Reasons for Concern Regarding Climate Change Risks.' *Nature Climate
Change*, 7: 28–37. Available at: https://doi.org/10.1038/nclimate3179.

O'Riordan, Tim, and Rupert Read (2017). 'The Precautionary Principle Under
Fire', *Environment*, 59(5): 4–15.

Oltermann, Philip, and Fiona Harvey (2021). 'Germany to bring forward climate
goals after constitutional court ruling.' [online] *The Guardian*, 6 May.
Available at: https://www.theguardian.com/world/2021/may/06/germany-to-
bring-forward-climate-goals-net-zero-after-constitutional-court-ruling.

Ophuls, William (1997). *A Requiem for Modern Politics*. Boulder, CO: Westview
Press.

Ophuls, William (2012). *Immoderate Greatness: Why Civilizations Fail*. North
Charleston, SC: CreateSpace.

Ord, Toby (2020). *The Precipice: Existential Risk and the Future of Humanity*.
London: Bloomsbury.

Oreskes, Naomi, and Erik Conway (2010). *Merchants of Doubt*. London:
Bloomsbury.

Parfit, Derek (1984). *Reasons and Persons*. Oxford: Clarendon Press.

Parry, Bruce [dir.] (2017). [film] *Tawai: A Voice from the Forest*.

Passmore, John (1974). *Man's Responsibility for Nature*. London: Duckworth.

Paul, Helena, and Rupert Read (2019). 'Geoengineering as a Response to the
Climate Crisis: Right Road or Disastrous Diversion', in John Foster (ed.),
Facing up to Climate Reality. London: London Publishing Partnership.

Phillips, Morgan (2021). *Great Adaptations*. London: Arkbound Press.

Phys.org. (2018). 'Permafrost: a climate time bomb?' [online] 5 December.
Available at: https://phys.org/news/2018-12-permafrost-climate.html.

Pinker, Steven (2018). *Enlightenment Now: The Case for Reason, Science,
Humanism and Progress*. New York: Penguin Random House.

Pistone, Kristina, Ian Eisenman and Veerabhadran Ramanathan (2019).
'Radiative Heating of an Ice-Free Arctic Ocean', *Geophysical Research Letters*,
46(13): 7474–80. Available at: dx.doi.org/10.1029/2019GL082914.

Pleasants, Nigel (1999). *Wittgenstein and the Idea of a Critical Social Theory: A
Critique of Giddens, Habermas and Bhaskar*. Abingdon and New York:
Routledge.

Pleasants, Nigel (2010). 'Winch and Wittgenstein on Understanding Ourselves
Critically: Descriptive not Metaphysical', *Inquiry*, 43(3): 289–317.

Power, Camilla (n.d.). 'The revolution which made us human.' [online] *Radical Anthropology*. Available at: http://radicalanthropologygroup.org/sites/default/files/pdf/the_revolution_which_made_us_human.pdf.

Powers, Richard (2018). *The Overstory*. New York: W.W. Norton.

Rao, Mala, and Richard A. Powell (2021). 'The climate crisis and the rise of eco-anxiety.' [online] *The BMJ Opinion*. Available at: https://blogs.bmj.com/bmj/2021/10/06/the-climate-crisis-and-the-rise-of-eco-anxiety/.

Rathor, Skeena, and Rupert Read (2021). 'How we will free ourselves – together', *Permaculture* 108.

Raymond, Colin, Tom Matthews and Radley Horton (2020). 'The emergence of heat and humidity too severe for human tolerance.' [online] *Science Advances*, 6(19). Available at: https://advances.sciencemag.org/content/6/19/eaaw1838.

Rawls, John (1971). *A Theory of Justice*. Cambridge, MA: Harvard University Press.

Raworth, Kate (2018). *Doughnut Economics: Seven Ways to Think Like a 21st-century Economist*. New York: Random House Business.

Read, Rupert (2007). *Philosophy for Life*, ed. Matt Levery. London: Continuum.

Read, Rupert (2007). 'The Enchantment of Words – book review', *Philosophy*, 82(4): 657–61.

Read, Rupert (2010a). 'Wittgenstein's *Philosophical Investigations* as a war book', *New Literary History*, 41: 593–612.

Read, Rupert (2010b). '*Avatar*: A call to save the future', *Radical Anthropology*, 4: 35–41.

Read, Rupert (2010c). 'Wittgenstein vs Rawls', in V. Munz, K. Puhl and J. Wang (eds), *Proceedings of the Kirchberg Wittgenstein Symposium 2009*. Frankfurt: Ontos.

Read, Rupert (2011a). 'Beyond an ungreen-economics-based political philosophy: three strikes against "the difference principle"', *International Journal of Green Economics*, 5(2): 167–83.

Read, Rupert (2011b). 'Why the ecological crisis spells the end of liberalism: Rawls's "difference principle" is ecologically unsustainable, exploitative of persons, or empty', *Capitalism Nature Socialism*, 22(3): 80–94.

Read, Rupert (2012a). *A Wittgensteinian Way with Paradoxes*. Plymouth: Lexington Books.

Read, Rupert (2012b). *Wittgenstein among the Sciences*. London: Ashgate.

Read, Rupert (2012c). 'Guardians of the future: A constitutional case for representing and protecting future people.' [online] *Green House*. Available at: http://www.greenhousethinktank.org/uploads/4/8/3/2/48324387/guardians_inside_final.pdf.

Read, Rupert (2013). 'How ecologism is the true heir of both socialism and conservatism.' [online] *LSE Politics and Policy*, 22 July. Available at: https://blogs.lse.ac.uk/politicsandpolicy/how-ecologism-is-the-true-heir-of-both-socialism-and-conservatism/.

Read, Rupert (2015a). 'How to End Our Love Affair with Evidence.' [online] *Philosophers Magazine*, 1 July. Available at: https://www.philosophersmag. com/opinion/49-how-to-end-our-love-affair-with-evidence.

Read, Rupert (2015b). 'Climate science is to geo-engineering as genetics is to GM food.' [online] *ResPublica*, 30 November. Available at: https://www. respublica.org.uk/disraeli-room-post/2015/11/30/climate-science-geo-engineering-genetics-gm-food/.

Read, Rupert (2015c). 'Green economics vs Growth economics: The case of Thomas Piketty.' *Radical Philosophy* 189. Available at: https://www. radicalphilosophy.com/commentary/green-economics-versus-growth-economics.

Read, Rupert (2016a). 'Wittgenstein and the Illusion of "Progress": On Real Politics and Real Philosophy in a World of Technocracy', *Royal Institute of Philosophy Supplement*, 78: 265–84.

Read, Rupert (2016b). 'The Rise of the Robot: Dispelling the Myth.' [online] *The Ecologist*, 13 December. Available at: https://theecologist.org/2016/dec/13/ rise-robot-dispelling-myth.

Read, Rupert (2017a). 'Why I had to tell my students that I fear for them: Being older, in the age of incipient climate disaster.' [online] *Medium*, 28 January. Available at: https://medium.com/@GreenRupertRead/why-i-had-to-tell-my-students-that-i-fear-for-them-64bf1625b878.

Read, Rupert (2017b). 'On preparing for the great gift of community that climate disasters can give us', *Global Discourse*, 7(1): 149–67.

Read, Rupert (2017c). 'THRUTOPIA: Why Neither Dystopias Nor Utopias Are Enough To Get Us Through The Climate Crisis, And How A "Thrutopia" Could Be.' [online] *Huffington Post*, 6 November. Available at: https://www. huffingtonpost.co.uk/rupert-read/thrutopia-why-neither-dys_b_18372090. html.

Read, Rupert (2017d). 'How whales and dolphins can teach us to be less stupid.' [online] *Open Democracy*, 19 December. Available at: https://www. opendemocracy.net/en/transformation/how-whales-and-dolphins-can-teach-us-to-be-less-stupid/.

Read, Rupert (2017e). 'Gaia is dead.' [online] *Medium*, 13 May. Available at: https://medium.com/@GreenRupertRead/gaia-is-dead-we-have-killed-her-you-and-i-bb040b1d1fff.

Read, Rupert (2018a). 'Some thoughts on "civilizational succession".' [online] *Truth and Power*, 9 February. Available at: http://www.truthandpower.com/ rupert-read-some-thoughts-on-civilizational-succession/.

Read, Rupert (2018b). 'Why is the Precautionary Principle needed in the case for action on Climate Change?' [Parliamentary Briefing] *APPG on Agroecology for Sustainable Food and Farming*, 6 March. Available at: https://agroecology-appg.org/ourwork/appg-briefings-on-the-precautionary-principle-climate-change-and-animal-welfare/.

Read, Rupert (2018c). *A Film-philosophy of Ecology and Enlightenment*. New York and London: Routledge.

Read, Rupert (2018d). 'Can There be a Logic of Grief?: Why Wittgenstein and Merleau-Ponty Say "Yes"', in Oskari Kuusela, Mihai Ometiță and Timur Uçan (eds) *Wittgenstein and Phenomenology*. London: Routledge.

Read, Rupert (2018e). 'Extinction Rebellion: I'm an academic embracing direct action to stop climate change.' [online] *The Conversation*, 16 November. Available at: https://theconversation.com/extinction-rebellion-im-an-academic-embracing-direct-action-to-stop-climate-change-107037.

Read, Rupert (2018f). 'I won't go on the BBC if it supplies climate change deniers as "balance".' [online] *The Guardian*, 2 August. Available at: https://www.theguardian.com/commentisfree/2018/aug/02/bbc-climate-change-deniers-balance.

Read, Rupert (2018g). 'After the IPCC report, #climatereality.' [online] *Medium*, 15 October. Available at: https://rupertread-80924.medium.com/after-the-ipcc-report-climatereality-5b3e2ae43697.

Read, Rupert (2018h). 'This civilization is finished: so what is to be done?' [online] YouTube, 9 November. Available at: https://www.youtube.com/watch?v=uzCxFPzdO0Y.

Read, Rupert (2019a). 'The end of globalisation and the return of localisation: How climate breakdown terminates developmentality.' [online] YouTube, 30 October. Available at: https://www.youtube.com/watch?v=JxIdhv2KHb8.

Read, Rupert (2019b). 'How a movement of movements can win.' [online] *Medium*, 13 August. Available at: https://medium.com/@GreenRupertRead/how-a-movement-of-movements-can-win-cfcfdad5151c.

Read, Rupert (2019c). 'Everyone knows our democracy is broken.' [online] YouTube, 23 April. Available at: https://www.youtube.com/watch?v=dcBZxqiqVfE.

Read, Rupert (2020a). 'Negotiating the space between apocalypse and victory.' [online] *Byline Times*, 19 June. Available at: https://bylinetimes.com/2020/06/12/negotiating-the-space-between-apocalypse-and-victory/.

Read, Rupert (2020b). 'What would a precautionary approach to the coronavirus look like?: A briefing.' [online] *Medium*, 7 March. Available at: https://medium.com/@rupertjread/what-would-a-precautionary-approach-to-the-coronavirus-look-like-155626f7c2bd.

Read, Rupert (2020c). 'The coronavirus letter you've just been sent by Johnson is a lie.' [online] YouTube, 29 March. Available at: https://www.youtube.com/watch?v=aKTwBbge4lQ.

Read, Rupert (2020d). *Extinction Rebellion: Insights from the Inside*. Melbourne: Simplicity Institute.

Read, Rupert (2020e). 'Smell the Roses.' [online] *Idler*, 23 May. Available at: https://www.idler.co.uk/article/smell-the-roses.

Read, Rupert (2020f). '24 Theses on Corona.' [online] *Medium*, 9 April. Available at: https://medium.com/@rupertjread/24-theses-on-corona-748689919859.

Read, Rupert (2021a). *Parents for a Future: How Loving Our Children Can Stop Climate Collapse*. Norwich: UEA Publishing Project.

Read, Rupert (2021b). 'Transformative Adaptation.' *Permaculture,* 107.

Read, Rupert (2021c). *Wittgenstein's Liberatory Philosophy: Thinking Through His Philosophical Investigations.* New York and London: Routledge.

Read, Rupert (2021d). 'An Open Letter to Michael Mann.' [online] *Medium,* 2 March. Available at: https://rupertread-80924.medium.com/an-open-letter-to-michael-mann-730205964d48.

Read, Rupert (2021e). 'The can stops now.' [online] *Brave New Europe* Nov. 12. Available at https://bravenew60urope.com/rupert-read-the-can-stops-now.

Read, Rupert (2021f). 'Will the whales inherit the Earth?' [online] *Dark Mountain.* Available at https://dark-mountain.net/will-the-whales-inherit-the-earth/

Read, Rupert, and Samuel Alexander (2019). *This Civilization is Finished: Conversations on the End of Empire – And What Lies Beyond.* Melbourne: Simplicity Institute.

Read, Rupert, Samuel Alexander and Jacob Garrett (2018). 'Voluntary simplicity: strongly backed by all three main normative-ethical traditions', *Ethical Perspectives,* 25(1): 87–116.

Read, Rupert, and Laura Baldwin (2021). 'The politics of paradox.' [online] *Green World,* 5 July. Available at: https://greenworld.org.uk/article/politics-paradox.

Read, Rupert, and Greg Craven (2017). 'The One Video to Watch on Climate, If You Have Just 3 Minutes.' [online] YouTube, 17 July. Available at: https://www.youtube.com/watch?v=pmcokyx6Tbk.

Read, Rupert, and Joe Eastoe (2021). 'The need for a moderate flank in climate activism.' [online] *Byline Times,* 18 June: https://bylinetimes.com/2021/06/18/the-need-for-a-moderate-flank-in-climate-activism/.

Read, Rupert, John Foster and Jem Bendell (2019). 'An open letter to David Wallace-Wells.' [online] *The Ecologist,* 4 April. Available at: https://theecologist.org/2019/apr/04/open-letter-david-wallace-wells.

Read, Rupert, and Aseem Shrivistava (2021). 'A Covidised world?' [online] *Open & Brave New Europe,* 3 July. Available at: https://openthemagazine.com/essays/the-permanent-pandemic/ & https://bravenew60urope.com/aseem-shrivastava-and-rupert-read-does-globalisation-make-covidisation-inevitable.

Read, Rupert, and Deepak Rughani (2017). 'Apollo-Earth.' [online] *Medium,* 10 March. Available at: https://medium.com/@GreenRupertRead/apollo-earth-a-wake-up-call-in-our-race-against-time-5f8121687966#.xqul7vjk0.

Read, Rupert, and Deepak Rughani (2020). 'Review: Michael Moore's *Planet of the Humans.*' [online] *Byline Times,* 14 May. Available at: https://bylinetimes.com/2020/05/14/review-michael-moores-planet-of-the-humans-heartbreaking-genius-of-staggering-over-simplification/.

Read, Rupert, and Kirsten Steele (2019). 'Making the Best of Climate Disasters: On the Need for a Localised and Localising Response', in John Foster (ed.), *Facing up to Climate Reality.* London: London Publishing Partnership.

Read, Rupert, and Timur Uçan, eds. (2019). Special Issue: Post-Truth?, *Nordic Wittgenstein Review.*

Read, Rupert, Thomas Wallgren, Aseem Shrivastava and Anat Matar (2021). 'Rupert Read on liberatory philosophy and politics in the time of civilizational crisis.' [online] YouTube, 29 January. Available at: https://www.youtube.com/watch?v=neclQ4-dd0M.

Rear, Rupert & Wolfgang Knorr (2022). 'This is not an 'Emergency'... It's Much More Serious Than That.' [online] *Emerge*, 21 February. Available at: https://www.whatisemerging.com/opinions/climate-this-is-not-an-emergency-it-s-much-more-serious-than-that.

Rockström, Johan, and Owen Gaffney (2021). *Breaking Boundaries: The Science of our Planet.* London: DK.

Rockström, Johan, Owen Gaffney and Joeri Rohelj (2017). 'A roadmap for rapid decarbonization.' *Science,* 355(6331): 1269–71. DOI: 10.1126/science. aah3443.

Roszak, Theodore (2002). *Voice of the Earth: An Exploration of Ecopsychology.* 2nd edn. Grand Rapids, MI: Phanes Press.

Rushkoff, Douglas (2018). 'Survival of the richest: The wealthy are plotting to leave us behind.' [online] *Medium*, 5 July. Available at: https://onezero. medium.com/survival-of-the-richest-9ef6cddd0cc1.

Samuel, Sigal (2020). 'If our governments won't stop climate change, should we revolt?' [online] *Vox*, 20 December. Available at: https://www.vox.com/future-perfect/2019/12/20/21028407/extinction-rebellion-climate-change-nonviolent-civil-disobedience.

Scheffler, Samuel (2013). *Death and the Afterlife*, ed. Niko Kolodny. Oxford: Oxford University Press.

Schlegelmilch, Jeff (2020). *Rethinking Readiness: A Brief Guide to Twenty-First-Century Megadisasters.* New York: Columbia University Press.

Scott Cato, Molly (2013). *The Bioregional Economy: Land, Liberty and the Pursuit of Happiness.* London and New York: Routledge.

Scott Cato, Molly, Rupert Read (2019). 'The Amazon burns: will the world learn' [online] *Green World*, 23 August. Available at: https://greenworld.org.uk/article/amazon-burns-will-world-learn.

Servigne, Pablo, and Raphaël Stevens (2020). *How Everything Can Collapse: A Manual for our Times.* Translated from French by Andrew Brown. Cambridge: Polity Press.

Servigne, Pablo, Raphaël Stevens, Gauthier Chapelle and Daniel Rodary (2020). 'Deep Adaptation opens up a necessary conversation about the breakdown of civilization.' [online] *Open Democracy*, 3 August. Available at: https://www.opendemocracy.net/en/oureconomy/deep-adaptation-opens-necessary-conversation-about-breakdown-civilization/.

Shareable (2019). 'The response.' [online] *Shareable*. Available at: https://www.shareable.net/the-response-film/

Sharrock, Wes, and Rupert Read (2002). *Kuhn: Philosopher of Scientific Revolution.* Cambridge: Polity Press.

Shine, Keith (2018). 'IPCC 1.5°C report: here's what the climate science says.' [online] *The Conversation*, 8 October. Available at: https://theconversation. com/ipcc-1-5-report-heres-what-the-climate-science-says-104592.

Shue, Henry (1993). 'Subsistence emissions and luxury emissions', *Law and Policy*, 15(1): 39–60.

Simard, Suzanne (2021). *Searching for the Mother Tree*. London: Allen Lane.

Sinclair, Ian, and Rupert Read (2021). *A Timeline of the Plague Year: A Comprehensive Record of the UK Government's Response to the Coronavirus Crisis*. [eBook] Available at: https://covidtheplagueyear.wordpress.com/.

Singh, Maanvi (2021). 'American west stuck in cycle of heat, drought and fire', experts warn.' [online] *The Guardian*, 12 July. Available at: https://www.theguardian.com/ us-news/2021/jul/12/wildfires-california-oregon-drought-heat-fire-cycle.

Smaje, Chris (2020). *A Small Farm Future*. London: Chelsea Green.

Solnit, Rebecca (2009). *A Paradise Built in Hell: The Extraordinary Communities that Arise in Disaster*. New York: Penguin Random House.

Solomon, Robert C. (2004). *In Defense of Sentimentality*. New York: Oxford University Press.

Solomon, Robert C. (2006). *About Love*. New York: Hackett.

Spratt, David, and Ian Dunlop (2018). 'What Lies Beneath: The Understatement of Existential Climate Risk.' Melbourne: Breakthrough – National Centre for Climate Restoration.

Spratt, David, and Ian Dunlop (2019). 'Existential climate-related security risk: A scenario approach.' *Breakthrough – National Centre for Climate Restoration*. Melbourne.

Steel, Daniel (2015). *Philosophy and the Precautionary Principle*. Cambridge: Cambridge University Press.

Steele, Kristen (2019). 'Disaster Localization: A Constructive Response to Climate Chaos.' [online] *Local Futures*, 22 October. Available at: https://www.localfutures. org/disaster-localization-a-constructive-response-to-climate-chaos/.

Steffen, Will, Johan Rockström, Katherine Richardson, Timothy M. Lenton, Carl Folke, Diana Liverman, Colin P. Summerhayes, Anthony D. Barnosky, Sarah E. Cornell, Michel Crucifix, Jonathan F. Donges, Ingo Fetzer, Steven J. Lade, Marten Scheffer, Ricarda Winkelmann and Hans Joachim Schellnhuber (2018). 'Trajectories of the Earth System in the Anthropocene', *Proceedings of the National Academy of Sciences*, 115(33): 8252–9.

Tabios Hillebrecht, Anna Leah and María Valeria Berros, eds (2017). 'Can Nature Have Rights? Legal and Political Insights', *RCC Perspectives: Transformations in Environment and Society*, 6.

Tainter, Joseph (1988). *The Collapse of Complex Societies*. Cambridge: Cambridge University Press.

Tainter, Joseph (2000). 'Problem solving: complexity, history, sustainability', *Population and Environment*, 22(1): 3–41.

Taleb, Nassim Nicholas, Yaneer Bar-Yam, Raphael Douady, Joseph Norman and Rupert Read (2014). 'The precautionary principle: Fragility and black swans from policy action.' [online] *NYU Extreme Risk Initiative Working Paper*. Available at: https://fooledbyrandomness.com/precautionary.pdf.

Taleb, Nassim Nicholas, Rupert Read, Raphael Douady, Joseph Norman and Yaneer Bar-Yam (2015). 'The Precautionary Principle (with Application to the Genetic Modification of Organisms).' [online] *NYU Extreme Risk Initiative Working Paper*. Available at: https://arxiv.org/pdf/1410.5787.pdf.

Tanuro, Daniel (2016). 'Specter of geoengineering haunts Paris climate deal.' [online] *Climate & Capitalism*, 25 January. Available at: https://climateandcapitalism.com/2016/01/25/the-specter-of-geoengineering-haunts-the-paris-climate-agreement/.

Tay, L. & E. Diener (2011). 'Needs and Subjective Well-Being Around the World', *Journal of Personality and Social Psychology*, 101(2): 354–65.

Taylor, Charles (1985). 'Atomism', *Philosophical Papers*. Cambridge: Cambridge University Press.

Taylor, Craig (2020). 'Winch and Animal Minds', in M. Campbell & L. Reid (eds), *Ethics, Society and Politics: Themes from the Philosophy of Peter Winch*. Berlin: Springer.

The Poetry of Predicament (2021). 'Transforming Activism exactly when we need it most.' [online] YouTube, 4 January. Available at: https://www.youtube.com/watch?v=IjP8oRPjV00.

Thunberg, Greta (2019). *No One Is Too Small to Make a Difference*. London: Penguin.

Tollefson, Jeff (2021). 'Covid curbed carbon emissions in 2020 – but not by much', *Nature*. Available at: https://www.nature.com/articles/d41586-021-00090-3.

Tolstoy, Leo (1904) [1869]. *War and Peace*. Translated from the Russian by Constance Garnett. Oxford: Oxford University Press.

United Nations (2019). 'UN emissions report: World on course for more than 3 degree spike, even if climate commitments are met.' [online] Available at https://news.un.org/en/story/2019/11/1052171.

Vaidyanathan, Gayathri (2015). 'How Bad of a Greenhouse Gas Is Methane?' [online] *Scientific American*, 22 December. Available at: https://www.scientificamerican.com/article/how-bad-of-a-greenhouse-gas-is-methane/.

Walker, Peter (2019). 'MPs endorse Corbyn's call to declare climate emergency.' [online] *The Guardian*, 1 May. Available at: https://www.theguardian.com/environment/2019/may/01/declare-formal-climate-emergency-before-its-too-late-corbyn-warns.

Wallace-Wells, David (2017). 'The Uninhabitable Earth.' [online] *Intelligencer*, 10 July. Available at: https://nymag.com/intelligencer/2017/07/climate-change-earth-too-hot-for-humans.html.

Wallace-Wells, David (2019). *The Uninhabitable Earth: A Story of the Future*. New York, NY: Penguin.

Ward, Michelle, Ayesha I. T. Tulloch, James Q. Radford, et al. (2020). 'Impact of 2019–2020 mega-fires on Australian fauna habitat', *Nature Ecology & Evolution*, 4: 1321–6. Available at: https://doi.org/10.1038/s41559-020-1251-1.

Weil, Simone (1952). *The Need for Roots: Prelude to a Declaration of Duties to Mankind*. Translated from French by Arthur Wills. London: Routledge & Kegan Paul.

Westra, Laura (2006). *Environmental Justice and the Rights of Unborn and Future Generations*. London: Earthscan.

Whitehead, Hal, and Luke Rendell (2015). *The Cultural Lives of Whales and Dolphins.* Chicago, IL: University of Chicago Press.

Wilkinson, Richard, and Kate Pickett (2010). *The Spirit Level: Why Greater Equality Makes Societies Stronger.* London and New York: Bloomsbury.

Wilkinson, Richard, and Kate Pickett (2017). 'Inequality and mental illness.' [online] *The Lancet.* Available at: https://www.equalitytrust.org.uk/resource/ inequality-and-mental-illness-comment-lancet-psychiatry-professors-wilkinson-and-pickett.

Williston, Byron (2015). *The Anthropocene Project: Virtue in the Age of Climate Change.* Oxford: Oxford University Press.

Williston, Byron (2020). *Philosophy and the Climate Crisis.* London: Routledge.

Wilson, E. O. (2017). *Half-Earth: Our Planet's Fight for Life.* New York: W.W. Norton.

Winch, Peter (1964). 'Understanding a primitive society', *American Philosophically Quarterly.* 1(4): 307–24.

Winch, Peter (1987). *Trying to Make Sense.* Oxford: Blackwell.

Winch, Peter (1990). *The Idea of a Social Science and its Relation to Philosophy.* 2nd edn. London: Routledge.

Winch, Peter (1997). 'Can we understand ourselves?', *Philosophical Investigations,* 20(3): 193–204.

Wittgenstein, Ludwig (1922). *Tractatus Logico-Philosophicus.* London: Routledge.

Wittgenstein, Ludwig (1958). *Philosophical Investigations.* Oxford: Blackwell.

Wittgenstein, Ludwig (1967). *Zettel.* Edited by Elizabeth Anscombe and Georg Henrik von Wright. Berkeley, CA: University of California Press.

Wittgenstein, Ludwig (1975). *On Certainty.* Oxford: Blackwell.

Wittgenstein, Ludwig (2014). *Lecture on Ethics.* Oxford: Wiley Blackwell.

Wittgenstein, Ludwig (2020). *The Mythology In Our Language. Remarks on Frazer's Golden Bough.* Edited by Giovanni da Col and S. Palmié. Translated from German by S. Palmié. London: Hau Books.

Wohlleben, Peter (2017). *The Secret Life of Trees.* London: William Collins.

Woodard, Christopher (2013). 'Classifying Theories of Welfare', *Philosophical Studies: An International Journal for Philosophy in the Analytic Tradition,* 165(3): 787–803.

Woodin, Mike and Caroline Lucas (2004). *Green Alternatives to Globalisation: A Manifesto.* London: Pluto.

Woods, Amanda (2019). 'Global carbon emissions rose at the fastest rate in seven years: report.' [online] *NY Post,* 11 June. Available at: https://nypost.com/2019/ 06/11/global-carbon-emissions-rose-at-the-fastest-rate-in-seven-years-report/.

Wright, Ronald (2012). 'A short history of progress.' [online] YouTube, 25 August. Available at: https://www.youtube.com/watch?v=sbQHe3d9_lQ.

Yunkaporta, Tyson (2019). *Sand Talk: How Indigenous Thinking Can Save the World.* London: The Text.

Index